Plays by Women in Irelan

Plays by Women in Ireland (1926–33): Feminist Theatres of Freedom and Resistance

Distinguished Villa

The Woman

Youth's the Season – ?

Witch's Brew

Bluebeard

Edited by

LISA FITZPATRICK and SHONAGH HILL

methuen | drama

LONDON • NEW YORK • OXFORD • NEW DELHI • SYDNEY

METHUEN DRAMA
Bloomsbury Publishing Plc
50 Bedford Square, London, WC1B 3DP, UK
1385 Broadway, New York, NY 10018, USA
29 Earlsfort Terrace, Dublin 2, Ireland

BLOOMSBURY, METHUEN DRAMA and the Methuen Drama logo are trademarks of
Bloomsbury Publishing Plc

First published in Great Britain 2022

Introduction © Lisa Fitzpatrick and Shonagh Hill, 2022
Distinguished Villa © 1926, John O'Brien & Donough O'Brien, Trustees of the copyrights of the
late Kate O'Brien
The Woman © Margaret O'Leary, 1929, courtesy of both the Abbey Theatre Archive and the
National Library of Ireland
Youth's the Season – ? © Mary Manning, 1931, thanks to her daughters
Susan Howe and Fanny Howe
Witch's Brew © Dorothy Macardle, 1931, reproduced with permission of Curtis Brown Ltd,
London, on behalf of the Beneficiaries of the Estate of Dorothy Macardle.
Bluebeard © Mary Devenport O'Neill, 1933, courtesy of both the Abbey Theatre Archive and the
National Library of Ireland

Cover design by Rebecca Heselton
Cover image: *The Woman* by Margaret O'Leary, Grace Plunkett, ink on paper. Courtesy of the
National Library of Ireland

A catalogue record for this book is available from the British Library.

A catalog record for this book is available from the Library of Congress.

ISBN: HB: 978-1-3502-3464-2
PB: 978-1-3502-3463-5
ePDF: 978-1-3502-3465-9
eBook: 978-1-3502-3466-6

Typeset by RefineCatch Limited, Bungay, Suffolk

To find out more about our authors and books visit www.bloomsbury.com
and sign up for our newsletters.

Contents

Illustrations

Acknowledgements

This project has been dependent on the support of many archivists and collections, and we would like to extend our thanks to all those involved. Barry Houlihan at the archives in the Hardiman Library, NUI, Galway has been unfailingly helpful and answered our many queries and requests. We would also like to extend our gratitude to: Mairead Delaney at the Abbey Theatre Archives; Ken Bergin, Sean Cafferkey, Anna Maria Hajba and Pattie Punch at the University of Limerick; James Harte at the National Library of Ireland; Selina Collard at UCD Archives; and Hugh Murphy at NUI Maynooth Archives. Thank you to Dayna Killian (PhD candidate at Waterford IT, working on women playwrights and the Abbey Theatre in the twentieth century) for generously sharing information and archival materials on Margaret O'Leary.

We are hugely grateful to the following individuals, archives and publishers for granting us permission to bring these scripts together in this collection.

The manuscripts of *The Woman* (Ms 21,437) and *Bluebeard* (Ms 21,440) are included courtesy of both the Abbey Theatre Archive and the National Library of Ireland.

Mary Manning's *Youth's the Season – ?* is included thanks to her daughters Susan Howe and Fanny Howe.

Thanks to Curtis Brown for permission to publish Dorothy Macardle's *Witch's Brew*, and thanks also to Tramp Press for their advice in this regard.

David Higham Associates and the O'Brien estate gave their permission to include *Distinguished Villa*; our thanks to them, and to Luci Gosling at the Mary Evans Picture Library for the review images from *The Sketch* of July 1926.

Every effort has been made to obtain permission to reproduce these materials. The editors/publishers will rectify any permissions in future editions if further information on the rights holder is received.

We would like to thank Dom O'Hanlon at Bloomsbury Methuen Drama for his continuous advice and support throughout this venture, and the scholars who reviewed our proposal and offered insightful suggestions as well as enthusiastic support: Charlotte Canning, Bishnupriya Dutt, Ondřej Pilný, Sean Richards and Denise Varney.

The scholarly networks of the Irish Society for Theatre Research and the International Federation for Theatre Research have been invaluable in offering opportunities for the development of the scholarship underpinning this project, and we offer our heartfelt gratitude for the many opportunities to discuss and debate with the members of both. Particular thanks to Cathy Leeney, a pioneer in research into Irish women's theatre of this period; without her earlier scholarship this collection might never have happened; and thanks to the late Christopher Innes who first sent Lisa to the archives to look for unpublished plays by Irish women, at the start of this century.

Lastly, we would like to thank our families and friends.

Introduction

'Ireland is in transition'

The plays gathered in this collection emerge from the years of the Irish Free State, 1922–37. Under the Anglo-Irish Treaty of 1921, twenty-six counties of Ireland were established as a dominion of the British Commonwealth, while the six counties of Northern Ireland remained in the United Kingdom. Playwright Mary Manning wrote in the Gate Theatre's in-house magazine *Motley*: 'Ireland is in transition; the nation is finding its soul. New forces are at work; new ideas are crowding in upon us' (Manning 1932: 5). Women had been integral to the events preceding the Free State's foundation, from the 1913 Lockout to the 1916 Rising, and were involved in suffrage, nationalist, labour and cultural organizations. Women were thus a vital constituent of the new forces and new ideas in circulation. However, as Cynthia Enloe points out, 'the history of a nationalist movement is almost always a history filled with gendered debate' (1990: 59). Indeed, feminism and nationalism did not always align in their pursuit for independence, and women's ability to maintain a public role was severely tested by the modern Irish state's predication on a highly gendered citizenship. The desire for stability following the state's foundation built on an existing conservativism to unleash a backlash against the gains that women had made during the revolutionary period. Culturally, these tensions were entangled with the negotiation between Irish nationalism and European avant-garde influences. The plays in this anthology reveal how, during the first two decades of independence, women continued to struggle for freedom and to offer resistance in the face of the conservatism of a patriarchal church-state.

The careers of these playwrights span a period of revolution and subsequent state-building. The eldest, Dorothy Macardle (1889–1958), was a Republican who participated in the War of Independence and spent a period in Kilmainham Gaol, while the youngest of the playwrights, Mary Manning (1905–99), describes her generation as 'raised in gunfire'. The revolutionaries fought for full and equal citizenship, and this was asserted in the 1916 Proclamation of Independence which guaranteed 'religious and civil liberty, equal rights and equal opportunities to all its citizens', as well as 'the establishment of a permanent National Government, representative of the whole people of Ireland and elected by the suffrages of all her men and women'. Suffrage was granted to property-owning women over thirty in 1918, and extended to all women over twenty-one in 1922. However, the new order was not radical: Kevin O'Higgins boasted that he and his colleagues were 'probably the most conservative-minded revolutionaries who ever put through a successful revolution' (quoted in Valiulis 2019: 45). As suffragist and nationalist Hanna Sheehy Skeffington noted: 'it may be said that, while the Free State has taken over from Britain, whereas the latter has advanced with regard to the position of women, we have either remained stationary – or have retrogressed' (Ward 2017: 336).

The promise of equality was crushed through legislation which restricted women's participation in the public sphere. In 1925 the right of women to sit all civil service examinations was curtailed; the 1927 Juries Bill excluded women from jury service unless they specifically applied; and in 1932, compulsory retirement on marriage (the 'marriage-bar') was imposed on all female teachers and later extended to the entire civil service.[1] The capstone of these laws was the 1937 Constitution; in particular Article 41.2 which defined woman's 'life within the home' and granted the role of mother dominance over other models of femininity: 'mothers shall not be obliged by economic necessity to engage in labour to the neglect of their duties in the home'.[2] Sheehy Skeffington clearly delineates between attitudes to women during the revolutionary period versus the Free State through comparison of James Connolly with Éamon de Valera: 'To the one, woman was an equal, a comrade; to the other, a sheltered being, withdrawn to the domestic hearth, shrinking from public life' (Ward 2019: 397). The Catholic Church bolstered the nascent state's definition of the pure and virtuous ideal Irish woman contained by a domestic identity. A range of women's groups refused this ideal through their activism, including the IWWU, Cumann na mBan, the Women's Prisoners' Dependents' League, the Women's Social and Progressive League, the Suffrage and Local Government Association, the Joint Committee of Women's Societies and Social Workers. The Women's Citizens and the women graduate associations of Trinity and the National University campaigned against the restrictions on jury service and employment for women, and against the marriage bar, and the National University Women Graduates Association played a leading role in opposing the draft constitution (Connolly 2003: 67).

Ireland was not isolated from the anxieties of the period, namely the rise of fascism across Europe and looming war. Manning's play *Youth's the Season – ?* captures the despair of these inter-war years:

> Raised in gunfire . . . one mysterious universe after the other . . . souls lacerated with psychoanalysis . . . censorship of literature . . . people putting their heads in gas-ovens all over Europe . . . the rest living from hand to flask . . . the Doctrine of Despair . . . the Philosophy of Hopefulness. Communism is coming . . . the Intelligentsia must die . . . Onward Christian Soldiers marching as to war. Oh, Mickey Mouse, where are you?

Moreover, Ireland was emerging from a period of civil war (1922–3) and the pressing need for stability was paramount. As Louise Ryan outlines, several feminine archetypes were utilized 'as scapegoats [which] attempted to simplify and obscure the many social and economic problems underlying the newly established state' (Ryan 2002: 294). These included the 'modern girl' with an interest in fashion and popular culture; the unmarried mother; the working woman; the emigrant woman; and women in public life in politics or culture. Examination of these feminine figures as they appear in the plays in this collection exposes the gap between the reality of women's lives and the official Church- and State-endorsed ideal woman. Through the act of writing plays and through the presentation of the lives of the women in the plays, the playwrights reveal that:

> Women's lives clearly transcended the single domestic dimension of the ideal constructed by ecclesiastical discourse. Increasing numbers were working

---

1   The marriage bar remained in place until 1973.

2   This article remains extant. The Recommendations of the Citizen's Assembly on Gender Equality were announced on 24 April 2021 and included: 'Delete and replace the text of Article 41.2 (woman in the home) with language that is not gender specific and obliges the State to take reasonable measures to support care within the home and wider community.' See https://www.citizensassembly.ie

outside the home. A significant number never married. Women continue to emigrate in increasing numbers. Women were exploring their sexuality, and were having children outside of marriage. Women were going to dances, wearing imported fashions and going to films – often enough for the complaint to be heard that they were never at home. Women were agitating for political rights, demanding a public identity. In essence, women were modern actors in a modernising society. (Valiulis 2019: 134–5)

Theatre, we argue, offered the potential for women to explore their role as modern actors, both through employment in the theatre and through the characters presented on stage. Macardle described the lack of opportunity available to women in the Free State: 'All life's realities seemed to be shut away as though by an invisible wall' (quoted in Lane 2019: 221). The plays collected here render these 'walls' visible, staging their protagonists' frustration and yearning for self-determination. They thereby offer a feminist theatre of freedom and resistance.

Experimentation and counterculture

Against the conservatism of the period, a counterculture of experimentation was evolving; most obviously evidenced through the establishment of the Peacock stage at the Abbey Theatre in 1927 and the Gate Theatre in 1928. However, both Mrs Cogley's cabarets and the Dublin Drama League pre-date these theatres. Elaine Sisson argues that the cabarets spoke 'to the desire for something expressive within the politics of the post-Civil War Free State' (2018: 23). Madame Desiree 'Toto' Bannard-Cogley was one of the four founders of the Gate, and her private members list formed the initial subscription list when it opened in 1928 (Sisson 2018: 13). From their first production in 1919, the Dublin Drama League was committed to experimentalism and introduced Irish audiences to European work. They welcomed expressionism and one of the regular directors, Arthur Shields, later directed Mary Devenport O'Neill's *Bluebeard*. The League had access to the Abbey on 'dark' nights and members continued their association through work presented on the new Peacock stage. Norah McGuinness embraced expressionism in her set design for the Peacock's opening production: Georg Kaiser's *From Morn to Midnight* (1927). At times, McGuinness collaborated with Dorothy Travers Smith, who worked as a set and costume designer at the Abbey during the 1920s and 1930s. Tanya Moiseiwitsch designed numerous sets and costumes at the Abbey in the years 1935–9, including the premiere and subsequent productions of Teresa Deevy's *Katie Roche*. These designers brought European innovations to the Irish stage and underline the importance of women's contributions to theatre across a range of roles.

Under the directorship of Hilton Edwards and Micheál Mac Liammóir, the Gate Theatre programmed European and experimental work, as well as new Irish writing. They had notable successes with Irish plays which drew on expressionism, from Denis Johnston's *The Old Lady Says No!* (1928) to Mary Manning *Youth's the Season – ?* (1931). Mac Liammóir's design for the Gate logo (see Figure 4) evidences a commitment to European experimental performance, both through the figure of the harlequin which references Nijinsky (see Pine 2018: 70–1), and the expressionist deployment of light and shadow. The Gate offered a theatrical home to several women playwrights of the period, including Mary Manning, Christine Pakenham (Countess Longford), Lilian Davidson (*Bride*, 1931, under the pseudonym Ulick Burke) and Hazel Ellis (*Portrait in Marble*, 1936 and *Women Without Men*, 1938). Dorothy Macardle had several plays staged at the Abbey in the 1920s before her play *Dark Waters* was produced at the Gate in 1932. Ria Mooney initially worked at the Abbey but left in 1933 to further her career at the Gate where she was offered 'elegant roles and romantic leads', in contrast to the more womanly figures she played at the Abbey (O'Dowd 2018: 141). The Abbey staged a number of plays by women during the 1920s and 1930s, including work by Dorothy Macardle, Margaret O'Leary, Teresa Deevy, Mary Rynne, Maura Molloy, Maeve O'Callaghan, Elizabeth Harte and Kathleen O'Brennan. Other writers left Ireland: Kate O'Brien, whose *Distinguished Villa* is included here, wrote for London's West End theatres in the 1920s and 1930s, as did Una O'Connor (*Love at First Sight*, 1931) and Helen Waddell (*The Abbé Provost*, 1935) (see Gale 1996).

The fate of Teresa Deevy's work is instructive. She was a prolific and very popular playwright, yet was forgotten for many years. Scholarship by Cathy Leeney has been central to efforts to counter this neglect. Deevy's plays have been published in two volumes by the Mint Theater Company (2017), and the Teresa Deevy archive, held at NUI Maynooth, is available online.[3] Deevy submitted her first play to the Abbey in 1925. It was rejected, but her third attempt was accepted, and *The Reapers* was performed in 1930, followed by *A Disciple* in 1931 (see Figure 1). In 1939 it was filmed for the BBC as *In Search of Valour*, directed by Denis Johnston. Other plays by Deevy which premiered at the Abbey include *Temporal Powers* (1932), *The King of Spain's Daughter* (1935), *Katie Roche* (1936), *The Wild Goose* (1936) and *Light Falling* (1948). Though we were unable to secure permission to include Deevy in this anthology, it is important to place her work in dialogue with the anthologized plays. Female characters are at the centre of all of Deevy's plays, as she experiments with theatrical strategies to stage women's interiority, against the backdrop of a limiting and closed society. The closing lines of *In Search of Valour* see Ellie Irwin left alone on-stage wailing, 'Wirra – why weren't I born in a brave time?!' (Deevy 1947: 16). Deevy's later characters like Annie Kinsella in *The King of Spain's Daughter* (1935) and the eponymous Katie Roche (1936) express similar longings for freedom and adventure, and rage against the restrictions placed upon them. Deevy's women advance vital performances of resistance and her collection of plays underscores her significant contribution to a genealogy of women's writing for the stage. To fully appreciate these playwrights' achievements, it is necessary to address the gendered confines of the Ireland they lived in, or indeed chose to leave; to address the limits placed on their capacity to work and on their artistic expression.

'The right to work'

The decades of the Free State encompass the post-Wall Street Crash years: the bleak and austere 1930s. Women's employment was a source of friction and blamed for the

---

3   https://repository.dri.ie/catalog/95944b38t

high levels of male unemployment. The Conditions of Employment Act (1936) enabled the Minister for Industry and Commerce to control and restrict women's access to industrial employment. In a letter to the *Irish Press* newspaper, Dorothy Macardle ardently expressed her support for women's right to employment: 'The right to work – not only to earn a livelihood but to work for work's own sake, is surely the inalienable right of every human being. It is not men only who, denied work, become restless, unhappy, unbalanced, unhealthy in body and mind' (13 May 1935, quoted in Lane 2019: 221). This contrasted with the idealized Irish woman: pure and modest, self-sacrificing and with no ambition of her own. Legislation that acted against women's access to properly paid employment, or that aimed to limit women's reproductive rights or their rights to autonomy, is often explained as in keeping with both Catholic social teaching and fascist ideology of the 1920s and 1930s. Ward comments that the conception of gender made explicit in the 1937 Constitution was 'indistinguishable from Nazi degrees' (1995, 240). Ireland's own fascist organization, the paramilitary Blueshirts, was founded in 1932.

Post-colonial nationalism, as in Ireland, often pits women's rights against the appeal to national custom and tradition, where the latter are part of the utopian rhetoric of the new independent state. Furthermore, an increasingly bourgeois model of Irish nationalist identity refused to consider the desperate economic situation of many poor families, which relied on both parents' incomes for basic survival. For most women at the time, work outside the home was an economic necessity rather than a career choice; most were factory workers, servants, seamstresses or shop assistants. However, from the early 1900s there was a growing number of women working as teachers, nurses and owner-shopkeepers, contributing significantly to the family budget. Conservative ideals of respectability coupled with anti-communist rhetoric limited sympathetic engagement with the plight of the very poor, who had very little political power and so could be safely ignored by legislators, but this developing women's middle class was systematically politically disempowered. The marriage bar and legislation about marital property and women's access to financial services combined to force women out of public life and into increasing dependence on male family members and husbands. Another consequence was that single women were often forced to share living accommodation. Hazel Ellis's play *Women Without Men* (1938) examines the tensions that arise among a group of teachers living and working in a boarding school: 'A small group of women all cooped up together with no release from each other save in the privacy of our bedrooms. Women brought together not by choice, not by liking, but by the necessity of earning our living.'[4] Rosamund Jacob's diaries offer a record of the tensions that arose between her and Dorothy Macardle, whom she lived with, over Jacob's late night visits from her lover Frank Ryan. The conflict between single women's private sexual needs and expectations of appropriate feminine behaviour was amplified by the necessity of sharing living space. Macardle chastised Jacob, highlighting how an 'almost childlike status [was] forced on unmarried women' (Lane 2010: 179).

---

4 Revival by the Mint Theater Company, New York, 30 January to 26 March 2016; streamed February to April 2021.

Emigration numbers peaked in the mid-1920s and gradually slowed in the early 1930s, when the US closed its borders; although emigration to England began to increase dramatically. Women emigrated in equal numbers to men – which was unusual – and were less likely to return (Rudd 1987); their mobility was enabled by high rates of participation in education,[5] and the lack of opportunities for work or marriage at home. Mary Manning left Ireland in 1935 for America, where she lived in Boston. There was concern that the state would be viewed as having failed to provide for its younger citizens, as so many were leaving for economic opportunities and the greater freedoms offered by life overseas. A recurring theme in the press coverage and in sermons from the time was the spiritual dangers – especially to young women – of moving to England, where they might fall away from religious practice and become pregnant outside of marriage. In 1936, Gertrude Gaffney's report on the plight of young Irish women in big English cities reveals the failure of the Free State to educate its citizens for the modern world. She notes that the women were often unprepared for city life, were naïve and easily taken advantage of, and many had neither money nor job when they set off from home. Some of the girls had effectively been exiled by their families because they were pregnant and unmarried (quoted in Ryan 2002: 118–19). An editorial in *The Examiner* from November 1936 asserts: 'It is all to the good that attention has been focused lately on the problem of young female emigrants or migrants from the Free State to Great Britain . . . If the money that had been wasted in the efforts to teach these girls Irish, and other subjects through Irish, had been applied to teaching them elementary housewifery, their position would not be so hopeless' (Ryan 2002: 115–16). As Ryan points out, *The Examiner* proposes relating girls' education more closely to domesticity, seeing this as a pathway to employment in Ireland and to marriage. However, girls were also reported to be uninterested in housekeeping or service: factory work paid higher wages for shorter hours. In Teresa Deevy's one-act play *In Search of Valour*, Ellie Irwin clearly resents her status as a servant and longs for passion, fame and power. Deevy vividly represents the entrapment of ambitious young women with limited education and no opportunities for self-fulfilment.

Women's experiences of employment and of emigration are a recurring trope in many of these plays, bridging the rural/urban divide and differences in social class and access to opportunity. Kate O'Brien's characters in *Distinguished Villa* are English, or living in England, and her protagonist is an independent working woman, but their lives are restricted by social mores and tight notions of respectability. Ellen Dunn in *The Woman*, like Deevy's protagonists, expresses a deep longing for escape from the dullness of her daily life, and the imaginative and cultural poverty of her surroundings. Ellen Dunn dreams of a utopia that she names as America, while Ellie Irwin (*In Search of Valour*) longs for the opportunities of England, where her heroine 'Miss Charlotta Burke' was making a career as an actress, until she committed suicide – although even this is heroic in Ellie's eyes. The play therefore points both to the desperation of many of the emigrants who could not find their way in the big, anonymous cities of England, and the plight of young women for whom no price was too high to escape from the

---

5   The majority of the playwrights included in this anthology were educated at third-level. O'Brien and Macardle attended University College Dublin, while O'Leary went to University College Cork and Devenport O'Neill attended the Dublin Metropolitan School of Art.

repressive atmosphere of 1930s Ireland. Ellen Dunn lives in the countryside, and marriage is the only option available to her; the protagonists in cities hardly fare better: the wealthy, Protestant young women in *Youth's the Season – ?* might study, but their professional lives will end with their marriages to suitable young men. Unlike their Catholic compatriots, their position is more tenuous and their links with England stronger, but their opportunities are still largely dependent on their choice of husband and the financial support of their fathers. Gertrude Gaffney criticized de Valera's Constitution for its attack on working women, which exacerbated the problems of emigration. Accusing de Valera of being 'a reactionary where women are concerned', and of aiming to keep women 'in their proper place' by extinguishing their rights, she argues that 'We are to be no longer citizens entitled to enjoy equal rights under a democratic constitution' (quoted in Ryan 2002: 131). She points out that if women lose their jobs in factories in Ireland, they will be more likely to seek work overseas. De Valera's ideal of domesticated motherhood was undermined by Ireland's long practice of emigration and his own policies.

'Strict definitions of permissible bodies'

It was thought that the foundation of the Irish Free State would curb immoral behaviour as the corrupting influence of British garrisons would be removed and this would end demand for prostitution. Historians Maria Luddy and Diarmuid Ferriter, amongst others, have demonstrated how mistaken these expectations were. Luddy highlights how, once the British garrison was gone, levels of sexual immorality appeared to rise; 'the real threat to chastity and sexual morality' was seen to reside 'in the bodies of women. Moral regulation, by Church and State, attempted to impose, particularly on women, standards of idealized conduct that would return the nation to purity' (2007: 80). Fears over public morality coalesced in the figures of unmarried mothers and '(f) ag-smoking, jazz-dancing, lip-sticking flappers' (*Kilkenny People*, quoted in Ryan 2002: 81). Bishops preached against the immodesty of modern fashion, and the Jesuit Michael Garahy published a pamphlet warning that 'in the great centres of progress the streets swarm with harlots' (Luddy 2007: 81). In contrast to these depictions of threatening women is Ferriter's assertion that there were few legal measures to protect young girls and women against sexual violence, and that rates of infanticide in the early decades of the state were shockingly high compared with other European countries (2009: 119–27).

Efforts to restore sexual morality were endorsed through the institution of several acts which placed restrictions on freedom of expression: the Censorship of Films Act (1923); the 1926 *Report on Evil Literature* which prohibited the circulation of material about contraception and abortion; and the 1929 Censorship of Publications Act, which banned 'indecent or obscene books'. Kate O'Brien's novels fell foul of the 1929 Act, but interestingly her 1926 play *Distinguished Villa*, which is included here, was written for the English stage and censored by the Lord Chamberlain's Office. Changes made to O'Brien's original script included the removal of,

> the lines that gestured towards the pleasure of sex and its potential to be
> enjoyed as part of a temporary rather than lasting relationship ('we were both

only having a bit of fun' 'it was only once') and . . . some of the lines that
emphasise how sex might lead to the birth of children outside of wedlock.
(Moran 2018: 13–14)

Theatre was not subject to a censor in Ireland; instead, public opinion, self-censorship
and the gatekeepers of cultural institutions prevailed. Of the plays included in this
collection, Marcardle's *Witch's Brew* was rejected by the Abbey and, following the
submission of O'Leary's *The Woman* to the Abbey, Yeats requested amendments to
the ending (see play introduction for further details). Deevy had six plays produced at
the Abbey but *Wife to James Whelan* was rejected in 1942, and apart from its production
of *Light Falling* in 1948, the Abbey ceased to support her work. The Gate took risks
and staged work – like *Youth's the Season – ?* – that was too daring for the Abbey. In
that play the son of the house, Desmond, is clearly gay and is referred to by one of the
characters as a 'pansy', while another nicknames him Flossie. Yet, his family,
neighbours and friends seem generally unperturbed by his sexuality. A surprising
feature of a number of these plays is the relative frankness of their depiction of sexuality
and sexual desire. Several of the plays depict women's passion and desire: notably
Distinguished Villa and *The Woman*. In the latter play, O'Leary represents the woman
of the title and her avid longing for love and passion, seeking it first in the men of the
village and finally in death. Although the villagers shun her and decry her as a 'jade'
and a 'black-eyed slut', the audience are drawn into sympathy with this otherworldly
young woman who seeks to draw her lover Maurice away from his family and his
motherless children, into her sole embrace. She is contrasted in the play with the
patient, gentle Kitty, who is also in love with Maurice.

The literary and realistic aesthetic of most of these plays appears to focus the
audience's attention on plot and dialogue. However, the characters' irrepressible
corporeal energies, as expressed in the stage directions, are undeniable. In *Witch's
Brew,* Blanid makes a startling entrance as she runs in, laughing, her '*black hair and
streaming rags wet and dishevelled*'. Likewise, Ellen Dunn's dynamic entrance on-
stage in Act Two: '*She is very agile, and moves with quick, rhythmic, feline grace.*' In
Act Three, Ellen is seen repeatedly jumping up from her seat; conveying the vitality
and defiance which characterizes Grace Gifford Plunkett's cartoon of the production
(see Figure 3). Ellen's defiant corporeal expression is placed centre-stage. In contrast,
Ilina's movements in *Bluebeard* are often contained: at times, limp and aimless. The
chorus of Ghosts gain power in the finale as they converge menacingly on Bluebeard,
but they are 'scattered' and 'crumple' in the closing moments of the play. Aoife McGrath
points to the period's 'strict definitions of permissible bodies' and that 'Yeats' dance
plays were a wonderful site of exciting experimentation and resistance to the status
quo' (2013: 51). Contemporaneously, *Bluebeard* captured the regulation of women's
bodies through the form of the ballet-poem, danced and choreographed by Ninette
de Valois, who had worked with the Ballets Russes and brought contemporary
European dance influences to the Irish stage. 'Foreign' influences were also evidenced
in social dance as jazz 'invaded' Ireland's dance halls; a space which offered
women relative freedom within the public sphere. The Public Dance Halls Act of 1935
confined dance meetings to licensed premises and imposed a government tax on
admission tickets. The Act was the result of pressure from the Anti-Jazz Campaign,

supported by the Catholic clergy and the Gaelic League, who highlighted the purity and authenticity of traditional Irish dancing, in contrast to corrupting foreign influences. These sentiments are captured in the *Kerryman* newspaper: 'The jazz spirit – in everything as well as dancing – is responsible for whatever decadence there is in the country' (17 March 1928, quoted in Ryan 2002: 183). The plays in this anthology relish this perceived decadence; 'inappropriate' corporeal expression persists in the 'silent' margins of the stage directions in the more overtly realist plays, and the creativity of women's bodily intention is explicitly presented, although ultimately defeated, in *Bluebeard.*

The boundaries of space and theatrical form

The space for women to explore their freedom and expression contracted in the Free State years. Nowhere is this more evident than the space of the home, private and institutional, as a framework through which to discipline women and enforce adherence to restrictive models of femininity. Women served the state through motherhood and her 'life within the home'; although the impossibility of embodying the Virgin Mother meant that all women were doomed to failure. The Carrigan Report (1931) presented evidence of rising illegitimacy rates and sexual crimes, undermining the project of national identity formation which rested upon the purity of women. James M. Smith outlines the newly independent state's response to what it deemed to be 'problem' women and children: the construction of 'Ireland's architecture of containment' which

1 Set photograph, *A Disciple* by Teresa Deevy. Premiere: 24 August 1931. Abbey Theatre Digital Archive, Hardiman Library, NUI Galway.

'encompassed an array of interdependent institutions: industrial and reformatory schools, mother and baby homes, adoption agencies, and Magdalen asylums, among others' (2007: 2). The punitive nature of this regime and the appalling treatment of the women and children in these homes is living history, and Ireland is still grappling with the legacy of stigma and shame.[6] Of the plays collected here, the only one which explicitly addresses the plight of the 'fallen woman' is O'Brien's play. Although the play is set in London, we are left in no doubt as to Gwen's fear of becoming an unmarried mother: 'I've always been respectable! I can't go wrong like that!' The threat of confinement to the space of the home threads through the plays in this collection, most violently with the bloody chamber of Bluebeard's castle. The impossibility of escape is captured in the conclusion to *Youth's the Season – ?* as Toots is left sobbing: 'I can't unlock the door! Help me, Desmond. Somebody. Let me out.'

Through the theatre, these women playwrights carved out a space for expression which refused confinement to the role of wife and mother, as endorsed by the Constitution; moreover, they refused to be restrained by dominant theatrical forms. Realism is notoriously difficult to define, but these plays – with the exception of *Bluebeard* and *Witch's Brew* – might all be described as kinds of stage realism. Visually, theatrical sets tend to be detailed and are often set in the drawing room or the kitchen. Of these plays, *Youth's the Season– ?* and *Distinguished Villa* are set in drawing rooms (Figure 2; see also the production shot from Deevy's *A Disciple*, Figure 1), while *The Woman* is set in rural 'peasant' interiors and the cultivated outdoor space of farmland. The urgent need to push the boundaries of space and form is articulated by Mary Manning: 'We are going through the difficult and hazardous process of becoming a nation once again. . . . We can never again be described as an Abbey kitchen interior, entirely surrounded by the bog!' (Pine 2018: 87). We could extend this metaphor to address how women's 'becoming' is hampered by the confines of the realist domestic space. Cathy Leeney suggests that the stage space in *Witch's Brew* 'works allegorically as a representation of the nation, sealed off from, yet not immune to, the huge cultural and political energies without' (Leeney 2010: 121). Eva Gore-Booth's *The Buried Life of Deirdre* (written in 1908 and published in 1930) brings a new dimension to the popular myth of Deirdre by presenting her as a reincarnated 'old and jealous king'. The utopian possibility of *The Buried Life of Deirdre* is associated with the god Mannanán, the underground passage and nature, and is made tangible through Deirdre's reincarnated body which evokes 'the freedom of the wind blowing through the world without barriers' (Gore-Booth 1930: 61). Gore-Booth's belief in an alternative future through the generation of spaces of possibility for women was a vital contribution in 1930s Ireland. It is the case that in many of the plays collected here, the realistic aesthetic is reshaped by the influences of expressionism (*Youth's the Season – ?*), the incorporation of pagan or folklore elements (*Witch's Brew*, *Bluebeard*), or innovations with genre (*Distinguished Villa*, *The Woman*). In *Witch's Brew* and *The Woman*, outside spaces,

---

6   Following the long-awaited publication of the Mother and Baby Homes Commission of Investigation Report in 2021, survivors of the system were appalled to discover that their oral testimony had been effectively silenced. See the 'rewriting' of the 'Executive Summary' by twenty-five academics who, through a feminist legal approach, re-examine the evidence available to the Commission: https://www.tudublin.ie/explore/news/rights-and-the-mother-and-baby-homes-report-launch.html

associated with the realm of the supernatural and folklore, offer an alternative to the domestic; Ellen chooses death in the waters of Poulgorm. *The Woman, Witch's Brew* and *Bluebeard* overlap in their interrogation of the convergence of femininity, death, beauty and punishment. Stasis, death and suicide (men and women) pervade the plays in this anthology.

Patricia Schroeder makes the case for feminist realism in the American theatre, in terms that are interesting to consider for these plays. She warns against ahistorical readings of women's plays, pointing to the radical potential of early realism and the opportunities it offered women to express their own realities, which were often at odds with those of the wider society (1996: 47). She notes that women writers often depicted 'the entrapment of women within domestic roles' and argues that critics like Sue-Ellen Case are correct to suggest that realism's family focus 'posits women as a dependent sexual "other"' (Case, quoted in Schroeder 1996: 48). However, 'such criticism sometimes overlooks . . . the protest agenda of many such depictions' (Schroeder 1996: 48). Schroeder also points out that issues that might seem simplistic to us may have been 'complex feminist issues' in their time (1996: 45). Writing to Lennox Robinson in September 1929, Margaret O'Leary expresses her anger and dismay at the Dublin critic's response to *The Woman*. She remarks that they seem to think that 'all peasant drama must be in the Synge or Murray mode, and therefore any drama in which new ground is broken is to them unintelligible' (O'Leary 1929a). The 'healthy normality of Kitty' and the passion of Ellen is 'lost on them' (O'Leary 1929a). O'Leary's innovation in the peasant drama genre, though appreciated by Yeats, Robinson and Joseph Holloway, was not admired by most of the Dublin critics. In December of the same year she again wrote to Robinson, this time to defend and explain the central character of Mona in an unnamed play that she describes as her 'second', and that the Abbey rejected. O'Leary argues that Mona is 'thirsting for life' and searching for something to believe in, but Robinson's feedback 'dismissed her summarily as "pert" and "unsympathetic"' (O'Leary 1929b). She sought to create a 'psychological analysis' of this complex character, but it was misunderstood. Interestingly, she also comments that the reviewers praised the character of 'Mrs Bailey' who O'Leary regards as an example of 'stock figures, with stock expressions, stock peculiarities, stock minds' (O'Leary 1929b).

O'Brien's play was innovative for its focus on a largely disregarded social class, the English lower middle class of the inter-war years. This play was acclaimed by the critics, though O'Brien in her letters notices that St. John Ervine criticized the work quite sharply; she feels that he intended to 'put me in my place . . . and took a column and a half to do it! I think he was unfair in spots' (1926). The review of the amateur Dublin production at the Abbey in January 1929 is mixed, describing it as 'by no means great work' but 'interesting' (J. W. G. 1929). The play also challenged social norms in its representation of extra-marital sex and pregnancy, though the resort to forced and unwilling marriage in the end was perhaps understood to preserve a sense of decency. O'Brien's evocation of despair is stylistically very different to Manning's, but their characters are similarly represented as trapped by the demands of middle-class respectability. As in her novels, O'Brien skilfully and delicately evokes suppressed love and sexual passion so realistically that it is startling to the audience. Like O'Brien, Manning's extraordinary play with its bleak and comic second act, and proto-absurdist figure of Horace Egosmith, found its stage outside the Abbey. It is tempting to see her

Protestant upper-middle class as existing on the margins of the nation that the Abbey was committed to staging, similarly to O'Brien's English characters. With their apparent focus on Irish peasant life, Deevy and O'Leary were produced at the Abbey, but there were attempts to 'correct' their innovations through revisions to the text.

The 'determined survival' of a women's theatre tradition

Women playwrights undoubtedly had some notable success in the 1920s and 1930s but increasingly struggled to get their work staged on their terms. Cathy Leeney argues,

> From the vantage point of the twenty-first century, one looks back to Irish
> women in theatre in the 1920s and 1930s with sympathy and admiration for
> their determined survival, and for their ingenious use of theatrical codes and
> devices to write dramas that could accommodate complex levels of meaning.
> (Leeney 2007: 23)

The rich collection of plays in this anthology navigates these 'complex levels of meaning' through the manipulation of theatrical form and space, and locates resistance in unruly and creative feminized bodies. But why is there not more awareness of the work? Theatre history, and the linear narrative of the male-dominated literary canon of Irish theatre, has not proven to be accommodating of women's voices and contributions, as Hill (2019) demonstrates. Thankfully, there is ongoing vital and innovative scholarship to correct these silences. In relation to the timeframe of this anthology, Leeney's *Irish Women Playwrights 1900–1939: Gender and Violence on Stage* (2010) is seminal. Later, Hill's (2019) reimagining of Irish theatre history as genealogical rather than chronological, and Melissa Sihra's work (2018) in reclaiming Augusta Gregory and bringing her writing into a new relationship with contemporary playwright Marina Carr, have advanced this process further. The work of forging the connections between women in Irish theatre is vital to the assembly of a women's theatrical tradition. In 1937, Hanna Sheehy Skeffington gave a talk on Irish women writers at the Minerva Club, the Women's Freedom League's social centre in London. It was 'crowded beyond its capacity' and Kate O'Brien chaired the meeting. Sheehy Skeffington detailed the work of contemporary poets and novelists, and with regard to theatre, she highlighted the work of 'the dramatists Dorothy Macardle, Margaret O'Leary and Maura Mallory' (*sic*, presumably Abbey playwright Maura Molloy; Ward 2017: 343), thereby publicly asserting a women's theatrical tradition.

These networks played an important role in sustaining the 'determined survival' of women writers of the Free State years and beyond. One such Irish network was the Women Writers' Club, established in 1933 by poet Blanaid Salkeld with Dorothy Macardle as Chair. The network met regularly and awarded annual prizes over the course of twenty-five years (see Figure 5). The Club offered a forum to discuss wider social and political matters, and its very presence asserted women's freedom of expression and their place in the public sphere. In her biography of Rosamund Jacob (who is included in the photo, Figure 5), Lane asserts the importance of the 'social and cultural events attended by Jacob [which] offered a sense of community and an outlet for a single woman' (2010: 202). These events and networks also nurtured feminist politics during a conservative period. In her history of the women's movement in Ireland, Linda Connolly corrects the narrative that feminism 'disappeared' in the 1920s and 1930s, as 'a core cadre of lifelong committed feminists continued to mobilise while experiencing alienation, marginalisation and isolation in the post-independence period' (Connolly 2003: 82). Connolly points to abeyance organizations which 'retained a structure capable of absorbing both intensely committed feminists ... and a much larger constituency of activists who did not necessarily refer to feminism' (Connolly 2003: 83). The Women Writers' Club encompassed committed feminists in its membership, including Sheehy Skeffington and Jacob. Many of the women associated with the plays in this anthology were connected through membership of this forum, including: Dorothy Macardle, Kate O'Brien, Mary Devenport O'Neill and Ria Mooney. Of the women in the photo, Sybil Le Broquy (writing under the name Helen Staunton) was a member of the Dublin Drama League and had a play produced by the New Players at the Peacock (*In Passing*, 1929), while poet Blanaid Salkeld had a verse play staged by the Dublin Drama League at the Gate (*Scarecrow Over the Corn*, 1941). Other theatrical women linked to the Club include Teresa Deevy, Christine Longford, Maura Laverty and Helen Waddell. During the conservative Free State years, these women encountered obstacles to asserting their theatrical voices and fought hard to be heard, yet their silencing is reimposed by neglect. It is our hope that making these plays accessible will lead to their revival, fuller inclusion in teaching and scholarship, and consequently, a reframing of Irish theatre history.

Distinguished Villa

Kate O'Brien

Premiere: 2 May 1926 in an amateur production at the Aldwych Theatre, London, performed by The Repertory Players.

Professional premiere: 12 July 1926 at the Haymarket Theatre, London; cast list given below. The Irish premiere took place in January 1929 at the Abbey Theatre in Dublin, but it was not produced by the Abbey.

'Natty' Hemworth	Ivor Barnard
Mabel Hemworth	Una O'Connor
Gwendolyn Tupman	Gillian Lind
Frances Llewellyn	Clare Harris
Alec Webberley	Henry Hoare
John Morris	William Stack

Kate O'Brien (1897–1974) was born in Limerick and educated at a French convent school there, becoming the youngest boarder at the age of five after her mother's death. She began her career as a freelance journalist and worked in the foreign language department of the *Guardian* newspaper. She travelled widely, spending time in the USA and Spain and living for many years in England. Her connection to Spain is evident in her novels and is commemorated by the University of Malaga with the Kate O'Brien Award.

O'Brien's literary career spanned five decades, and *Distinguished Villa* is her first work. It was apparently written in a couple of weeks, as a bet, and it was first performed by the amateur company The Repertory Players at the Aldwych Theatre in London, in May 1926. It was very well received and was given a professional production at the Haymarket Theatre the following July. The play was not produced by the Abbey Theatre, Dublin but an amateur production directed by Mrs Kirkwood-Hackett played there on 28 January 1929.[1] O'Brien followed this with two more plays on a similar theme of sexual dissatisfaction in the English middle class: *The Bridge* (1927), which was critically panned, and *Gloria Gish* (1931), which was never produced. *Gloria Gish* coincided with the publication of her first novel, *Without My Cloak*, in 1931, which won the Hawthornden Prize and the James Tait Black Memorial Prize, and established O'Brien as a promising novelist. Her best-known works include *The Ante Room* (1934), *Mary Lavelle* (1936) and *Land of Spices* (1940), which draws on her childhood experiences at convent school. The latter two novels were banned in Ireland by the Censorship Board.

---

1 See Moran (2018), also review by J. W. G. (1929), 'Distinguished Villa', *Irish Independent*, 28 January 1929.

Distinguished Villa is set in Brixton in the lower-middle-class family home of Natty and Mabel, where they live with Mabel's younger sister Gwen and the refined and well-educated lodger Frances Llewellyn. Two men provide the love interest: John Morris, unhappily engaged to Gwen but really suited to Frances, and Alec Webberley, who fruitlessly pursues Frances but engages in a flirtation with Gwen. Produced concurrently with Sean O'Casey's *The Plough and the Stars*, the plays were inevitably compared, and O'Casey wrote O'Brien a supportive letter after her play's premiere. *Distinguished Villa*'s focus on lower-middle-class life was unusual at the time on the English stage. Realistic in style, the work explores female sexuality and contrasts Mabel, who implies that she does not have a physical relationship with her husband Natty because of the 'delicate state' of her health, with her younger sister, who at the play's climax is pregnant outside of marriage having slept with both John and Alec. Gwen's pregnancy destroys the potential happiness of Frances and John, when Alec refuses to admit that the pregnancy is his responsibility and John (believing the child to be his own) is forced to marry Gwen. Meanwhile Natty's quiet desperation, which is traced delicately through the play, culminates in his off-stage suicide in the closing scenes.

The work was censored by the Lord Chamberlain's Office to remove Gwen's explicit statement, 'I'm going to have a baby' and her references to her short relationship with Alec being only for 'fun'. Moran (2018) argues that O'Brien had intended to more fully represent female sexual agency and choice to incorporate the notion of sexuality as pleasurable, and the concept of regret. Some critics, including Eibhear Walshe and Ailbhe Smyth, argue that O'Brien's representation of female sexuality is radical in its assertion of women's capacity for sexual pleasure and autonomy outside of marriage or monogamy. However, Cronin (2010) argues that she must be located within her historical moment, taking the individual in modern society as her topic. O'Brien treats sexuality as a vital force, examining in all her writing the tensions for the free individual regulating her own conduct within a set of externally fixed norms and mores, which can trap her characters into dishonest actions, or conversely into honourable self-sacrifice.

Though set in England, *Distinguished Villa* sits alongside the other work in this collection in its thematic focus on the intimate and underexamined lives of women. Like the work of Teresa Deevy, it illustrates the potential for a feminist dramaturgy, in its detailed portrayal of the quiet misery of respectability and its realistic representation of female desire and sexuality.

Plays of the Moment: "Distinguished Villa," at the Little Theatre.

THE AFFECTION-STARVED NATTY FINDS SYMPATHY WITH FRANCES: MR. IVOR BARNARD AND MISS CLARE HARRIS.

THE TRAGIC FINALE: JOHN MORRIS (WILLIAM STACK) PREVENTS MABEL (MISS UNA O'CONNOR) FROM ENTERING THE KITCHEN WHERE NATTY HAS COMMITTED SUICIDE.

MABEL HEMWORTH ARRANGES HER LODGERS' LOVE AFFAIRS: L. TO R., ALEC (HENRY HOARE), FRANCES (CLARE HARRIS), MABEL (UNA O'CONNOR), AND GWENDOLINE (GILLIAN LIND).

" Distinguished Villa," by Kate O'Brien, the young Irish playwright, has just been produced at the Little Theatre, after having been given in the spring by a Sunday play-producing society. It is an interesting piece of work. Mabel Hemworth, the châtelaine of " Distinguished Villa," Brixton, is the epitome of acid gentility, and her husband, Natty, has been starved for want of affection all their married life. The arrival of Frances, the charming lodger, gives him an inkling of what life might be with a sympathetic companion. Troubles then overtake all the Brixton circle. Gwendoline loves Alec not wisely but too well, and when John is accused of being the cause of her trouble, he is quixotic enough to marry her. Natty seeks the happiness denied him at home by going in for a common intrigue, and the play ends with his suicide.—[Photographs by Sasha.]

THE CHÂTELAINE OF " DISTINGUISHED VILLA ": MISS UNA O'CONNOR AS MABEL HEMWORTH.

2 *Distinguished Villa* by Kate O'Brien. *The Sketch*, 28 July 1926, p. 180. 'Plays of the Moment: "Distinguished Villa" at the Little Theatre.' Photographs by 'Sasha', image © Illustrated London News Group. Courtesy of Mary Evans Picture Library.

Characters

'Natty' Hemworth
Mabel Hemworth
Gwendolyn Tupman
Frances Llewellyn
Alec Webberley
John Morris

Time – Present day.
Scene – Sitting-room in the Hemworths' house in Brixton.

Act One – A Sunday afternoon in early spring.
Act Two – Saturday evening, four months later.
Act Three – Next day.

Act One

The sitting-room in the **Hemworths***' house is small and noisily furnished. It has been cleaned and polished to an intense degree. The floor is covered in red Brussels carpet of an uncompromising floral design. The walls are treated with a glossy cream-coloured paper – satin striped, of the Ideal Home variety – and the frieze that finishes it off under the white picture rail is a neat thing of apples and pears. In the centre of the back wall there is a spotless white door which leads into the hall of the house. To the left of the stage a similar door goes on the kitchen and back premises. Further down on the left side is a fire-place of coloured marble, and over it an oak overmantel, full of little shelves and mirrors. All the little shelves are filled up with vases and jugs. The fire-place itself is neatly filled with white paper frills. The fender is magnificently polished, and in front of it lies a snowy sheepskin rug. The right side of the stage is filled by a large bow-window, each pane tidily screened half-way up, and with long curtains of cream lace, looped back at each side with brass chains. Between these curtains three well-grown aspidistras flourish on an oak stand. In the right-hand corner of the stage there is a cabinet gramophone. There is an oak dining-table in the middle of the room, and in the centre of this a little pot of maidenhair, with some small white swans, on a piece of mirror. A number of stiff oak chairs are ranged about the room, but there are one or two more or less comfortable ones drawn up near the table and a well-used rocking-chair near the fire. Birmingham gas-fittings with pink glass shades are a characteristic item. When the curtain rises the bright sun of an April afternoon is flooding in from the bay-window. The gramophone is at work and is already nearing the end of the refrain of Tosti's 'Parted'.*
'**Natty' Hemworth** *is standing facing the window, listening with attentive pleasure. He is a small, slightly built man in his middle thirties with sleek mouse-coloured hair and a small pale face. He is, in fact, rather boyish-looking. His eyes are sunken and gentle. His cheap blue suit is of a very new cut, and his stiff butterfly collar gleams immaculately. His tie, of light blue poplin, matches his socks. A white piqué slip is arranged under his waistcoat. His cuffs are well pulled down, and he wears a ring. His entire appearance suggests a very neat man and one who enjoys his clothes.*

The door on the left of the stage is open, and as the song proceeds **Mabel Hemworth** *skips briskly to and from the kitchen on trivial housewife's business.*

Mrs Hemworth *is taller than her husband. Sparely made, she moves about cheerfully on neat blackshod feet. Her hair is frizzed, but in moderation, as becomes a matron. Her face is small and colourless, and there are no lashes and no shadows about her little wide-open eyes. Her mouth has no colour, but she smiles easily and often. Her chin is very firm, and her nose, though of course it never does sniff, seems somehow to suggest a vague superiority in its wearer. Sometimes one would swear to an actual sniff. One would be wrong.* **Mrs Hemworth** *never powders her nose. This Sunday she wears a spotless and frilly blouse of pale pink crepe de Chine, and her dark skirt is protected by a small Sunday apron. She wears some jewellery, discreet earrings, a brooch, a few rings and a gold wristwatch. Her speaking voice is high and clear, and her accent very careful, especially with strangers. Her husband's voice is very soft, his accent Cockney. Once as she moves about,* **Mrs Hemworth** *pauses to listen more attentively, shaking her head dubiously at what she hears; then she resumes her trotting and humming.* **Mr Hemworth** *remains dreamily by the window until the conclusion of the song, when he goes towards the gramophone and stops it, still looking thoughtful.*

Mabel   There's something about that record that doesn't seem becoming on Sunday, Natty.

Natty   But why, Mabel? It's one of our very best.

Mabel (*who has just been galvanised by catching sight of the open window*)   Good gracious! The window wide open! The Smithsons have heard every word – and Mr Smithson's such a refined man, and so religious. Yes! I can see Mrs Smithson in her drawing-room.

Natty   Glad the poor dear's had a treat. Why, what's wrong, Mabel?

Mabel   How stupid of you, Natty! I wouldn't offend them for the world. The best connected people on the Avenue, and always so attentive to me!

Natty   How are we offending them?

Mabel   Well, I don't like to refer to it, but it does make me go hot and cold to think of Mrs Smithson hearing such advanced words from our gramophone. I never did approve of that second verse.

Natty   There's no harm, Mabel, really. Only a bit of strong feeling.

Mabel   No harm in a bit of strong feeling? What's coming over you, Natty Hemworth? No harm in all that talk about the night? Oh, I'd blush to quote it, I would indeed.

Natty   Well, I know you don't care for that subject, Mabel, but it's only a song, you know.

Mabel   You can't be too delicate for me, in songs or in anything else. I was brought up in nice ways, and I'll never turn from them. Anything coarse upsets me, Natty, as you know. Oh, I do hope Mr Smithson wasn't listening! He has such a high opinion of me.

Natty   Never mind, Mabel, I'll do away with the record; maybe people are a bit too outspoken nowadays.

Mabel   Refined people are never outspoken.

Natty   Want another record?

Mabel   No (*Sitting down by table and unfolding* Sunday Pictorial.), I'm tired, I'll read.

Natty (*coming nearer*)   . . . You look done up. Why do you work so hard, Mabel?

Mabel   I hope I know what I owe to my home.

Natty   If you don't, who does?

Mabel   Who does, indeed? That's what Mrs Barwell was saying to me. What a model my home is to the Avenue. She is a nice woman. Not so well connected as the Smithsons, but she has a smart husband.

Natty   Barwell's a good chap.

Mabel   Mrs Barwell tells me that he thinks the world of me. Oh well, I'll be getting vain, I declare, if I listen to the people round here. Oh dear me! There's that pain again! Oh! Oh!

Natty   There you are, Mabel!

Mabel (*gulping it down*)   Ah! That's better. Instant relief it gives me. I really must say that Dr Broad understands my constitution. No easy matter.

Natty   Really better? Poor Mabel, you work too hard at this blooming house. I wish you hadn't to work so hard.

Mabel   And what would become of your nice home, I wonder, if I didn't work hard? I hope that whatever I do will always be a credit to me. Mr Smithson – I never told you this, I declare! – was joking me again last evening. He always has a joke for me. He said, 'I'll cut you dead if you don't put up the name I've given your house, "Distinguished Villa".'

Natty   'Distinguished Villa'! Why! we'd hurt everyone's feelings round here. It'd never do.

Mabel   But it *is* a nice name, and this *is* the most refined home on the Avenue. It does me as much credit, Mr Smithson says, as my husband's happy face every morning going to the train.

Natty (*edging nearer and touching her frizzed hair*)   Take off that apron, Mabel, will you?

Mabel   What for?

Natty   Dunno! Just because I'd like you to.

Mabel   That's the only reason, silly? (*Very brightly.*) I never take off my apron at home, and you know it. Don't fiddle at my hair, Natty. Sit down. What makes you so fidgety lately?

Natty   Dunno. Am I fidgety? I say, Mabel, give a chap a kiss?

Mabel (*laughing gaily*)   You are funny! I wish the Smithsons heard you. It isn't every man wants to kiss his wife after eleven years in harness! You certainly are lucky.

Natty   Well, kiss me, won't you?

Mabel   In the middle of Sunday afternoon. Be off with you! Supposing my sister Gwen came in – or our nice Miss Llewellyn?

Natty   It'd be fine encouragement for Gwen now she's thinking of fixing up with John – and I don't believe Ethelberta would mind!

Mabel   Why ever do you call Miss Llewellyn by those fancy names of yours? Ethelberta indeed! And yesterday I heard you calling her Mildred – and Daisy, if you please!

Natty   Oh, she don't mind, she's a real sport in her quiet way. She knows my little tricks by now. It only makes her laugh. She's a real nice one.

Mabel   Indeed she is that, I must say. And anyone can see that she's highly connected. Her way of speaking reminds me of Lady Ulverston and her friends – whom I used to meet at the Red Cross depot. That's why you'd please me by treating her more respectfully, Natty. I like having such a refined person lodging in my home.

Natty   She's a queer fish; she told me this morning that she likes Ethelberta best of all my names for her.

Mabel (*coyly*)   Oh well, we shan't have her long, I'll be bound. Her young gentleman was here this morning. He has a nice way with him! I shouldn't wonder if they were looking for a new librarian soon. He is mad about her. That's plain.

Natty   It takes two to make a match. Ethelberta's in no hurry, I'll bet.

Mabel   Well, what girl would choose to go on listing up books in a Free Library when she could be married to a smart young gentleman? Woman's true sphere is in the home. I've always held to that, Natty, and always will. That sounds like Gwen!

Enter **Gwendolyn Tupman** *from hall. She is tall and slim, and twenty-one years old. Exquisite to look at, fairhaired with white skin and with wide childish eyes. Carefully and showily dressed, addicted to strings of beads and cosmetics, she is yet unable to suppress her 'blessed damozel' beauty. She speaks in a high ill-educated tone, but her manner is quiet on the whole. She is a silly sort of girl, but there is a very young appeal about her, and her great beauty disturbs and interests most people for a time. She drifts in now, looking vaguely sulky.*

Natty (*smiling*)   Well, Gwendolyn my child, all dolled up for John?

Gwen (*smiling back*)   He's due round any time now. (*Sits down near fire.*) Said he'd take me to the Olympic to-night.

Natty   They tell me there's a great film on there this week. Any chance you'd come along one night, Mabel?

Mabel (*with a bright laugh*)   How often have I told you, Natty, that Dr Broad won't hear of my sitting in such an atmosphere! Goodness knows, I find it hard to deny myself that little pleasure – but my health is important to us both, I presume?

Mabel *has become interested in the paper;* **Natty** *surveys the beautiful* **Gwen** *kindly for a minute – then laughs.*

Natty (*to* **Gwen**)   You are a beauty, Gwen, and no mistake. When's the happy event?

Gwen   Oh, I don't know. John doesn't seem to know exactly. Some time in the summer, I suppose.

Natty   I've noticed he gets moody-looking at times. Poor chap! Bet it's the money that's worrying 'im. His bookshop can't be doing too well, I should think. I'll lend a hand with the money business, old girl. Just give him a hint of that. You can mention it easier than I can.

Mabel   Well, Natty Hemworth, of all the oddities! Afraid of hurting him, I suppose! You're always thinking of people's feelings. Where you get such rum notions, I can't think. I've no wish to pry, Gwen, but it *has* struck me lately that John might be getting a move on. But if you will keep company with such an odd individual as John Morris, of course it's no business of mine. Nowadays we must all manage our own affairs, eh, Natty?

Natty   H'm. Funny how hard it is to talk about one's own affairs!

Gwen   You're queer, Natty. Whenever you've nothing to do, if anyone makes an ordinary remark, you answer just like you did now. Sort of sad.

Natty   Good reason for keeping me occupied, then!

Mabel   Finding out his secret sorrow, eh, Gwen? Well, I can answer for him – he hasn't got one, of that I'm sure. It's the pictures are getting you, my girl – making you pay attention to casual remarks. It's a bad habit. By the way – is Miss Llewellyn in?

Gwen   She's in her room writing. I've just been talking to her. I never saw such a place for books. She's awfully nice – says I can borrow any I want. But they are all so dull, worse luck!

Natty   Don't you think she might like to come and sit here? Must be pretty lonely for the poor girl upstairs. Shall I call here down?

Mabel   She has sat here chatting to me before now. I must say I like her company. But we mustn't be too pushing, Natty!

Natty   She doesn't say much, but I think she likes to be with people.

Mabel   Well, perhaps if you like to ask her nicely, she might care to sit down here with us and do her writing.

Natty *goes out.*

Natty   Ethelberta! Ethelberta!

Mabel   Don't call! Go and ask her politely.

Natty   Righto, Mabel.

Gwen   Through with the *Sunday Pictorial*, Mabel?

Mabel   Yes; not that I think it suitable reading for a young girl like you, nor any of the Sunday papers.

Natty (*coming in*)   She'll be down in a minute.

Mabel   Put that chair up to the table for her, Gwen. She'll want to sit there to write.

Natty *jumps across very briskly and sets a chair close to the end of the table. He then selects a cushion, shakes it, and places it carefully on the back of the chair.*

Natty (*musing*)   I wonder which record she likes best?

Gwen   I don't think she's overstruck on any of them. Funny thing, you know, John doesn't like any of my pet records. I can't make out what's wrong with 'Pale hands I loved'. He shouts at me if I put it on!

Mabel   Shouts at you indeed? Well, I'm bothered! A gentleman may shout at his fiancée nowadays! No gentleman ever shouted at me. I knew what was owing to my dignity – of that I'm sure.

Gwen   Oh, John don't mean it, Mabel.

Mabel   I heard Miss Llewellyn's door shut. Don't start the gramophone now, Natty; we want a little peace.

Enter **Frances Llewellyn**. *She looks about twenty-eight, and is slim and tall. Her dark brown hair is closely shingled. Her face is leanly cut in noble lines. Her eyes are gentle and merry, her skin pale. She is dressed rather boyishly, too, with a rakish, Bohemian touch, and in luminous colours. Her colourful distinction strikes out shrilly in the little room, but her movements and general air are very quiet, and her voice is always low. She carries one or two books and writing materials, and seems a little diffident.* **Natty** *goes to her at once, and takes her belongings out of her hands, closing the door for her, and indicating a chair. While she talks to* **Mabel**, *he busies himself placing her things on the table, taking quick pleased glances at her as he does so.*

Frances (*to* **Mabel**)   You are very good to let me come downstairs like this, Mrs Hemworth.

Mabel   Not at all, Miss Llewellyn. If there is one thing I do like to feel about this house, it is that everyone in it is at home. You mustn't look on it as lodgings. It's your home, for as long as you care to stay in it.

Frances (*moving towards her own chair and speaking shyly*)   You take wonderful care of me, Mrs Hemworth. (*As she says this, she sits down and plays with her writing things.*)

Mabel   Well, I try to make people comfortable. It's very nice to know that you are satisfied, Miss Llewellyn. But we must not chat to you now. You want to write.

Frances (*suddenly eager*)   No, please – please talk to me. I like voices. I never hear any in the library.

Mabel   Indeed, it must be trying for you to be shut up there all the week. Books! Books! My nerves could never stand them: of that I am sure. By the way – I almost forgot – I beg your pardon, dear Miss Llewellyn – it's something most important! (*Very coyly.*) Can you guess? No? Well, then, I'll tell you. Mr Webberley called on you this morning in his smart little car. He was most disappointed you were out! He stayed quite a long while chatting with us. He is a good-looking gentleman. Said he'd call again this afternoon. I do call that attentive!

Frances (*vaguely, but embarrassed*)   Ye-es.

Gwen   He's very like a new man I've seen on the pictures. I've forgotten the name. I'll find out for you, Miss Llewellyn. I can easily. Wears his hat the same way, too. Mr Webberley does dress well, doesn't he?

Frances (*writing, and looking dimly amused*)   Excellently, I should think. What was he wearing this morning?

Natty   Sorry, I didn't see him. Clothes is where I shine, you know! Show him to me, Ethelberta, and I'll put him through his points. I wasn't named Natty for nothing.

Frances   Natty?

Mabel   Yes, don't you see – everyone calls him 'Natty' because he is always so well-dressed.

Frances   Natty? Ah! Of course.

Mabel   Yes, I must say that in that respect he does me credit. My husband must be smart, Miss Llewellyn.

Natty   Oh, I like to be well turned out.

Frances   Yes, you must live up to your name. May I call you Natty?

Mabel   Certainly, Miss Llewellyn – of course. If it's not too free and easy for you. Everyone round here knows Natty Hemworth.

Natty   Bit of a celebrity, you see!

Mabel   Well, although I do say it myself, Miss Llewellyn, we are rather famous round here. Especially in the Avenue (*Looking bright and coy and mysterious.*) people often ask me how I do it, and all the rest of it!

Natty (*moving away and looking a little weary*)   Ah, Mabel, cut out that rot. Ethelberta wants to write.

Mabel (*bridling good-humouredly, and with an appeal to* **Frances**)   Rot, indeed! Natty and I are known round here as the model of what a married pair should be. We've been married over eleven years, and yet everyone remarks on what a success we are, and what a nice refined home we keep. We never quarrel. I never was quarrelsome. I consider it beneath a woman's dignity. Everyone thinks us a wonder! Our friends the Smithsons were all for christening our house 'The Abode of Love' a little while ago. Very pretty and complimentary. But lately Mr Smithson wants to call it 'Distinguished Villa'. The atmosphere of the house is such a credit to me, he says.

Frances   Unwise to call it 'The Abode of Love'. There are so many interpretations. It's a rare thing, I suppose, for married people to be pleasant to each other after eleven years?

Mabel (*coyly*)   Nothing rarer, Miss Llewellyn. Believe me. And it's always the women's fault – of that I am sure. They've no hold on their husbands.

Natty (*laughing nervously*)   You're frightening our Gwen. She's got to tread the mill herself soon.

Gwen *looks up from paper and laughs.*

Mabel   Well, it's not my fault, Gwen, if you make a hash of it. My little sister's been in my care, Miss Llewellyn, ever since she was nine, and I brought her up strictly – you might say old-fashionedly; but I don't hold with any of this new nonsense for young girls. She's had a good example set her here – of that I'm sure! But everything depends on herself, of course.

Frances (*smiling at* **Gwen**)   Nothing on John? Nervous, Gwen?

Gwen   Of course not!

Frances (*stretching and looking out of the window*)   What a day it is! By the way, Natty, I bought some records yesterday. Like to try them?

Natty (*with radiant face*)   My hat! Ethelberta, you're a good sort!

Frances   They're on my table upstairs.

Natty *goes eagerly to the door.*

Mabel (*smiling self-consciously*)   I don't know if you – if – perhaps it's quite the thing, Natty! A lady's room, you know!

Frances (*laughing*)   Oh! That's quite all right, Mrs Hemworth. A flat package, Natty; thank you very much.

Exit **Natty**.

Silence falls. **Frances** *writes; the others continue to read. After a minute a motor-horn is heard.*

Gwen (*lifting her head*)   There's a car coming down the Avenue.

Mabel (*rising and peering over aspidistras*)   Here? Oh yes – why, it's Mr Webberley. Run and let him in, Gwen.

Gwen *goes slowly towards the door.* **Frances** *lifts her head and smiles vaguely towards the twittering, interested* **Mabel**, *who continues to peer.*

Mabel Ah! I can see that spying Mrs Drayley pretending not to look out of her window. You can't be too close with your own business round here. People are so vulgar-minded. No refinement at all, no dignity. I must say he does look distinguished! (*Very gay now.*) He reminds me of a nephew of Lady Ulverston's! I'm sure he's very highly connected. I really mustn't be seen peeping at your friends like this, Miss Llewellyn. Whatever do you think of me? Well, well!

She fusses about tidying the frenziedly tidy room. **Frances** *remains at the table at her work.* **Gwen**'*s voice and* **Webberley**'*s sound vaguely in the hall. After a minute they enter.* **Alec Webberley** *is what one expected to see – a handsome, well-dressed, self-assured man about town. There are so many of him everywhere that it would be fatuous to describe him now. He is young and gay and conventional. Very well-dressed. Nothing more.*

Frances (*looking up*)   Hullo!

Alec   Hullo! Glad you're in this time. (*Turning very gaily to* **Mabel**.) Turned up again, you see, Mrs Hemworth. Dreadful blighter, aren't I? You must be sick of me.

Mabel (*very bright and pleased*)   Now then, Mr Webberley, you mustn't fish for compliments from me. I was never any good at paying them, indeed! But I need not tell you that Miss Llewellyn's friends are welcome at all times, of that I'm sure!

Frances   You spoil me, Mrs Hemworth.

Mabel   While you're here I want you to be happy; but who knows when we'll be losing you!

Frances   Funereal though – for this divine day.

Alec   Yes – the divine day is responsible for my bright idea. Thought you'd like –

Mabel (*drawing ostentatiously to kitchen door*)   Well, well, we must leave you to yourselves now. You'll want to chat together, of course. Come along, Gwen.

Alec *goes to the door and opens it, bowing with particular politeness to* **Gwen**, *who goes out behind* **Mabel** *and looks at him rather deliberately.*

Gwen Thank you so much, Mr Webberley!

Exit **Mabel** *and* **Gwen**.

Alec (*coming towards* **Frances**, *and laughing*)   Good sort that woman seems to be – in a chatty style. Jolly nice for her class.

Frances (*sitting on the edge of the table*)   Ah! Then you are highly connected. Any relation to Lady Ulverston?

Alec (*irritated*)   Good beginning, Frankie. It may be that only in heaven I shall find all your lost jokes.

Frances   If I married you, you'd see them all in one, Alec.

Alec   If – does that mean – Frankie?

Frances   F-R-A-N-C-E-S – I spell it.

Alec   What harm does it do you if I call you Frankie?

Frances   Works like a blunt saw across my vertebral column, that's all.

Alec (*laughing*)   Nonsense! It suits you. Why, you're just like a boy.

Frances (*edgily*)   I'm not an atom like a boy. (*Enter* **Natty** *from hall with a flat parcel in his hands.*) Thank you, Natty. (*Going towards him and looking towards* **Alec**.*) This is Mr Webberley – Mr Hemworth. (*The men bow.* **Alec** *rather amusedly.*)

Natty   Very pleased, I'm sure. (*Sets down records and walks over to shake hands with* **Alec**.) Just been having a squint at your car, Mr Webberley. She is a beauty.

Alec   Useful little runabout. Interested in cars?

Natty   Well! I'm not up in them, you know, but I always have hoped –

Mabel (*popping her head round the kitchen door*)   Come along, Natty.

Natty   Righto, Mabel, I'm coming. Ta-ta, Mr Webberley. (*Goes towards the kitchen door.*)

Frances   We'll try the records later on.

Natty   Right you are, Ethelberta.

Alec (*with a start*)   What did that little merchant call you?

Frances   Ethelberta.

Alec   Damned cheek!

Frances   It's a joke.

Alec   And you let it go with him?

Frances   I like it.

Alec   Good Lord!

Frances   I like him to do as he likes.

Alec (*growing ironical*)   May I ask why?

Frances   Because he so seldom does.

Alec   Upon my soul, that little worm may call you pet names, but if I do it's – What did you say it was?

Frances   A blunt saw across my vertebral column, Alec.

Alec   What is a fellow to do with you?

Frances   Don't you see the difference between Frankie and Ethelberta?

Alec   No.

Frances   There's an immense difference. (*Repentant.*) I can't imagine why you keep on coming to see me. I simply don't know how to be nice to a man. But cheer up, there are heaps of girls who do.

Alec   Frankie! Oh, sorry, but really you know, you're very rough on a fellow. I came down here in such a ripping mood, but somehow that greasy little bounder seems to have got on my nerves. I can't understand why you live in this place, anyway. Of course, the women folk aren't half bad. Your little comedian's got a jolly nice wife.

Frances   Do you think so?

Alec   Rather! She's tons too good for him. He looks like a bookie's clerk. (*Good-humouredly again.*) Funny old Frankie! You're a strange girl! But you haven't answered me. Why do you live here? This room is awful.

Frances   I have my own things upstairs. It's charming.

Alec   But you're not a one-room person.

Frances   No, but I'm a lazy person. I like to be near my work, and I like to think I'm the only wage-earner in the world who hasn't a season ticket.

Alec   Well, the whole thing is idiotic – that confounded library is bad enough, but these rooms!

Frances   They are most immorally clean – and there the immorality ends. I quite agree with you about this room, or rather I did about three weeks ago when I first came. Now it's just a part of the whole. These people are kind to me, Alec. I like kindness and to be well looked after, and I'm not a millionaire. Those reasons do?

Alec   Are there any more?

Frances   Yes, there are – now. The household has begun to interest me – and I like Natty. I want to stay and look on, that's all.

Alec   You're always so keen on looking on. Surely there's nothing to look on at here?

Frances   I'm not so sure.

Alec   Well, I expect these little people have their own affairs, but I'm dashed if I can see any fun in watching them. They're no business of yours, in any case, my dear young Nosey Parker!

Frances   It's because they're no business of mine that I'm interested. I loathe my own business. I like problems in which there is no danger of my becoming involved. In fact, I'm a good old-fashioned gossip.

Alec (*yawning a little and looking casually round the room*)   Oh! (*Pause.*) Smoke? By the way, who's that girl?

Frances   That's Gwen Tupman – Mrs Hemworth's sister. Lives here. Types in Basinghall Street, Smiles & Co.

Alec   Is that a croak?

Frances   No, only a statement.

Alec (*amused, and coming close to her*)   Oh! Mustn't a man admire a pretty face?

Frances   Some men can.

Alec   Have you seen her young man?

Frances   Yes, often.

Alec   He's got a good eye for beauty. What's he like?

Frances   He's not like Natty, and he's not like you. He's not even like the cinema star that Gwen says you're like.

Alec   Gwen! When did she say that about me? When did she see me?

Frances   Oh, they peep though windows at you. They all admire you here.

Alec   Bless their hearts! Then perhaps they're better company for you than I thought. Perhaps they'll teach you to appreciate me.

Frances   Don't worry. Mrs Hemworth knows quite well that with your fascinations it's only a matter of time. She's got her shirt on you!

Alec (*very eagerly*)   Is she right? Frances darling – for the hundredth time – will you marry me?

Frances (*wearily but gently*)   Oh, I did think the Hemworths, the weather and the Hemworths' furniture might have got us through this interview without a lapse.

Alec   Be serious for one minute. I love you. I love you. I want you, Frankie. I must have you.

Frances (*shrinking away*)   Please don't say that, please!

Alec   I will. I want you to kiss me. You must!

Frances   I won't. It's idiotic of you to behave like this here. Be quiet. Let me go.

Alec   Why won't you marry me?

Frances   All over again. There are so many things it's no good saying. But this I will tell you. If I were a man I'd tell no woman I loved her until I knew beyond asking that she wanted me. I have tried to be polite, but it's unpleasant to hear a grown-up man shouting vigorously for what he can't have.

Alec   But darling, I –

Frances   Oh, I know what you're going to say. You want to give me everything and take me everywhere. But I don't love you. We don't belong together. We don't even drift towards each other. We share nothing. Don't look so wretched; if you would only realise things once and for all it would be better for us both.

Alec   But I'm unhappy, don't you see? I want you. I can't live without you. Without you everything is useless and miserable.

Frances   Because you've never before done without anything you've wanted. Isn't it amazing, when you come to think of it?

Alec   Don't be a brute, Frankie. Pulling a chap's leg like this is a bit thick, you know, in the circs.

Frances   Well, there it is. Put me out of your head. I'm sorry you've persisted in bothering about me for so long. You've had a lot of unnecessary sadness, but this won't hurt you for long, I know, and honestly I'm not the kind of wife you want.

Alec   Rot! You're the kind of wife every man wants.

Frances   Ah! I'm not simple enough to enjoy that colossal compliment. But in the end, even if it were true, there would remain my side of the business.

Alec   What do you mean?

Frances   Merely that you're not the kind of husband I want.

Alec (*with eagerness*)   What sort of husband do you want?

Frances   I wonder! I don't know. Someone rather sulky and fussy, I think. He'd be childish and groping, and very good and very bad. He'd be very uncertain sometimes, and sometimes very wise.

Alec (*sharpened*)   Were you describing anyone in special?

Frances (*very much amused*)   Good Lord, I hope not; what a knock-kneed individual he'd be! (*Vaguely, her eyes on the window.*) There is Gwen's young man at the gate. Alec, they'll want the parlour.

Alec   Right, I'll clear. Good-bye, old Frankie. But remember I'll stay the course!

Frances   Oh! I'll go to the gate with you. Come along.

Exeunt through the centre door into the hall. Their voices echo vaguely. After a second **John Morris** *comes in by the same door. He does not shut it to at once, but holding it slightly ajar, looks back towards the receding voices with diffident curiosity. After a second he jerks his head impatiently, shuts the door and walks slowly about the room. Vaguely his steps take him to the aspidistras, and there he pauses, staring through the window. From without comes the throb of a motor-engine and, vaguely still, the voices of the two who have just gone out.* **John Morris** *is tall and strongly made, but he carries himself carelessly. He stoops as a rule, and his movements are either very swift and nervous or too slow to suggest any purpose or power. His dark head is rather fine and a bit shaggy. He is pale and serious-looking, with nervous sensibility beginning to be written too plainly about his restless mouth and brows. His eyes are sombre and young, his hands nervous. He wears dark flannels and, except for his wind-tossed hair, his general appearance is neat. He carries great heaps of yellow primroses under one arm. Some of them fall about the carpet as he moves. After he has stared through the window for a minute* **Morris** *turns with an effort and walks slowly towards the kitchen door. As he moves* **Mabel** *comes in, followed by* **Gwen**.

Mabel   Good afternoon, John. We didn't know you had arrived. Has Miss Llewellyn gone out?

John   No! At least I think not. I believe her friend has just gone. (*To* **Gwen**.) Sorry I'm late. Do you like these? (*He goes over and holds his primroses close to her face.*)

Gwen   Ye-es, John. Oh, they're wet, dear. Don't rub them on my jumper. They're very pretty. I saw hawkers selling them at the 'Elephant' yesterday. Did you get them there?

John   God! No! Not at the 'Elephant'.

Mabel (*who has been spying over the aspidistras all this time, now turning round in bright reproval*)   Tut, tut, tut – who's swearing in my house, and on Sunday too? Careful, John, if you please!

John (*ignoring* **Mabel***, who resumes her spying*)   I gathered every one of them myself, Gwen. I thought they were so like you. Your little sisters.

Gwen (*laughing vaguely, more embarrassed than pleased*)   What ideas you do have, John! (*She touches one or two of them vaguely and smells them.*)

Mabel   Most poetic, of that I am sure! (*While she prattles she continues to gaze and dodge round the aspidistras.*) But I shouldn't relish being compared with a common little primrose, Gwen, if I were you. I must say he's most lover-like. Seems as if he can't go. Giving the Avenue plenty to talk about too. Well! (*Sighing sentimentally.*) She's a lucky girl!

John (*turning round and speaking hesitatingly*)   Do you mean Miss Llewellyn? She's not engaged to that man!

Mabel   Oh well, she hasn't given us her confidence yet – but it's only a matter of time, of that I'm sure. And she's just what I'd select for him. (*Still bobbing round the window.*) Now I think he's off. Oh yes. (*To* **Gwen***, who has been having a peep too.*) Be careful, Gwen, it's not refined to be too prying and curious. Keep well back.

Gwen   He does drive splendidly, doesn't he?

John (*who has been left disconsolate with the primroses*)   Won't you take them, Gwen? Don't you want them? The poor little beggars want a drink.

Gwen   Oh, yes, John, of course – I forgot. Put them on the table and I'll get something to put them in.

Mabel (*with a scream*)   *Not* on my polished table, please. How can you, Gwen? Don't attempt to put those wet things down there, John.

John   Oh God! Where *may* I put them? I can't hold them like this for the rest of the day!

Mabel (*brightly, spreading layers of newspapers*)   Not so short with me, if you please. I'm not as mild as Gwen, of that I'm sure. You can put your flowers down now and Gwen will arrange them for you.

Gwen (*a bit sorry for him, and helping him to lay them on the paper*)   Wherever did you pick them all?

John   Long miles from here, little lady. I came on them suddenly, all by themselves in a little wood.

Mabel (*who is busy picking up stray primroses and tut-tutting good-humouredly at the mess they have made*)   So that's how you spent the morning! Picking all those things to make a mess of my nice tidy drawing-room? Well, you are an oddity. Where's the waste-paper basket?

Throws a handful into it and goes on picking up and fussing – always good-humoured. Meanwhile **Frances** *and* **Natty** *come in together.*

Natty   Hello! John! Gwen and I were wondering where you were since dinner-time.

John, *who has been standing rather dejectedly by the table and watching* **Mabel**'s *activities, now smiles very pleasantly at* **Natty** *and continues to finger his flowers.* **Gwen** *has gone to the kitchen.*

Frances (*coming impulsively to the table and gathering primroses eagerly in her hands, pressing them to her face*)   Oh, lovely, lovely, lovely, lovely things! All wet and muddy, too! Real primroses – real dirty rascals!

John (*suddenly eager and vigorous, with husky voice*)   You love them?

Frances (*looking at him straight, but with shy eyes*)   I had forgotten them since last year. It's great to see so many together!

Natty (*who has been watching her very kindly, comes nearer and touches the stems*)   Spare a chap a buttonhole, John?

Frances *arranges his buttonhole for him, and he watches her, looking enormously pleased about it; then she turns back again to the table.*

Frances   Where did you find them?

John (*very gay and happy*)   I had been travelling a long time when I came on a whole troop of them by the river-bank in a little wood; they looked glorious.

Frances   But where?

John   Guess! Falstaff was tumbled out of a clothes-basket not far from there!

Frances   Datchet?

John   Right! Ate my bread and cheese all among the little ladies – and then – I suppose it was mean of me – I just had to bring some of them home.

Frances   It wasn't mean of you, was it, Natty?

She gathers great handfuls of them to her face and walks slowly from the table, purring, with her mouth on the flowers. A few of them fall, but she passes them, unnoticing. **John**'s *eyes, which have been fastened on her, fall to the dropped flowers. He steps nearer to them, with a furtive hint of purpose in his movements. As he hesitates and stares, the inexorable bright energies of* **Mabel** *seize the primroses. They are picked up and carried out of sight.* **John** *sits down slowly near the fire-place. Meanwhile* **Frances** *has drifted over to* **Natty** *with the flowers.*

Frances   Natty, don't you love them?

Natty (*smiling*)   They're beautiful, Ethelberta. I'm fond of a flower, especially my little decoration! (*Pointing to his buttonhole, sees* **Gwen** *enter with a large bowl full of water.*) Look, Gwen, you don't grudge a few of these beauties to your kind old brother-in-law, do you?

Gwen   Of course not, Natty –

Mabel   Be careful, please, with my beautiful bowl.

Frances   We'll be very careful, Mrs Hemworth.

Gwen *helps* **Frances** *to arrange the flowers.* **Mabel***, seating herself near the window with a newspaper, keeps an eye on the bowl, and tut-tuts whenever a flower falls on the carpet.* **Natty** *moves vaguely round the room, fidgeting at the gramophone, aspidistras, etc.* **John** *stands very still, interested in the arranging of the flowers, and happy apparently for the nonce.*

Frances   Lovely long stems! (*Laughing suddenly, and holding one at arm's length.*) Gwen, they're like you! (*As she says this, she holds a flower near* **Gwen***'s head and looks questioningly towards* **John***, who starts and nods, with eager understanding.*)

Gwen (*laughing and rather shy*)   Oh! I don't know! John said that too. Seems silly to me. Too high-flown, I suppose.

John   They reminded me of her this morning. That's why I gathered them.

Frances   Do you often go tramping on Sundays?

Gwen (*plaintively*)   Every single Sunday, Miss Llewellyn; don't know from Adam what he sees in it. It would bore me stiff.

John   I have to. I'd stifle if I didn't. Once a week isn't too often to see green fields. Of course, Gwen couldn't stand it, not at my pace. It would kill her. I go alone every Sunday. I'm gone before the milkman's out. If I start early, I can get back in time to take Gwen somewhere.

Gwen   Isn't he queer, Miss Llewellyn? Fancy trudging off like that with bread and cheese and books – and no Sunday dinner!

Frances   Sounds good to me. Not the bit about the milkman.

John (*smiling at her*)   I'd wait for a friend.

Frances   There! They're all fixed and drinking away like Prohibitionists. (*Standing back from them and smiling whimsically at* **John***.*)

Gwen   I suppose I had better put my hat on now. Isn't it rather late, John?

John   Well, Gwen, that depends on what we are going to do?

Gwen (*hurt*)   Oh, don't you remember? The Olympic.

John   Cinema! But it's an exquisite day!

Gwen (*sulky*)   Well, you promised, you know. And it's the *Lure of Lust*.

John   Rightho! So I did. Run and get your hat on.

Exit **Gwen***, quite happy now.*

Frances   The *Lure of Lust*. That ought to be worth one and threepence.

John   Oh! I've seen them with names that beat that hollow. They're never as good as their promise.

Frances   Surely this one sets a stiff pace.

John   A cinema's a fair place to rest in, Miss Llewellyn. I'm getting used to thinking things out at the pictures.

Frances   What things?

John   Nothing great, only the things I want, Miss Llewellyn. Not worth talking about.

Frances   Only worth silence.

John *bends very earnestly towards her, but as he would answer,* **Natty** *interrupts him.*

Natty   I say, Ethelberta! What about the records?

John   Records?

Frances   A few I bought yesterday. I'll put one on now. Do you mind, Mrs Hemworth?

Mabel (*looking up from the picture paper*)   On the contrary, Miss Llewellyn, I'll be delighted. It must be the very latest thing when you buy it. Of that I'm sure!

Frances (*going towards the gramophone, where* **Natty** *is already opening the parcel*)   I'm afraid it's nothing very up to date this time. Thanks, Natty, I'll put it on.

Natty   What is it, Ethelberta?

Frances   Just a song I used to like.

She walks away from the gramophone, which has started, and stands near the fire-place. The record begins. It is 'Voi che Sapete'. The room is very quiet, and the song is broken only by the rattle of **Mabel**'*s paper. The latter lifts her head perkily now and then to listen, but reads complacently most of the time.* **Natty** *stands at the back of the stage, near the gramophone, his head on one side. He seems uneasy, although the music vaguely pleases him. He casts troubled glances at his wife, and once or twice looks towards* **Frances**, *whose back is turned to him. Towards the end of the verse,* **John** *rises abruptly, strides to the gramophone, and stops the record. Then, without a word, returns to his chair.* **Natty** *looks amazed,* **Frances** *mildly surprised.* **Mabel** *alone is unaware of the happenings. There is a painful pause.*

Mabel   Sounds very nice indeed, Miss Llewellyn, of that I'm sure. Quite a cheery little tune, in fact. (*She resumes her reading.*)

Natty (*softly to* **Frances**)   It's queer, Ethelberta; it's a queer song.

Frances   Did you like it, Natty? (*Turning round.*)

Natty   Well, it's new to me. But there is something catchy about it. Who's it by?

Frances   Mozart.

Mabel (*who had been getting up and folding her paper*)   Hark at him! Catchy, he calls it. Shows all you know, Mr Hemworth! It's by Mozart! (*Laughs at* **Natty**.)

Natty   I'd like to hear it again. (*Whistle.*) There's the Barwell kids come out with their scooter. (*Goes to the window and leans out.*) Hi, Bobbie! Hi, there!

He leans out of the window, laughing and calling out to the children, then climbs out. **John** *looks at* **Frances**. *She returns the stare.*

Mabel (*going to window*)   Dear! dear! I wish he wouldn't do that (*Turning.*) I'm afraid Gwen's keeping you waiting, John. Young girls do take a time to beautify themselves nowadays. I'll go and help her if you'll excuse me. (*Goes out.*)

John   I stopped your record.

Frances   I had observed that.

John (*more angrily*)   I suppose you think I did it out of sheer boorishness?

Frances   Well, the politeness of it hadn't struck me.

John   That's where you're stupid. I stopped it because I am polite – because I couldn't stand the impudent priggishness of it. I call it rude of you – rude – to bring that record here!

Frances   What do you mean? How dare you!

John   I couldn't stand it. Things are ugly here. God! I know how appalling it is! No need to rub it in. But Mozart! Mozart in this room! I couldn't stand it, I tell you, I couldn't stand it!

Frances   Priggish and impudent to play a tune I like on the gramophone! I don't even dimly see what you mean. And how dare you – an utter stranger – attack me like this?

John   I'm not an utter stranger – I've known you three weeks. But don't you see? Mozart's incongruous and out of place here – and cruel! Don't you see?

Frances   Please stop glaring at me. I bought the records for Natty's amusement, and my own. He liked that unhappy little song. Do try not to behave ridiculously about something that has nothing to do with you.

John   But it has something to do with me. I could not bear to hear that music here. Oh, I know I'm behaving like an idiot, but I can't help that. I thought you were sneering at this room and these people.

Frances   Sneering! Oh, you foolish, foolish man! Were you sneering when you brought the primroses?

John   It's not the same thing.

Frances   Mozart for me, primroses for you, Distinguished Villa for Mrs Hemworth. We're all chasing the same thing.

John (*softly*)   What?

Frances   God knows! We won't, unless we catch up with it.

John   Shall we ever?

Frances   You know, you and I are talking nonsense.

John   Not quite! We both *mean* something.

Enter **Mabel** *with* **Gwen**.

Mabel   Here she is, John, and worth waiting for, of that I'm sure.

Gwen   Sorry I was so slow, John.

John   Ready? Then let's go.

Frances (*looking up*)   Good-bye, Gwen, Enjoy yourself. You do look nice.

Gwen (*from the door*)   Thanks. My favourite actor's starring. Good-bye.

Exeunt **John** *and* **Gwen**.

Mabel (*sitting near the table*)   Well now, Miss Llewellyn, you'll be able to get on with your writing in peace at last. But I must move all these messy flowers out of your way.

Frances   Please leave them, Mrs Hemworth, I love them; and anyway – I'm feeling lazy.

Mabel   Oh well, just as you please. It is most pleasant for me to have your society, Miss Llewellyn. I must say that when Mr Webberley called I did not expect he would leave me this pleasure.

Frances   He did, you see!

Mabel (*coyly*)   Not his fault if he did – of that I'm sure. You're not at home on Sunday for the want of being asked out! But a lady must be self-contained, of course. I always was most self-contained myself. I really do not understand what has come to girls nowadays. Gwen, of course, is like me – all that a lady should be; I've seen to that. You wouldn't believe, Miss Llewellyn, how exceptionally careful and reserved I always was, and I always had a very great number of admirers. A most flattering number, if I may permit myself a trifling vanity. If a woman knows what's owing to her dignity the men will know it. That's what I've dinned into Gwen, and though she has many faults, in that way she certainly does me credit!

Frances (*interested but lazy*)   I've noticed you don't think much of girls nowadays, Mrs Hemworth. Are we so very bad?

Mabel (*laughing consciously*)   Well now, Miss Llewellyn, I've no wish to be hard, or to set too high a standard; there's coarse and fine in this world, we all know; I don't hold with criticising people. And I can at least pride myself that I have brought Gwen up to my own refined standards with men.

Frances   That is helpful, I suppose! If you know what it means. It sounds as though men were one kind of animal and women another, and as if there were no meeting-ground.

Mabel (*stiffening*)   I am afraid that I am at a loss, and, in any case, I do not allow the word 'animal' to be applied to my fellow-creatures, Miss Llewellyn. I beg you to be more delicate!

Frances   I'm awfully sorry, Mrs Hemworth. But what I mean is, suppose a girl grows fond of a man?

Mabel   It's his business to grow fond of her.

Frances   I see – different species. Supposing he doesn't grow fond of her?

Mabel   Very well – if she's a ladylike and refined girl, she's none the worse. She may be thankful she hasn't shown her hand.

Frances   The good old conspiracy! But if people – well, for instance, Gwen and John Morris. How did they become engaged?

Mabel   Oh, that was all very nice and as it should be. They met at a friend's house in the neighbourhood. You may take it from me that Gwen never forgot herself.

Frances   Have you ever forgotten yourself, Mrs Hemworth?

Mabel (*astonished*)   I really think, Miss Llewellyn – goodness gracious! – only that I know you – I really can only think that you're not feeling well.

Frances   Ah! But really – not about men, and all that; but really and truly to forget oneself! I've never done it, I think –

Mabel (*relieved, and laughing a little*)   I should trust not indeed!

Frances   I should love to!

Mabel   Miss Llewellyn, I must beg of you not to speak so foolishly. I really cannot bear to hear such a refined young lady say things that I can only call indelicate – I really cannot bear it!

Frances   Once more – I'm very sorry, Mrs Hemworth. (*There is silence for a minute.* **Mabel** *taps her feet and hums nervily, looking at her paper.* **Frances** *watches her with amused perplexity. Then she leans forward and speaks coaxingly.*) Am I in disgrace?

Mabel (*smiling with kind condescension*)   Oh no, I'm quite willing to pardon mistakes.

Frances   Thank you!

Mabel   I haven't been married eleven years for nothing. Natty, of course, does me credit in many ways.

Frances   He is very devoted.

Mabel   Of course he is – but I kept him in his place. Kept myself to myself, Miss Llewellyn. And he respects me all the more for it. So will John respect Gwen. I'm surprised at her, to be frank, Miss Llewellyn. I'd have thought her taste would have been for someone smart and gentleman-like. And I'm afraid that he has very strong feelings. In fact, I don't care for him.

Frances   He certainly does give himself airs!

Mabel   Between you and me, he's a very passionate young man, Miss Llewellyn. When he first met Gwen he went wild – poetry and flowers and letters by every post. I should have put a stop to it at once, but Gwen actually liked it! All the same, I don't allow too much of his nonsense. I know how to keep him at a distance!

Frances   What distance?

Mabel (*giggling*)   Now, Miss Llewellyn, you're poking fun again; but I won't get angry with you. You know very well how an engaged couple should behave. When I was engaged to Natty, I sometimes – *sometimes* allowed him to kiss my hand. (*With coy sentimentality and unction.*) He never kissed my lips until I was his wife.

Frances (*awestruck with the solemnity, and suppressing a smile*)   Poor Natty – dear little Natty! (*Laughing towards the window.*) There he goes, flying past on the Barwells' scooter!

Mabel   Yes, he's never done with that young Bobbie Barwell. It gets on my nerves to see a grown man spend his Sundays so foolishly.

Frances (*still watching, turning from window and speaking gently*)   You must be sorry you have no children.

Mabel   Ye-es. Of course, I never was strong; never equal to much.

Frances (*musing, her eyes towards the street*)   Natty would have *enjoyed* a baby so.

Mabel   Well, of course, my health has been a great worry to him always; and Dr Broad has said it would be a great risk for me – a terrible risk!

Frances   Ah! Of course, it is a risk.

Mabel   Oh, but my case is quite exceptional. My nerves are extremely sensitive; I'm very highly strung, and can't stand anything. I must say that Natty has been most careful of me always.

Frances (*hesitating*)   Ah! Oh –

Mabel   You see, I'm not an ordinary woman. Perhaps I'm too refined. I – I – ahem! Well, I – marriage has not suited me. Of course, I have every care, but I don't spare myself!

Frances (*timidly*)   I've often thought that you waste a good deal of your strength on household duties!

Mabel   Of course I do. I hope I'll always do so. I know my duty, Miss Llewellyn, and I think I've the right to be proud of my home.

Frances   Of course. What does Natty think of it?

Mabel   Why, he's proud of it and proud of me.

Frances   But it tires you very much, doesn't it, and can't leave you much time for him?

Mabel   Time for him? We're always here together when he's not in the office! What do you mean?

Frances   Natty's a friendly soul; I suppose he wants a lot of companionship? His office must be deadly!

Mabel   That's why I'm so particular, so that he'll love his home.

Frances (*looking round the room slowly*)   Has he – has he always been as nice as he is now, Mrs Hemworth? Does he ever – has he ever – got drunk?

Mabel (*shrilly*)   Really, Miss Llewellyn! I can hardly believe my ears to-day. That's the last straw indeed! Of that I'm sure. Drunk! Drunk!

Frances   Supposing Natty got drunk? Or ran wild somehow?

Mabel (*with tight lips*)   It would never happen again. Why should he?

Frances   Anything can happen to anyone. There are no certainties.

Mabel   To-day is the first time since you came here that I have doubted your good sense, Miss Llewellyn.

Frances   I've just as little sense as anyone else. I believe you think I'm mad! Perhaps I am, Mrs Hemworth. Certainly, I am very talkative. Have you always been delicate; highly strung?

Mabel   From the very beginning, Miss Llewellyn. But people like a bright face and I always try to show one. You may have noticed, and it's only to you I'd remark it, that Natty is moody now and then. I have hard work sometimes trying to rouse him. No cause whatever; but no one is perfect, I suppose.

Frances   No, only now and then one begins to think that a few get near perfection.

Mabel (*playfully*)   Oh, you must not think too highly of me, Miss Llewellyn, you must not indeed!

Enter **Natty**.

Mabel   Now just go back, Mr Hemworth (*Playfully.*) and dust your boots properly. I should hope my drawing-room is worth that attention!

Natty   Course it is, Missus! (*Withdraws and speaks from outside, while scraping boots on the mat.*) What have you and Ethelberta been talking about?

Frances   Were your ears burning, Natty?

Enter **Natty**, *smiling and rather dishevelled.*

Natty   So you've been gossiping, have you?

Mabel   I have my faults, but gossiping I never do tolerate, of that I'm sure!

Frances   Did you enjoy yourself?

Natty   Top hole! Why didn't you come out and play?

Mabel   Well, Natty, what an idea to be sure!

Frances   To tell you the truth I was too lazy. How dark it's growing; must be getting latish. (*Leisurely begins to rummage among writing things on the table.*)

Mabel   The evenings aren't very long yet. (*Resumes her paper.*)

Natty (*standing by aspidistras and smoothing the leaves*)   – Any more records?

Frances (*absentmindedly, without looking up from her writing*)   No, we'll have them to-night if you like.

Silence falls. **Natty** *remains fingering leaves and staring out. Sunset light falls about him. The room is full of the intense brightness of closing day. There is no sound but the scratch of* **Frances**'*s pen and the rustle of* **Mrs Hemworth**'*s paper. After a moment the pen-scratching ceases.* **Frances** *raises her head and watches* **Natty** *quietly. He does not turn round.*

Natty   What a sky there is! Never seen it lovelier. Makes me sad somehow, the sunset, and still I love to watch it fading.

Mabel (*brightly, without looking up*)   Don't watch it, stupid, if it makes you sad. Leave it alone!

Silence again.

Natty (*pensively*)   I dunno! (*Half turning his head.*) Funny thing. (*Pause.*) There's John strolling down the hill alone. Looks rottenly glum.

Mabel   Nonsense! No gentleman would come out and leave a young lady alone in a picture-house, of that I'm sure. It can't be he!

Natty   Oh, it's him all right! Most likely they're had a tiff. He looks like that. Staring at the sky – he seems fearful glum. Poor old John! (*Pause.*) Ethelberta, what's it for?

Frances   What, Natty?

Natty   Feeling so rotten! Why does the sky make a chap feel rotten?

Frances   Don't know! Wonder if anyone knows!

Natty (*his eyes still westward*)   Ethelberta! It's damned queer.

Mabel *starts in horror at the words.*

Mabel   Natty! Your language! Please! Please!

Curtain

Act Two

Same scene. Four months have passed and it is Saturday evening – nearly six o'clock. The room is as neat as ever – the windows are open; outside the weather is very fine and hot. When the curtain goes up **Mabel** *is standing between the window and the table. She is wearing a frock of shiny taffetas and many jewels. Her feet are adorned with high-heeled patent leather shoes and light stockings. She is vigorously brushing a long black overcoat, and talks towards the kitchen door all the while in a shrill and irritated voice. In the pauses of her talk she purses her lips angrily. There is no trace now of her former coy good humour. She is a woman who is, to her own amazement, failing to force her will on a usually docile victim. Her cheeks are flushed, but not prettily. Every now and then her foot stamps a tiny little stamp of sheer irritation.*

Mabel (*continuing in a jerky style what has obviously been a lengthy address*)   But when I do make an effort, and in spite of my poor health insist, against my doctor's opinion, in doing what I consider to be my duty to the Avenue – I expect in return the considerate attention which a husband owes to his wife – of that I'm sure! (*Pause.*) Oh, don't trouble to answer! It's come to this now that my remarks are not worth a reply! (*Pause.*) Don't trouble! (*Pause.*) Natty! Natty! Will you have the kindness to come here at once and tell me that you will do as I wish and come to the whist drive?

Natty (*who looks tired and worried, emerges from the kitchen*)   Mabel dear, I'm dog tired. I don't feel social to-night. It's no great matter if I don't show up. You're the important one.

Mabel   It's no great matter to disobey and displease your wife? You know very well that I must attend this whist drive. I have promised our dear curate, Mr Cuthbertson, to be present.

Natty   Right you are, Mabel. Go ahead, dear – and have a good time.

Mabel   Of course, I'll go ahead. But you'll come too.

Natty   I'm tired, Mabel. Don't be hard on a chap. You know everyone – and you'll have Gwen – and John says he'll call to bring you home. I'll do that too – if you like. I'm sorry if I've disappointed you, Mabel – I've got a queer fit on – don't you know, old girl – one of those fits when you can't be pleasant?

Mabel   Can't be pleasant, indeed! I'm afraid that's painfully evident, Mr Sulky. What's come to you lately I cannot think. Up and down, up and down – like a see-saw. I'll admit you never were as even-tempered as I'd like, but in the last three months you've tried even my patience too far. Why, you're even depressed in my very presence, and it isn't as if you were the only one. I declare that Gwen's sulks lately are enough to upset my health! It's very hard on me, as Dr Broad says, to have to contend with a sulky husband and a sulky sister all at once – to say nothing of John stalking in and out with a face of doom. Dr Broad thinks it may have very serious effects on my internal system, and I begin to notice every day that he is right. Where's Gwen? Gwen! Are you ready? Gwen!

Gwen (*upstairs*)   Not yet, Mabel.

Mabel   Good gracious! What's coming over you? I promised Mr Cuthbertson that I would not fail him at six o'clock. He cannot manage to receive without me – of that I'm sure!

Gwen (*still upstairs*)   I say, Mabel, must I go?

Mabel   Well, I never! Natty! Did you hear that? Now I suppose Gwen thinks she can't be pleasant. (*Screams up to* **Gwen**.) Of course you must go. I'm starting at once. Come along!

Gwen (*coming downstairs and coming in in a cotton dressing-gown*)   I say, Mabel, don't you think –

Mabel (*shrieks with horror at the négligé condition of* **Gwen**)   What are you about? I'm due at the Assembly Rooms now.

Gwen   I loathe the whole show. I'd give my soul to go to bed, Mabel.

Mabel   Well – your selfishness is only matched by Natty's. I know now, since he can't trouble to appear in public with me, how little he values my sufferings. But you, Gwen! I expected more of you – *my* sister. Well, – I suppose I must sit down and wait for you, and then arrive late and explain that my devoted husband felt that he couldn't be pleasant this evening – couldn't be pleasant to my friends!

Natty   It'd never do for you to be late, Mabel dear. Hadn't you better go on and let Gwen follow you?

Gwen   Do, Mabel. I'll be along in a few minutes. I came down to look for that camisole I made.

Mabel   Well, I suppose I owe it to Mr Cuthbertson to be there in time. You know that is your duty to appear at my side in public. If you insist on failing in the respect you owe me it's your disgrace – not mine.

Natty   I'm tired, Mabel, I'm tired.

Mabel   And, of course, your poor wife is never tired. Oh, no! Never! What do you know of the headaches I endure with a smile?

Gwen (*who has been rummaging in a chest of drawers*)   I say, Mabel, you get along. Maybe you'll meet the Smithsons and walk there with them. If I could find that cammy I'd be with you in a tick.

Natty   The new pink one you were working at yesterday? It's in the kitchen, Gwen.

Gwen (*nodding and trailing towards the kitchen*)   Right you are.

Mabel   Well, I'm off then. (*Getting into her coat with* **Natty**'*s assistance.*) You are causing me great pain this evening, Natty, but of course you'll call to fetch us home with John, and you'll see that Miss Llewellyn has her supper. It's all ready on a tray in the pantry. What she thinks of all the sulky faces lately I can't imagine! But she can have no criticism to make of my behaviour, of that I am sure. (*Much ado of departure* *and turning back from door to call through to* **Gwen** *in kitchen.*) Don't dilly-dally, Gwen, I must not be left long in public without a member of my own family, though indeed you're not much support to anyone of late. You look as if you had a secret sorrow. (*Laughter at her own sally and a return of good temper.*) Doesn't she, Natty?

Natty   Oh, she's all right. It's the hot weather, I expect. We're all feeling it a bit, but you look fine, Mabel.

Mabel   Well, I do feel that I look as I should, without yielding to vanity.

Natty   Give a chap a kiss.

Mabel   No. You're out of favour, Mr Hemworth. Call for me at eleven.

They go out. **Natty**'s *voice and hers can be heard in the hall and at the hall door.* **Gwen** *comes back from the kitchen with the camisole in one hand. Now that she is alone she drops into a still greater listlessness and, unwilling to go upstairs and dress for the whist drive, she sinks for a minute into the arm-chair near the fire-place. The camisole falls off her arm and she leans forward wearily, staring at nothing. Her eyes look very worried. After a minute or two tears gather in them; she covers her face, remaining very still. From her reverie she is startled by the voice of* **Alec Webberley** *in the hall talking to* **Natty**. *The latter opens the sitting-room door and shows* **Alec** *in. He does not come in himself but speaks to* **Alec**, *who has entered the room, from the hall.*

Natty   She won't be long, Mr Webberley. Gone to the post, I believe.

Alec (*who still faces towards* **Natty** *and does not see* **Gwen**)   It's quite all right, thanks. No hurry. Hope you're all well here?

Natty   Fair to middling. Heat's affecting us a bit. You're quite a stranger lately.

Alec   Oh, busy you know.

Natty   I see. Cheerio, Mr Webberley. Miss Llewellyn won't be long. (*Exit and closes door.*)

Alec *moves round slowly, opening his cigarette-case. He gives an impression of being a little uneasy and not too pleased to be left alone in the room. He does not look towards* **Gwen**, *being engrossed in watching the road for* **Frances**. **Gwen** *looks at him wearily and calmly.*

Gwen   Hello!

Alec (*wheeling around*)   Good Lord! I say! Why didn't you speak sooner? (*His manner is uneasily friendly, but very cautious.*) How are you, Gwen?

Gwen   Fair to middling; heat's affecting us a bit. You're quite a stranger lately.

Alec   What's the matter, Gwen?

Gwen (*listless again*)   Nothing much.

Alec   Well, then, you might have a civil word for a fellow. I'm glad to see you again, you know. (*Puts out his hand.*) Won't you shake?

Gwen   Too hot.

Alec (*huffily*)   Sorry, Touch-me-not. There was a time – But look here, little girl – you're not peeved that I haven't rung you up lately, are you? Fact is, I've been busy, and after that bout of flying round with you I've had to get down to things. My old boss is a bit of a Tartar. I've been sorry not to see you – was going to ring you up on Monday.

Gwen   So was I going to ring you up.

Alec   Funny thing. Telepathy, I expect. But you haven't apologised for your négligé, little lady. Supposing anyone came in? Hadn't you better cut along and dress?

Gwen   Oh! I'll be gone before Miss Llewellyn gets back. Don't worry.

Alec (*with forced gaiety*)   I'm not worrying. You look stunning like that.

Gwen (*relaxing*)   Alec! Isn't it queer that you should walk into this room just when I was wanting you? Don't you think it's queer? Like a sort of answer to prayer?

Alec   Oh, I say, little girl – I've been called names in my time, but – well – an answer to prayer!

Gwen   Alec – listen to me. I – I –

Alec   'Pon my word, you look quite worried. What's gone wrong, old Gwen? Never do to have you wilting up, you know. There aren't enough of 'em that can look like you!

Gwen   That's hard lines for you.

Alec   Sympathy out of order? Oh, well – sorry and all that. This heat really is the devil! (*Hums softly, looking bored; walks towards window.*) Wish Frankie would come along.

Gwen (*grown timid suddenly, and appealing*)   She won't be long. That's why I do want you to listen to me now. I mustn't waste this chance to settle everything. Alec! Please don't look so bored. Two months ago you were keen enough on anything I had to say! (*Standing up and going to him.*) Oh, I'm frightened! Help me to tell you!

Alec (*very stiff, and choking back sudden alarm*)   But what on earth – my dear girl? No, don't paw at me, Gwen – anyone might come in. No, no! Let my hands go. I've just told you I was sorry I hadn't rung you up for so long – I swear I was going to look you up on Monday. I'd no idea: but you don't mean you're – anyway, you always pretended that you cared more for Morris! (**Gwen** *has turned away again and is standing motionless with her back to him.*) You and I always understood each other; that was why I was so keen on you – I thought you such a sportsman. Gwen – I still think it. I'll look you up on Monday. That do?

Gwen   I'm going to have a child, Alec.

Dead silence, in which **Alec** *stiffens in every muscle.* **Gwen** *does not move. After a few still seconds* **Alec** *licks his lips and leans forward.*

Alec   I didn't hear you. What did you say?

Gwen (*wheeling round and wailing*)   I'm going to have a child – I'm going to have a baby! I'm going to have your baby! It's no good looking like that. How's it going to hurt you – my having a baby? You ought to be glad! It'll be all right for you – when you've married me! Alec, Alec – I tell you, it's true! But it'll be all right if you marry me soon. I'll like having a baby when we're married, Alec!

Alec (*untwining her arms from his neck and speaking very nervously, with uneasy glances towards the window*)   Gwen! Stop it, stop it, I tell you. Stop this nonsense! Have you gone mad? We're both ruined if anyone comes in! You're not going to have a baby, you silly little fool! Stop crying! Just because you're feeling flapped with the heat you go off the deep end like this! That's all it is. Ssh, ssh – there's a good kid! Ssh, Gwen, old girl!

Gwen (*suddenly quiet again*)   I tell you I'm going to have your child, and all you can do is gasp at me that it isn't true! What good is that going to do? Oh, Alec, Alec! I was sporting with you. I know we were both only having a bit of fun – I meant it just like you did. I wasn't a bit huffed when you didn't ring up. You gave me a good time, and I liked you – but I wanted to stick to John. I'm fond of him – I am, honestly – and I know you're fearfully sweet on Miss Llewellyn. You never made any bones about that. But it's all different now. We've got to see it through! We must stick together, Alec. We will, won't we?

Alec   Gwen, I beg of you to talk quietly. I don't believe, to begin with, that you are going to have a child. It's hysteria. And, secondly, if you are, I deny that I am responsible. You are engaged to a man whom you like far better than you ever like me, and – well, I don't want to be rotten – but you know – well, you once admitted to me, when we were friends . . . that he . . .

Gwen   Oh, I know. But that was long ago. And I know – I swear to you, Alec – that it's you. I'm telling the truth!

Alec (*in command at last, and growing more comfortable*)   My dear little Gwen, I'm quite sure you are trying to tell the truth, but the fact is that you are not telling it. You're frightened, and I quite understand. But I don't see why you should unburden it all to me. This is Morris's affair. Ssh, ssh! Don't cry. Even if this thing is going to happen, Gwen, there's absolutely no reason for hysterics. Morris is quite ready to marry you, I take it. He'll see you through – he's bound to, if he's any sort of a white man.

Gwen (*standing back and staring at him*)   But I can't ask him to see me through – don't you see? It's not his affair!

Alec   I tell you it is his affair. Anyhow, it's not mine. Of course, if you're short of money, or there's any crux of that kind – well, you know what I mean, Gwen.

Gwen   Money's no good to me. I can't have a baby unless I'm married. How can I? Alec, how can I?

Alec   No one's asking you to. You can marry Morris tomorrow, if you like.

Gwen   No, I can't.

Alec   For God's sake, why?

Gwen   Because I'm not a liar. I'm no saint, but you know I'd draw the line at cheating John like that. John's as straight as straight. Oh, Alec! you couldn't ask me to foist a child on him that isn't his?

Alec   Who's asking you to do anything of the kind? I'm simply stating that if you are as you say, I am not to blame, and therefore I know that the responsibility is Morris's. I'm only asking you to be sane, and to believe me that it's all right.

Gwen   You're clever, but I'm not taken in. You're a cheating beast, that's all you are! And I'm not so bad as you, but I'm a funk. Oh, is it no good if I beg you not to make me miserable for the rest of my life? I tell you I want to be straight with John – I want to tell him everything straight, and be done with it. I can't face such a big lie – I'd never be rid of it – I'd never have peace again!

Alec   Oh, God! Oh, God!

Gwen   I'm cheating someone decent, and I can't go on with it. I hate going to bed, because in the dark I cry and cry – think of the pain that's going to be; and when I wake every morning I turn hot and cold when I think of what I've got to face. But I hoped you'd be straight, Alec. In spite of doubting you most times, I thought you'd see that it was up to you. Oh! won't you put it right? I know you don't want to marry me. I'm not your sort for marrying, but I'd be decent to you –

Alec   If you won't listen to reason I've got to go – right away. I've told you what I think of this scene, and what I think of your accusations of me. You've got one man – for the Lord's sake stick to him. Cut heroics, and forget about me. You'll be all right, little girl. I know you will.

Gwen   Thanks for being so plain spoken. A girl knows where she is with a man like you. I'll never forgive you – Oh, God! Oh, God! What am I to do? I can't go on alone! I can't have a baby unless I'm married! I can't! I'm sick, I'm frightened, I tell you, and I can't tell anyone . . . I've always been respectable! I can't go wrong like that! Mabel would die of it! I'd die of it! I shall die! I know it! Oh – (*Sobs, sobs, sobs – and collapses on the floor.*)

Alec   I say, don't cry! You're tired, I know; but there's nothing wrong really. Tell John you want to marry him, and the trick's done! There, get up, Gwen. Don't cry – don't cry, I say!

Gwen   (*crawling against the arm-chair by the fire*)   I'm afraid! I don't know anything about a baby! I can't have a baby all by myself. I must be married – I must, I must! I'm a respectable girl, I tell you! You said it would be all right. Alec, you swore it was all right!

Alec   Hush! I tell you. Don't rave at me, Gwen. I can't help you; it's up to Morris, you see – and he'll do it. It'll be quite all right. Face it squarely, and chuck this nonsense about lies – you're not going to tell any lies.

Gwen   Go away – I'm sick of you! Leave me alone – (*Getting up.*)

Alec   I'm going now.

The gate clangs harshly. He starts and looks about him cautiously. Flustered, he loses all control and, seizing **Gwen** *by the arm, speaks huskily.*

Alec   I'll get out through the back door. I can't see Miss Llewellyn now. Don't say I came.

He darts through the kitchen door.

Gwen *leans heavily against the mantelpiece, drying her eyes. After a minute* **Frances** *comes in, her hat in her hand.*

Frances   Hello, Gwen! Not going to the whist drive?

Gwen (*trying not to turn right round*)   Got to go. Should be there now. Mabel's gone.

Frances (*sitting down rather wearily and looking critically at* **Gwen**)   You don't want to go, do you?

Gwen (*turning round suddenly*)   I loathe going, Miss Llewellyn. I'm dead tired.

Frances   You look it. Why not go to bed instead?

Gwen   It's not worth it. Mabel would carry on.

Frances   But surely, Gwen – when you really are not well. You haven't looked well for weeks now –

Gwen (*shrinking*)   Oh! I'm all right.

Frances   No, you're not. The heat wave and the city are a bad combination, Gwen. It's none of my business, I know – but I wish you'd see a doctor.

Gwen (*turning away*)   I've seen a doctor.

Frances   Oh, I'm glad. I didn't know.

Gwen   I'm all right. Really I am. And I must fly. I'm dead late.

Frances   Wait a minute, please. I'm going to be very rude. Why are you crying? Oh! Don't be offended. I shan't ask you again. But you can't mind my wanting to help you? We've known each other five months now.

Gwen (*with tears in her eyes, but backing away*)   I don't mind, of course, of course. I don't. It's terribly kind of you, Miss Llewellyn. But there's nothing, really. Just the heat – and things in general. Good night, Miss Llewellyn.

She goes out. **Frances** *looks after her musingly, then crosses to the fire-place. Sinking into a chair, she becomes wrapped in her own thoughts. Enter* **Natty** *from the hall. He drifts in looking forlorn and unhappy, potters about the room without a purpose.* **Frances** *makes a movement, acknowledging his presence, and remains folded in abstraction.*

Natty (*fidgeting with the aspidistras*)   I suppose you think it's rotten of me to have made Mabel so unhappy? (**Frances** *has not been listening, and looks round vaguely.*) Do you, Ethelberta?

Frances   What is it, Natty?

Natty   Well, I was due to go to this here church whist drive with her and I just took a fit and couldn't go. Poor Mabel was most unhappy. I didn't ought to have displeased her so.

Frances   I shouldn't think that it mattered much.

Natty   It's no joke to upset Mabel, Ethelberta. She's not like other people. She's very sensitive, you know. I'm afraid she'll be unhappy for a long time over this!

Frances   Oh dear, I hope not. (*Relaxes wearily again.*)

Natty   So do I, Ethelberta. When she's unhappy she takes on so. I did ought to have been kinder. I'm a rotten moody chap, I am!

Frances   You're nothing of the sort. You're terribly kind.

Natty   I'm not, Ethelberta, I'm just a beast – that's what I am, a mean, depressed beast, if you only knew. Poor Mabel! She picked a dull one all right!

Frances   Don't talk like that. I want to be cheered up, and you're never failed me before.

Natty   You think I'm cheery? Honest, Ethelberta? Do you really think me a decent sort of chap?

Frances (*turning round and looking at him*)   Natty, I do; indeed I do. I thought you knew that. But I believe you're very unhappy to-night. What is it?

Natty   Oh, nothing. I tell you I'm a gloomy sort always. That's why I liked it when you called me cheery. You're a judge, you know. If you think me cheery, seems as though I can't be too bad after all!

Frances   Too bad! You're very good. Rarely and amazingly good is what you are, Natty.

Natty (*pleadingly*)   Don't make fun of a chap, Ethelberta.

Frances   I'm not making fun. I think it's great that you're staying in. I've got a headache and I'm very tired. I don't know what I'd do here all by myself. I'm awfully glad you were so wicked as to dodge the parish whist drive.

Natty (*who has been visibly reviving under her spell*)   That pulls a chap together and no mistake. Got a headache? Then you've got to rest awhile. Yes, that's not a bad chair. Lean back, Ethelberta, and close your eyes. I'll go away and leave you in peace; maybe you'll go to sleep.

Frances   Oh no! You mustn't go away. I'll be very good if you will stay and talk, Natty. I don't want to be alone.

Natty (*delighted*)   Right you are, I'll stay. But I'm rather chatty you know. It'ud be better if I went away. I say, that's a rotten cushion you've got there. Here's a real good one. (*He hurries across the room, selects a cushion from another chair and comes to* **Frances**.) Lift your head, Ethelberta. That's right! There now – better?

Frances (*sighing and shutting her eyes*)   Lovely! Talk to me, Natty, or would you like to start the gramophone?

Natty (*laughing scornfully*)   Gramophone! While you've a headache? I should hope not. Besides, I'd rather talk.

Frances   Talk's a good thing. Reams and reams of talk.

Natty   It must be fine to be able to say what you mean.

Frances   I wonder who can?

Natty   Can't you, Ethelberta? (**Frances** *shakes her head.*) Then I oughtn't to worry myself trying, ought I?

Frances   All depends. What do you want to say?

Natty   Oh, nothing much. And who would I say it to?

Frances   Any friend.

Natty (*sitting down suddenly after much restless plodding round the room*)   It's like this. When I get one of these attacks of being a beast and not wanting to please anyone – not even Mabel – I feel rottenly sick. Any chap would. And I know that every decent person – even if they're as kind as Mabel – thinks that I'm just simply being rotten, and that I don't mind upsetting them, and all that. But, you see, I do mind, and every time I get so depressed I feel that I shall go mad if someone doesn't see that I can't help it. And no one does see. Why should they? There's no reason for it. Other chaps don't get like this; they don't seem to mind doing the same thing in the same way every day for eleven years. They even like it, Ethelberta. At least that's what I say to myself when I look at them in the train. But I suppose they think I like it – the jolly old eight forty-five.

Frances   Have you ever asked them?

Natty   They'd say I was mad!

Frances   What do you most want to know?

Natty (*shy again*)   Oh nothing really. I suppose there is nothing to know. I suppose we're all the same – under our bowlers.

Frances   Your bowlers do resemble each other rather.

Natty   Look here! We all do the same things. If we were different, would we all do the same things?

Frances   You mustn't set me such posers. There are hundreds of answers I could give you – all inadequate.

Natty   Do you think all those chaps round here are happy? Seems to me they can't be.

Frances (*musing*)   Well, you see –

Natty   Ethelberta, they must get sick of it. Take this Avenue! Take any of the chaps I know. Same old life eternally. Eight forty-five train every morning regular. – Same fellows in the carriages. – Same newspapers. – Same jokes. – Same office. – Same slogging. – Same lunch. – Home again. – Same station. – Same walk. – Same gossip on the Avenue. – Ethelberta, do'ye think they're happy?

Frances   They probably don't like it in the sense of enjoying it, but I expect they like it because getting through it represents the endurance of other things. I suppose they're not all happy. None of them are always happy. But if they have to catch the eight forty-five every morning they do come home again at the end of the day. That's the meaning of it, Natty! That's why they bear up. The reason, I suppose, is in the coming home; the secret life at home where we can't follow them explains it all. That's my guess.

Natty   The secret life at home. That's why they stand it!

Frances (*tentatively*)   Do you grow tired of it, Natty?

Natty   I? Oh no. Not more than most, I expect. I was only thinking about the other chaps really.

Frances   You've seemed rather less bright in the last month or two. When I first came you were so gay, Natty. Always calling people new names, always starting the gramophone –

Natty   When you first came I was gay. That's true, Ethelberta. Ever since I've been a little chap I've been one for a bit of fun. Always on the look out for it, and found it mostly, in those days. Spent all my money on fun and clothes and going courting – and always thought that something great would happen one day. Even when I got the dumps I thought that because I felt blue so often I was bound to have a good time. Couldn't last, I thought. And then – I married Mabel. I was very young; a bit thoughtless like, and not refined or sensible enough – not good enough by half for Mabel – but she said 'Yes' when I asked her. I was very lucky, Ethelberta. Since then Mabel's looked after me, and run this house, and been a trump, and never grumbled at my small pay. Everything's been right except her health. I think maybe it's because of Mabel's health that I get the blues.

Frances   I'm quite sure that's why.

Natty   Do you think so, Ethelberta? You see, she's never had a day's proper health since we've been married. Even when we were courting, things easily upset her, young as she was – she's not like other people, poor old Mabel. But she's always kept bright, although she's had to deny herself so much. Ethelberta, maybe it's wrong of me to bore you like this?

Frances *shakes her head kindly at him.*

Frances   Go on, Natty!

Natty   That thing you said just now – about the other fellows – about their 'secret life' – what was it?

Frances   I don't remember it exactly.

Natty   I think it was 'their secret life at home explains it all'. You said something about our not being able to follow them there, Ethelberta.

Frances   Yes; looking on at this alarming business of catching trains, and balancing ledgers, and listening in – one loses hope – one knows that it is all too dreary to be borne, too futile. But that's because we forget the miracle; the chance of a miracle. It may be – it just may be that everyone who crossed London Bridge this morning is, or has once been, or once may be, luminously, unutterably happy. It's possible, since they are alive. And they know it. That's why they finish crossing London Bridge. Isn't that splendid, Natty? Aren't we a brave and tragic people – who will live eighty years in patience, groping towards that little hour, and then remembering it?

Natty (*huskily and in distress*)   I'll never get there, Ethelberta.

Frances (*distressed in her turn and very kind*)   What nonsense, Natty. How silly of me to talk like this when you're depressed. I'm awfully sorry – I really might have known better. But you mustn't look so miserable.

Natty   I can't help it, Ethelberta. I feel miserable!

Frances   But surely you couldn't be as wretched as this because of the whist drive fuss. Surely Mrs Hemworth –

Natty (*interrupting*)   Oh, it's not that. It's nothing to do with that. Mabel was quite decent about that, really. It's not Mabel's fault at all. Nothing to do with her. Nothing to do with anyone!

Frances   But what is it then?

Natty (*miserably embarrassed and wretched*)   Oh, nothing. I'm no good at explaining, and there's nothing to explain.

Frances   But we're such friends, Natty. I'd like to cheer you up.

Natty   You do; you cheer me up no end. It's been – oh! (*He paces up and down, stares through the window, looks nervously at her over his shoulder, and turns suddenly again to face her.*) I can't rest, Ethelberta – honest I can't. I must explain things a bit. I've never been happy, really. All that about us being a model pair – Mabel and me – it's – it's, well, it's all due to her. Mabel's a marvel. I'm not such a gay bloke really. Never was. Life's always seemed a bit lonesome like. I can't help it, Ethelberta, sounds rotten, but I've always felt a bit left. I haven't been left – you see how decent everyone is. You see what everyone thinks of Mabel, and how everyone envies me! Must be something rotten in me that I could never settle down and be cheery about things. I've put a sort of face on it – especially to Mabel, of course. Couldn't be quite so low down as to worry her, with her health what it's always been – and all that. Never satisfied! Always wanting more than I've got. Was even beginning to think lately that there was nothing strange about life about all.

Frances   Have you changed that opinion, Natty?

Natty (*wringing his hands and pleading with her*)   I have changed it. Things have been different lately. Oh, 'different' is not the word. It's just all turned queer inside. I used to be fidgety before, but now – it's like madness – I can't explain it; I seem to be hurrying always, hurrying through things that must be done so as to get back to something – something that isn't there. I can't explain any more. (*Drops into moodiness.*)

Frances   But is it better like this – are you happier?

Natty   Better? Happier? Oh no. Oh, God, Ethelberta, no! It's madness, I tell you. Sometimes it makes me want to die. I never wanted to die before, Ethelberta, not at my worst. I always thought it'd be a frost to die without something happening. Now I'm not so sure. And still I *am sure*, Ethelberta. I want to go on – I can't die – but I can't go back to being just dull, dull, dull! I'm glad about it all, really. I don't care how restless it makes me. No one need ever know – not Mabel or anyone – it's no one's business – it'll do no one any harm. And I'm glad it's happened, even this way. It sort of explains things. Oh, don't look so sorry! I'll shut up now. It's all over. I'm all right really, honest I am!

Frances   You're not all right; you're sad and wretched. I wish I knew what to say. But I am glad you used me as a safety valve. That's all. (*Standing up.*) It's cruel of me to say this, but listening to your sadness made me forget my own. I was feeling beastly this evening, Natty!

Natty (*who is still distraught by the outburst, is struggling to be natural*)   Oh, I know, your poor head!

Frances   Well, it wasn't just the head. I've been worried because of something I wanted to say to you and Mrs Hemworth – something I hate saying. Perhaps I ought not to say it now. I'm sure you will be sorry to hear it, and you're quite sufficiently depressed to-night as it is.

Natty   Bad news, Ethelberta? I'm sorry!

Frances   Oh, well, I think you'll be disappointed – but I can't help it, Natty.

Natty   Why, what is it then? Let's hear it.

Frances   Oh, it's nothing tragic – don't look like that. It's simply that I have to leave, Natty – and I dislike the idea.

Natty (*catching his breath and after a long pause*)   Have to leave, Ethelberta? Leave this house?

Frances   I'm afraid that's it. I'm sorry!

Natty   For ever?

Frances   Oh, well –

Natty   Leave here? But why? Oh, why? Haven't you been happy?

Frances   Very, very happy in a way!

Natty   Is there anything you want altered? We'll do any mortal thing –

Frances   It's nothing like that. I've been beautifully looked after. It's hard to give a reason, but – I have to go.

Natty (*almost wailing*)   Ethelberta! I can't see why! I can't see why!

Frances   It's not my fault. Oh! It's good of you to dislike the idea so much: I knew we were friends. It's simply not my fault. I've got to go.

Natty (*staring out of the window*)   So it'll be like it was.

Frances   I shall hate changing.

Natty (*timidly, and without looking round at her*)   Don't answer any questions that you think I shouldn't ask, Ethelberta. But is it – er – has a man anything to do with it?

Frances   It's because of a man that I'm going.

Natty (*turning slowly and looking full at her*)   Oh! he's lucky.

Frances (*starting as if hurt*)   It's not that! I mean, I'm not being married, Natty.

Natty (*delicately*)   Not being married? (*Hesitates.*) Never mind, whatever you do is right.

Frances   Ah! Bless you! But I am not going away to be happy, I tell you – I'm going away because I must!

Natty   Going away! Going away! Funny that I had never thought of that! Going away!

Frances   How it seems to distress you, Natty. I was a beast to talk of it to-night. I don't know why I did. Forget about it now. (*After a pause.*) May I read down here for a while? (**Natty** *makes a dumb gesture, but cannot look at her. She turns to the door. Suddenly he wheels round as if to cry out to her but represses himself. As she goes out she speaks without turning round.*) I'll fetch my book.

Exit **Frances**. **Natty** *stands very still for a long time. At first his eyes rest on the door through which she has vanished. There is nothing alert or intense in his stare or in his attitude. He is all limp and desolate and his eyes are dazed. Slowly they move from the door and travel to the chair where* **Frances** *has sat when she talked to him. Life comes ebbing back to him, and dreary little efforts at movement show his rising pain. He tries to swallow. Suddenly with a great sob he runs like a child to the rocking-chair and snatches the cushion which he had placed under her head. He buries his face deep in it and yields himself to frantic sobbing. The hall doorbell rings sharply through the house. He does not hear it. In the after silence his cry is heard.*

Natty   Ethelberta! Ethelberta!

Silence again except for the sobbing. Slowly it subsides and his form relaxes. But again he cries out –

Ethelberta! Ethelberta!

Sharp on the name comes a second peal of the bell. He starts at that and lifts his head. Heavily he draws himself upright and drops the cushion. As he looks about the room listlessness falls on him again and the last shred of his passion that broke through him falls away. He trails wearily towards the door, a crumpled, seedy little fellow. As he goes out into the hall the bell rings again. After a minute **John Morris**'s *voice is heard in the hall. Then there is a pause. He speaks again, and there is the sound of the hall door shutting. He enters the sitting-room alone; he seems puzzled and uneasy. He goes at once to the window and looks out intently, still with baffled eyes. While he is at the window* **Frances** *comes in, moving listlessly towards the chair by the chimney. Looking round the room for* **Natty**, *she is surprised to see* **John** *by the window. He half turns in silent greeting and she nods casually at him, still drifting onwards towards her chair.*

Frances   Did Natty let you in?

John   Yes!

Frances   Where is he?

John   Gone out.

Frances   But he was going to spend the evening here.

John   I can't make him out. When he let me in he looked ghastly. Couldn't open his lips when I asked him what was up! Just shook his head at me! Looked as though he'd been through fever! Why did he look like that?

Frances   He seemed awfully depressed just now – but not as bad as that. Some silly row with Mrs Hemworth about the whist drive. But he wasn't really upset, I think. Are you sure he was as miserable as you say?

John   Never saw him in such a state, honestly. His wretched Mabel often rows him – but he's a great little fellow – it never knocks him over. Poor old Natty, he took no hat with him either. He's generally so fussy about his hats!

Frances   But what can have distressed him enough to make him forget his hat? Oh, Natty, Natty, why won't you talk to people!

John   Proud and remote as an eagle – that funny little beggar!

Frances   I wish he'd stayed home. He's such a child.

John   He's cutting a wisdom tooth to-night!

Silence. **Frances** *leans forward, her elbow on her knees, staring at the paper frills in the fire.* **John** *fidgets with the window-screens, glowering dejectedly at the twilight. What a street it is. Silence.* **Frances** *remains motionless, still staring at the paper frills.* **John** *leans on the window-sash, his head on his arms, staring into the garden. There is no sound anywhere. At last* **Frances** *speaks without moving.*

Frances   If you're looking for Gwen, she's gone to the whist drive at the Assembly Rooms.

John (*also without moving*)   I know. I believe I'm to call for her there to-night.

Frances   Did you come now to take her along? You've only missed her by a very little while.

John (*turning round slowly and looking very straight at her over the aspidistras*)   No, I didn't think of it. (*Silence. He moves round from behind the plants. He has suddenly grown straight and alert, and there is a quiver in his voice.*) I came because you and I wanted to see each other. I came because this house holds you. I came because I hoped you'd be alone. You stay quite still. That is right. You stay quite still because you are noble and strong. It does not frighten you – this shaking of my voice. You have known long ago that my voice would shake when I tried to tell you that I loved you. Your voice would not shake, I think, Frances! Frances Llewellyn! Your name is like cool water and mountain bells! For four months now it has been my song! Frances, I love you! Oh, stay quite still – I want to go on telling you for a long while yet – I love you! I love you! You stay quite still. That is right. I knew your hands would stay as they are now, and that your grave dear face would be graver than ever. I knew that when I spoke to you all the ugliness of this poor place would fall away, and that I'd see only you. I love you! I love you! Frances, I'm waiting for your voice! Oh! I'll come near! Only speak to me now! I love you!

Frances (*turns round slowly and stands up very straight to meet his eyes*)   My voice is shaking just like yours. (*He stretches out his hands and she puts hers into them.*) My hands are shaking too. I love you!

John (*standing back to look at her, still holding her hands*)   Before I heard you say it I knew it must be like that. But now I'm afraid. How can you love me, lovely, quiet lady? Are these your own two hands? And are you giving them to me? Frances! What can I say? However am I to tell you what it means?

Frances   I love you!

John (*catching her face in his hands*)   My heart is pounding – bursting. All I can think of is your lovely mountain name! Frances Llewellyn! Only kiss you, quiet, sweet!

Frances (*laying her hands about his neck*)   Your eyes burn me.

John   I will close them when I kiss you. But I'm afraid. How can it be that I am holding your head in my two hands? How am I to dare to kiss you?

Frances *lifts her face nearer, and as he bends, searching its lines with wondering joy, her brows suddenly contract as though in pain, her eyes open, her voice, when she speaks, is husky with sudden misery.*

Frances   This is Gwen's house – the house of Gwen's people.

John (*dropping his arms with a quick breath which seems almost a sob*)   Gwen! Gwen's house! I had forgotten that!

Frances   So had I.

John   I had forgotten that, and, since I first said I loved you, I had forgotten Gwen, I swear I had!

Frances   John, I had forgotten too!

John (*suddenly alive again*)   You called me by my own name! Oh, sweet, sweet, sweet! You simply did not think of anything else. You called me by my own name. That's because you know that I belong to you, and that I'm bound to you, body and soul, for all our days. Oh, love, love, love, come back to me! Give me your hands. Nothing can ever matter again. No one can ever matter. There are only us two to-night and always.

Frances (*in his arms again, but uneasy*)   That's true. I've said I love you. I'm not going back on that, but, darling, don't look like that – not yet – not ever, perhaps.

John   Little fool! When two people love each other, two people as young and as wise as we are, nothing can stop them. I tell you I belong to you; I have forgotten everything but you – Frances Llewellyn!

Frances   Wait! There is Gwen. We must face that question.

John   I know; I've faced it by myself already. Gwen won't mind. She'll understand. We're not good companions, she and I. We've done our best. A week after I had seen her face we were engaged – as they say – and a week after that I think we must both have known what fools we were. But we drifted on with it. Lately Gwen has hardly noticed me at all. For two months now I have scarcely seen her. And just when I was beginning, this last week, to think of asking her to let me go, I thought that she seemed sad and wistful – almost ill, in fact, and I let well alone. But as I watched you, every day more and more, my beautiful, I saw that you were unhappy too. I knew that something was wrong. And when I met your eyes – oh, how solemn the air would grow, and how grave your glances were! Frances! I was conceited, I was mad; but I knew that you loved me! And so I came to-night because I had to come, and because I knew you wanted me!

Frances   I wanted you. I shall want you always.

John   You will have me always. You've got to marry me! You've got to keep a bookshop in the Camberwell Road!

Frances   What fun it will be! Us two selling books in the Camberwell Road!

John   Us two! Us two! You must give up your lovely name like mountain bells! Frances Llewellyn! Frances Morris!

Frances (*laughing*)   It's unlucky to call me that until it's time.

John   It will be time soon, my darling. As soon as I've told Gwen. I'll tell her tomorrow.

Frances (*dreamily*)   Gwen won't mind. She hasn't looked well lately. I honestly think she's worrying about being engaged to you. You're mine, you see, not hers.

John   I'm yours, am I, and for always! I am going to marry you, do you hear? Aren't you afraid?

Frances (*laughing*)   Yes, I'm afraid – and so are you, my darling. (*Looking about her.*) Queer how I loved this ugly little place from the very start! Queer how I couldn't go away! And now I'm going, with full hands!

John   They'll miss you here, poor devils.

Frances   I was leaving, you know.

John   Leaving?

Frances   Yes, I couldn't stand it any longer. I was getting too fond of you.

John (*laughing outright*)   So I was only in the nick of time! Oh, you must kiss me – but not here! Come away; come out! I'll take you miles away to fields where I dreamt of you on many, many Sundays! Come free of all this – my flower, my love!

Frances   I'll come.

John   Give me your hand.

Frances (*laughing towards the window*)   There's the little new moon! But I've seen her through glass – for bad luck.

John   We're beyond luck, good or bad. We have love. Oh, come!

He draws her into his arms and they run out of the room together. A second later the hall door bangs, there are steps on the path and the clang of a gate. They are gone.

Curtain

Act Three

The same scene – in early afternoon of the next day. The parlour looks less neat than usual, but brilliant sunlight streams in over the aspidistras. When the curtain rises, **Mabel Hemworth***, neatly dressed and coiffed, is pacing the room in a frenzy that is compounded of amazement, cruelty, outraged conventionality and total ignorance of the reality of her situation. Her unrelieved egoism makes the hour easy for her – something has happened which strikes at her dignity – the citadel has never been threatened before, and she rages and sets her lips, awaiting her inevitable victory. Since nothing can strike at her soul – supposing she has one – she has no tears now, and she is not afraid. But, for all her power, she is for the moment a little less mistress of 'Distinguished Villa' than it is her pride to be. After many restless journeys about the room and much fidgeting, she sits down for a minute near the table and endeavours to read a Sunday paper. But her lips remain drawn in their awful cruel line – it is plain that she does not see the print. She starts on her pacing again, at last turning to the kitchen and looking in there as if it might yield her victim. Turning back from surveying it she sees* **Natty** *standing in the other doorway of the room. He wears yesterday's clothes – but all the creases are gone, and his collar is seedy, his tie badly arranged. He wears no hat and his hair is ruffled. He wants a shave, and much else besides, to judge by his miserable shadowed eyes. He droops with misery, but his gaze meets* **Mabel***'s without fear or cringing, only with a piercing plea in them.* **Mabel** *stares in rage that is now edged with triumph. Her citadel is safe again – only remains her vengeance. She becomes mistress of the situation.*

Mabel   Come in and shut the door. (**Natty** *obeys. Looking at her again, he makes a weary effort to come nearer, stretching out one hand.* **Mabel***, still without moving, stares witheringly at it.*) How dare you? Stand further back, if you please. As far back as possible.

Natty *withdraws, but is still determined to be allowed to speak. He seems to have difficulty in articulating.*

Natty   Mabel!

Mabel   Not a word! Not a word. You have forfeited your right to address me by that name. You will speak only when I question you. There are questions which I must ask you. It must indeed amaze you that with my health I have survived the shock of last night and this morning. Oh, don't trouble to interrupt me, thank you. Only my natural self-control has helped my delicate constitution in the last fifteen hours! But you have no reason to congratulate yourself. Your conduct has most certainly done my whole system a permanent injury, of that I'm sure! And so will Dr Broad be sure. You have succeeded in ruining what health I still possessed! You have insulted me. You have insulted the home, before my own sister – and you have broken down my health. No, I do not want you to speak to me – not yet. Not as you like. You will answer my questions in my time. A pretty figure you cut, of that I'm sure! (*Laughs at him.*) A nice match you are now for a lady of refinement! Not even shaved! A pretty figure indeed, of that I'm sure. (*Laughs very fiercely and long at him.*)

Natty (*covering his ears*)   Don't laugh, Mabel! Don't laugh!

Mabel   Must I repeat that you have forfeited your right to call me by that name? And since when have you taken to instructing me as to what I'm not to do? (*Laughs again.*)

Natty   Laugh then! But while you're laughing I'll talk, and you'd better listen. Oh, listen, Mabel, listen!

Mabel   Listen indeed! I will listen to the answers you give to my questions.

Natty   Don't ask me that way, Mabel. Help me. Sit down and listen and I'll tell you everything. Honest I will, Mabel.

Mabel   I should hope so, indeed. You owe me a full account of this, and I mean to get it. Not only has your conduct been an insult to me, and an injury to my poor health, but you may not be aware that your callousness – and John Morris's, I may add incidentally – in not calling for Gwen and me at the whist drive last night, has disgraced us in the eyes of all our friends in the Avenue! I cannot expect you to understand the humiliation I had to suffer when at eleven o'clock neither of you had arrived! You are of too coarse a fibre to realise a woman's sensitiveness – you always were, of course, of that I'm sure! Had it not been for the kindness of the Smithsons we would have had to come home unescorted! I shall never recover from that public humiliation. I am not of the fibre that can weather indignities. I shall never recover.

Natty   Mabel! Will you let me talk? Please, Mabel! I'm tired.

Mabel (*laughing*)   Tired? Oh, no doubt. I expect you're tired. I'm tired too. Answer this question: Where did you go when I left for the whist drive last evening?

Natty   Nowhere – that's to say – oh, Mabel – here's what happened. After you left for the whist drive I suddenly felt rotten about not going with you – honest I did, Mabel! I knew I'd been a selfish beast again – only worse than usual this time. I was even thinking of going after you, only – well, I thought that you'd have made some excuse for me by then, and if I arrived it would have been awkward for you. So I stayed fooling about here – and met Miss Llewellyn. She'd a bit of a headache and seemed depressed like. We just sat and talked – and – oh, well, I don't know – her talk sort of upset me, Mabel! I can't remember very well, but I must have walked out of the front door – I don't know why – but I must have walked miles and miles without stopping, or remembering anything. I don't remember the streets or the crowds or a blessed thing. I lost my hat. I think I walked by the river – seem to remember boats. Suddenly I was tired all over and I leant on the wall by the river. The water was so black that looking at it was like being asleep – there wasn't a sound except the splash on the water steps. So I thought I was asleep, and then I thought I was dead. And it seemed hard lines to be dead without ever having been – what was it she said? (*With sudden startled anguish.*) Oh, then I remembered – then it all came back – and I was sorry that I wasn't dead after all. (*Quicker.*) But I was miles away from everything I knew – and it seemed to be fearfully late – only boatmen on the water. I was hungry. I went into an eating-house – open all night, they said. It was a rotten place, but they gave me coffee and stuff. Did me good. There were only two people in the place besides the owner – they said it was half-past two.

Mabel (*who has listened with a kind of fascinated horror*)   Did they tell you where you were?

Natty   Rotherhithe, they said.

Mabel   Rotherhithe? At half-past two? I presume you did not try this fancy story on them? Anyone who had had the pleasure of meeting you – without your hat – at Rotherhithe at that point in your adventure, would realise without much trouble what my intelligence has found out without your assistance. (*Laughing savagely.*) Of that I'm sure!

Natty (*dazed*)   How do you mean, Mabel?

Mabel   Kindly keep my Christian name out of this.

Natty   But, but, Mabel – don't you believe me? Honestly, Mabel, it's dead true.

Mabel   You may have got to Rotherhithe – but what reason had you for behaving like you described? What were you doing on the journey? I don't wonder that you are ashamed to tell your unhappy wife (*Savagely.*) that you were drunk.

Natty (*astonished*)   But, Mabel, I wasn't. I've never been drunk. Never. You know it.

Mabel   Neither have you ever before been out all night.

Natty   I tell you honestly, I drank nothing. I wasn't drunk.

Mabel   Very good. Very good. Do you imagine that I expect the truth from you now?

Natty (*desperate and drooping with fatigue*)   I wasn't drunk. I said to myself coming home to-day that I would tell you the whole truth about last night, every word of it – as well as ever I could – so that the slate would be clear. I knew that that was the only way of fixing up. Only just listen; I'm telling the truth.

Mabel   Will you remember that I am not to be instructed? I will listen when and to what I choose.

Natty (*who has fallen abstracted again*)   They were awfully decent – the two in the eating-shop. She wanted to give me brandy.

Mabel   She? To whom do you refer?

Natty   The lady – the young girl I met there.

Mabel (*laughing*)   You met a lady in a Rotherhithe eating-house at two a.m?

Natty   I don't know what you call a lady, but she was a real good sort.

Mabel   And she was carrying brandy about with her? It is very plain what she was –

Natty   How do you mean, Mabel?

Mabel   Do you expect me to defile my lips by mentioning her profession?

Natty   Oh, I dunno. She was that all right, I suppose. Kind little kid – and down on her luck she seemed.

Mabel   How do you know? However far gone you were, I must do my husband the honour of presuming that he did not speak to such a person.

Natty   'Course I spoke to her. Spoke for over an hour there in the shop.

Mabel (*screaming*)   You spoke – you spoke for over an hour to – to – to a wretched creature of the streets! You, whom I married, *my* husband, married to a woman of my nature for eleven years – could speak to – speak to – such a wretch as you have described! And for an hour! You were drunk; if you weren't you couldn't have done it!

Natty (*very quiet and forlorn*)   It's no good carrying on that way. I shan't rest until you know it all. I spoke to her and she took me home. I stayed with her until I came back here. She was very kind.

Mabel (*hoarse*)   She took you home? You stayed with her? A strange woman; a bad woman? What do you mean?

Natty   I can't say any more. I was mad and miserable, and she was very nice to me. You know what I mean. You know it all now, Mabel. I couldn't rest if you didn't know.

Mabel   Rest? Rest? And do you think you'll rest now? Do you think I'll rest – ever again? Never, never, never! I cannot bring to my lips the things that I think you are. You were always too coarse and horrible for me. But that you should bring your cruelty to this! That you should callously go out and in a drunken madness wrong me and insult me with a – a – a fallen woman! That you should sink to such a level – even you! I will never forgive you, never. I will never forget all this. But because I know my duty I shall continue – just as usual. I will not have it known that my husband could have stooped to the lowest of all crimes! I owe that much to my self-respect. The outside world will never forget it. As long as you live you will suffer for this, of that I'm sure!

Natty (*vaguely*)   I'm sorry. But she was very kind. I couldn't help it.

Mabel (*going to the door that leads into the hall*)   I am going to lie down. You are not to address me again until I speak to you. You are vile and low and sinful. Keep out of my sight. To see you makes me think of the evil thing that you have done – and makes me sick. (*Opens door.*)

Natty (*stretching his hands to her*)   Mabel! Mabel! Say one kind word! Say only one kind word to me! I'm sorry, I tell you! I can't bear any more to-day, Mabel.

Mabel   I believe you are still drunk. You look like a scarecrow. Go and get a wash – you need one, of that I'm sure! (*She goes out with a horrible laugh.*)

Natty drops his hands and turns from the door. He is absolutely listless and looks round the room as if trying to remember things. He goes to window and looks out, turns back, fidgets with the gramophone, puts on 'Voi che Sapete' without paying the least attention to it. As it proceeds, however, anguish seems to steal over him. At last, the record still playing, he walks with a kind of lurching resolution into the kitchen and closes the door. After a minute or two the centre door opens again, and **John**

Morris *comes in. He is straight and broad-shouldered now, and moves with a swing of joy. He looks years younger, and a touching change in him is that he is much more carefully groomed than usual. He sings softly with the gramophone, moves about the room, goes back to the door and, holding it open, looks eagerly upwards where the staircase is, still singing. There is the sound of a door opening above and his frame seems to tighten, but it relaxes quickly, and the singing stops.*

John   Hello, Gwen! Coming down?

There is a vague murmur and steps on the staircase. **John** *holds the door open and* **Gwen** *enters. She looks wretchedly tired and harassed, and more burdened than ever with cheap jewellery and trimmings, which spoil her beauty.* **John** *looks thoughtfully at her, seems reassured by some reflection, pulls himself together, and enters the room, closes the door and stops the gramophone. Although a slight nervousness has come over him since seeing* **Gwen***, he is quite unable to suppress his new vitality.* **Gwen***, glancing sideways at him, seems interested in his air of joy and takes heart. She smiles vaguely and comes near to him.*

Gwen   Taking me out?

John   Mayn't we talk first? There's something I want to say to you.

Gwen   Funny – I want to talk to you too, John. How nice you look to-day!

John (*eagerly*)   Do I look nice?

Gwen   Ripping. What's up?

John   Never mind. You get ahead and say your say.

Gwen (*growing nervous and wretched again*)   I can't. It's not easy to start! I – I can't tell you, John.

John (*gently*)   Are you worried about anything that's got to do with you and me?

Gwen (*hopefully*)   Yes – Yes.

John   Ah! You've looked worried lately, Gwen. I thought I was beginning to guess at it, you know. Any easier now?

Gwen (*breathing deeply*)   Oh, much easier, much easier. How kind you are, John. And I've been nearly mad with fright. Near mad!

John (*laughing*)   Nearly mad? But, Gwen, surely that's a bit extravagant? What kind of wild ogre to you take me for?

Gwen (*shy and wondering*)   Well, you know, it isn't easy – some men might –

John   Go on – get it off your chest. I swear I know what you're going to say!

Gwen (*hiding her head on him and almost happy now*)   I can't, I tell you, I can't. You must tell me how you guessed it. How did you know? How did you know that I was going to have a child?

Silence. She remains calmly buried on his shoulder. He does not move his limbs, only his face contracts in a slow ghastly spasm. Once he tries to repeat her last words, but they only come in a whisper. He shuts his eyes a minute. **Gwen** *stirs restlessly, but does not lift her head.*

Gwen   Why don't you say something, John? You knew, didn't you?

John (*huskily*)   Going to have a child, Gwen? But how? How do you mean?

Gwen (*startled*)   But you said you guessed. You know, I mean – you remember – once – we were sorry afterwards – but you remember! John – you said you knew! And then I wasn't afraid anymore – not a bit afraid! Why did you say you knew?

John   I know now, anyway. I remember. But are you sure? Oh, Gwen, Gwen, Gwen, for God's sake, are you sure? How could it be?

Gwen   I know, I tell you. I've nearly been mad with knowing. But why have you turned so queer again? Why did you say you knew if you didn't?

John   Oh, nothing. I just thought you were going to tell me something else, that's all.

Gwen   What?

John (*laughing*)   I thought you were going to say that you didn't want to marry me.

Gwen (*crouching back*)   And you were gay about it! I've never seen you so happy! That means you don't love me any more!

John (*gently*)   You are the mother of my child.

Gwen (*triumphantly*)   And you'll marry me? (*Eager and coaxing.*) Even if you're not keen on me much – you'll marry me for that? It'll be all right, won't it? You'll marry me at once? It'll be all right, won't it? Won't it?

While speaking she has pressed herself against him and now buries her head in his neck. He has never once touched her with his hands, nor does he put his arms round her now. He stands very still, staring over her head at nothing. His face is miserable. Suddenly it contracts with pain.

John   My darling! My darling!

Gwen *nestles closer when she hears the first cry, but something in the voice, and the stiffness of his attitude, startles her, for she looks up in wonder. Fear of what she sees in his face makes her creep away from him. He falls back into listlessness.*

Gwen (*huskily*)   Who are you talking to? Who is she? (*He shakes his head. In sudden beautiful pity she comes to him and takes his hands.*) Oh, John, my poor John! My dear, my dear!

John   S-sh! It's my fault, not yours, not yours.

Gwen (*trying to kiss him*)   But I'm sorry; I'm dead sorry. I'll make up for her. I'll try – John – I swear.

John (*shaking off her hands and turning from her*)   Go away, Gwen – please, please.

Gwen   I'll put on my things – take me out – will you? (**John** *does not answer. He is staring over the aspidistras.* **Gwen** *moves towards the door and then turns backwards.*) But it'll be all right now, won't it? It'll be all right! (*She goes out gaily, almost her old self again.*)

John *remains by the aspidistras, staring, staring. Into the silent room comes* **Frances**, *transfigured as he had been transfigured, only more subtly. Her eyes shine towards him where he stands, still motionless. She closes the door, leans against it, and laughs very quietly.*

Frances   Can you guess who's here? Do you know this voice? (*Coming to him swiftly with a ringing laugh and flinging her two hands across his eyes.*) Whose are these hands? Tell me! Tell me! No, I'll not set you free. I'm punishing you because you wouldn't turn to see me come! John, why didn't you turn to look at me? You have missed something that will never come back. I shall never again be beautiful, as I feel beautiful now, since I shall never again be so happy. I'm almost glad. (*Leaning against his back.*) I couldn't bear it if it were to last for ever. How I shall rest and be lazy in revenge for this uprooting! No, be still! I don't want to see your eyes yet. I don't want you to see mine.

John (*dreamily*)   Don't move your hands. Keep my eyes dark and let me hear your voice!

Frances   Strange, shaky words! Almost as if you were unhappy! John, John darling! (*Drawing her hands away quickly in reproof.*) Not tears on my hands! There can be nothing to cry for to-day? (*As he covers his face and will not turn to her, she catches at his hands and forces him to look up.*) Darling! Darling! Why is your face so white? (*Wailing.*) Why do you look afraid? Who has hurt you? My dear, my sweet! Who has hurt you?

John   Why did you bring me back from the dark? I asked you to keep my eyes dark! (*Catching her in his arms.*) Oh, flower! Oh, sweet! I cannot bear this light! Give me more darkness! Only one second more of peace – and then I'll tell you who has hurt me.

Frances   Tell me now.

John (*dropping her from his arms*)   I must move away. Oh, Frances!

Frances (*very gently*)   I beg of you, tell me quickly what has happened. Once we both know, we can put it right; you know we can. It will be all right when I know, John.

John   No, it won't.

Frances   What is it then? Be quick.

John   Gwen has been here. I wanted to tell her about us two, but she had news for me. She told me her news first.

Frances   Go on.

John   She is going to have a child.

Frances   Going to have a child?

John   That was her news, that was what she said. My child!

Frances   But –

John   It's incredible; one night about two months ago.

Frances   Is it hysteria?

John   Gwen's not hysterical. And her whole manner – Oh, it's true enough!

Frances   Was she frightened?

John   Terrified. I was slow about understanding her.

Frances   Poor Gwen! Then that was it? You told her you would marry her at once?

John   I said nothing.

Frances   You will tell her that to-day.

John   I tried to say it – but I couldn't. Frances – is there no way? Must it be this?

Frances   There is only this way. Gwen and your child will need you.

John   And you – you and I?

Frances   You and I. – No.

John   But we are young and strong, and full of love!

Frances   The right thing is the best thing. My dear, I love you. You shall never hear me say it again, but you will remember that I said it often. I will go away to-morrow, grateful to you – content.

John (*with a cry*)   Frances Llewellyn!

Frances   Hush! That song has ended.

John   That song never can end.

Frances   Then let that comfort us. My dear – good-bye.

They break apart. Into the silence enter **Gwen** *and* **Mabel**.

Mabel (*stiffly*)   Where's my husband? Has he made himself fit to appear in my presence yet?

John (*wearily*)   Perhaps he's in the kitchen.

Goes to the kitchen door and stands stock still on the threshold. His figure stiffens as he stands. The others look interested. **Frances** *is frightened and starts towards him.*

Frances   John! (*He turns quickly and shuts the door, standing against it.* **Frances** *stares hard at him.*) John! Where is Natty? What is it?

John   Natty's all right – at last.

Frances What's he done?

John A good thing, and easy thing. He's done it with a knife.

Gwen (*screaming*) You mean he's dead! Oh, God! Is Natty dead? Did Natty kill himself?

John Natty is dead.

Mabel Natty is dead. Natty has killed himself. It could not happen! He knows the delicate state of my health! He couldn't do this. It did not happen. It's all a mistake, John. I tell you it's a mistake – this thing could not happen to me.

Mabel *rushes into the kitchen. After a pause a terrible scream is heard.*

John Things like this are done slowly. Our methods are refined in Distinguished Villa.

Frances (*reprovingly*) Hush! It's all over now. Oh, Natty, Natty! (*Sobbing.*)

THE END

The Woman

A Play in Three Acts

Margaret O'Leary

Premiere: 10 September 1929 at the Abbey Theatre.

Kitty Doyle	Mairead Bonass
James Deasy	Michael J. Dolan
Mrs Dunn	May Craig
Ellen Dunn	Eileen Crowe
Jer Murnane	F. J. McCormick
Stranger	Denis O'Dea
Maurice	Arthur Shields
William Dunn	John Stephenson
Tim Murnane	Michael Clarke
John O'Hara	P. J. Carolan
Mrs O'Hara	Maureen Delaney
Musical Director	Dr J. F. Larchet
Produced by	Lennox Robinson
Assistant Producer	Arthur Shields

Margaret O'Leary, originally from Cork, came from a family deeply engaged with the Gaelic Revival: her brother J. F. O'Leary was one of the founders of the GAA in the city. She was educated at St. Vincent's Convent and University College Cork, where she completed a BA. She taught in Ireland and Scotland for a number of years, and travelled in France, before moving to Dublin to focus on a career as a writer. She wrote two plays that were produced by the Abbey Theatre: *The Woman* (1929) and *The Coloured Balloon* (1944). She also published two novels: *The House I Made* (Jonathan Cape, 1935), which won the Harmsworth Prize for best fiction by an Irish writer in 1937, and *Lightning Flash* (Jonathan Cape, 1939), which is based closely on the story of *The Woman*, adapting the stage play to the novel form.

First staged at the Abbey on 10 September 1929, *The Woman* was well received and was praised by Joseph Holloway, who wrote that 'The Abbey was booked out for the first night of *The Woman* . . . It was a great night.' He praised the 'clever characterization' and 'easy flow of dialogue' and notes that 'The house was very interested in the piece, and the players were recalled several times at the end as also was the author' (quoted in Hogan and O'Neill 1968: 52). *The Woman* returned to the Abbey stage later the same year for a further run and played in Cork in early 1930. The text was never published, and the script here comes from the manuscript in the National Archives.

Despite Holloway's enthusiasm, the critics' response to the play was mixed. In a letter to Lennox Robinson in September 1929, O'Leary asks how the Irish critics could have so little understanding of her work that 'everything of value in the play was lost on them'. She writes that she has already submitted a second play to the Abbey but is now unsure about proceeding: 'I feel now that I could never again let a play of mine be submitted to [the critics] for vandalism.' She thinks she will ask for the play back and will 'turn my back on Ireland' to return to London or Paris. In fact, the Abbey rejected this second play. O'Leary wrote an impassioned defence of its central character to Robinson late in 1929 (see Introduction), and as with the reception of *The Woman* it is possible that the female characters were simply incomprehensible to the Ireland of the time (O'Leary 1929a, 1929b).

There is some evidence that an earlier draft of *The Woman* was submitted to the Abbey sometime before April 1929. That month, W. B. Yeats wrote to Lennox Robinson stating that the ending of the play – which had the heroine Ellen leaving to wander the roads – would have to be changed. Yeats wrote, 'the heroine must die and we must know she dies; all that has been built up is scattered, and degraded, if she does not come to the understanding that she seeks something life, or her life, can never give'. In the same letter, he writes, 'Miss O'Leary should be the best realistic peasant dramatist who has yet appeared', who (pending edits) has written 'a most powerful play'. O'Leary's note on the letter implies that the changes were made (reproduced in O'Leary 1939: 7–9).

The Woman is a three-act, realist, family drama set in rural Cork. The action centres on the themes of marriage and the land: Maurice O'Hara is a farmer and a widower with two small children, who is discovered to be courting Ellen Dunn, the eponymous woman. She is from a poor family and has a bad reputation. Men become obsessed by her and pine away: Maurice, who cannot eat or sleep, is no exception. Gentle and virtuous Kitty is an alternative wife for him but he believes that Ellen was 'made for me from the beginning of the world'. Inevitably, he cannot live up to Ellen's dreams of passion, and she leaves, hinting that she will drown herself in a nearby lake. The last page is missing in the printed text in the National Library of Ireland, but it is preserved in the microfilm and reproduced here. In the final moments, Mrs O'Hara likens Ellen to the heroines of legend, 'Helen the beautiful and Deirdre of the Sorrows', while the men revile her; Maurice, suddenly realizing where Ellen is going, remembers that her grandmother drowned herself in the same lake and 'dashes for the door'.

Holloway likens Ellen to a female Christy Mahon, but she also resembles Teresa Deevy's heroines: they long for excitement and passion, but their ambitions are entirely incongruent with their time and place. For a woman of the time, romantic love is the only possible avenue to such emotions and experiences, yet Ellen realizes that passion will be overwhelmed by domesticity and childrearing. The local people regard love as a kind of madness or illness. Land is what matters; Maurice's father tells him 'a dirty trick it would be to turn your back on the land for the sake of a woman . . . The land that is more to you than a mother . . . the darling land . . .' In contrast, he describes Ellen as 'a jade' and a 'black-eyed slut'.

Yeats's remark that Ellen must realize she wants something 'that her – or her life - can never give her' is particularly poignant in the context of the works presented here. The local society's ostracism of the character points to the closed and repressive nature of Ireland at the time, and the inexplicability of a woman like Ellen in that cultural context. Her dialogue is out of joint with her world; her actions, and attempt to assert her individuality, are dismissed as lying or madness. She resorts to sexual relationships to find expression for repressed passions which are not, of themselves, primarily sexual. Trapped by her poverty and her gender, her plans of emigration to America give way to thoughts of suicide and the embrace of the lake's waters.

3 Cartoon by Grace Gifford Plunkett of Margaret O'Leary's *The Woman*. Courtesy of the National Library of Ireland.

Characters

John O'Hara, *a farmer*
Mrs O'Hara, *his wife*
Maurice, *their son*
James Deasy, *brother of Mrs O'Hara*
Jer Murnane, *brother-in-law of Maurice O'Hara*
Tim Murnane, *brother-in-law of Maurice O'Hara*
Kitty Doyle, *a young girl, a neighbour of the O'Haras*
Mrs Dunn
William Dunn, *her son*
Ellen Dunn, *her daughter*
Stranger

The action takes place in County Cork. Act One in the **O'Haras**' *kitchen; Act Two, a few weeks later, in the* **Dunns**' *kitchen; Act Three, a week later than Act Two, in the* **O'Haras**' *kitchen.*

Act One

A large comfortable farm kitchen; walls creamy yellow, woodwork and furniture deep brown. On left, a large open fireplace: brass candlesticks and copper utensils on mantlepiece: stool on right of fire, and on left a comfortable rush-bottomed armchair: on each side of fireplace a door leading into bedrooms. In the background a neatly curtained window and door opening on farmyard, the half-door closed, the big door open. Along wall, perhaps between window and door, a table covered with a white cloth: tea things a little in disorder, as if after meal. At least two chairs, one at each end of table. On the right front, a door leading into parlour; back, a settle; between the settle and door a dresser well laden with ware.

Evening.

John O'Hara, *in great anger, is walking up and down, now addressing his wife who is seated on the stool near the fire, now his brother-in-law who is seated on the settle.* **John** *is a powerfully built energetic man, somewhere in the sixties. His face is round, healthy, rather heavy but good-natured. His blue eyes are a shade prominent, his mouth is full and wide. His voice is sonorous, deep and rich, kind but authoritative: the voice of a man who gets his own way.* **Mrs O'Hara** *and her brother resemble each other in being gentle and unassertive. They are of medium height and rather pale-faced. They are more refined than* **John**. **Mrs O'Hara** *is fuller in figure and face, and more gracious in speech and manner than her brother.* **James**'s *voice is rather high-pitched and thin, his manner self-effacing and almost deferential.*

John   No, it's no use talking, I won't have it. And I'm master in this house with a good many years before me yet with the help of God. I won't have it, and I'm going to put my foot down on it. Getting himself talked about. What courting he wants. A man with two little children, and his wife dead only six months. Is there any shame in him at all? Getting his name coupled with that black-eyed slut.

James (*nodding*)   Yes indeed: slut. Carrying on with every man that comes her way.

John   Ha, a nice wife she'd make for any man, let alone any of the O'Haras (*With arrogance.*): a family that always had their heads high – a family with a long line of ancestors – a family that never owed a penny to anyone – and that had respect from everyone high and low, from king to beggar.

James (*humbly*)   That's true, John. And you'll see too that Maurice isn't an O'Hara for nothing –

John (*not heeding*)   And now, he – he – with everything he wants, can't be satisfied without gallivanting with that wan – the seed and bread of tinkers and twisters! Her father born in a ditch the son of a gipsy! And her grandmother, the gipsy woman, drownding herself in a bog-hole! A grand pedigree! A grand pedigree![1]

Mrs O'Hara (*sighing*)   Well, maybe we are fretting ourselves about nothing. Maybe 'tis only a passing fancy.

John (*scornfully*)   Passing fancy indeed. I want no passing fancies in my house. Passing fancy. What right has he to have any passing fancy? Tell me that. Hasn't he two children? And his farm?

Mrs O'Hara (*sadly*)   Ah well, the lad is young; and the girl good-looking.

John (*further incensed*)   And in the name of God, what has that to do with it? Good-looking indeed. So is the devil, and all his damned spawn.

James (*gently*)   Wouldn't it be better now to talk to Maurice himself? He's a good lad, and always biddable.

Mrs O'Hara (*warmly*)   He is so a good lad.

John   Till she put her spells on him – the jade. Bet I know what she's after, and I'll put a spoke in her wheel. I will, so I will. Good looks indeed? Ay, good looks, good looks. It's her and her likes that do the devil's work – going round destroying any bit of family peace there's in the world.

James (*nodding slowly*)   That's the devil's work indeed and make no mistake.

John   But I know what she's after: a fine comfortable house to walk into. (*Speaking towards the door.*) It's that you're after. But I tell you, you can stick in your bohawneen[2] up the mountain – stick there until you rot – before you ever put foot inside this door. Yourself and your cadging brother that never looked an honest man straight in the face. And as for the old mother – my God! – that wan – (*He stops, choking with anger.*)

---

1   The language used here reflects long-standing racist discrimination against Travellers and Roma people in Ireland and across Europe. While these terms are not acceptable, they are reproduced here as they are part of the original script. For information on Irish Travellers, see for example The Irish Traveller Movement (www.itmtrav.ie), and Pavee Point (www.paveepoint.ie).

2   Bohawneen means little hut; the use of a double-diminutive indicates contempt. 'Both' is an Irish word for a hut or shed, and bothan means a small hut or shed. The further suffix 'een', meaning little, is used here to exaggerate the poverty of the living accommodation.

James (*nodding*)   She's mane sure enough.

John (*turning to him fiercely*)   Mane? Mane? My God, man, she'd skin a flea for his hide.

Mrs O'Hara   They say that's why her man had to fly off to America from her.

James (*with some heat*)   Indeed he too was no great shakes. Drinking and carousing at every fair in the country he used to be.

John   Arra, what could you expect? A gipsy's brat that he was!

James   And making love to the young girls, he used to be, and he a married man – the blackguard.

John   Oh, a nice lot, a nice lot. And to think it's there our son must go looking for a wife. Our son. There – there – there – (*He stops again choking with anger.*)

Mrs O'Hara (*warmly*)   The boy himself is all right.

John (*turning on her*)   Of course you'd take his part.

James   He is, John. Maurice is all right. He hates maneness and dirt as much as any of us.

Mrs O'Hara (*reflectively*)   There's one thing anyhow: he's fond of his home and his children – terrible fond.

James (*hopefully*)   And he won't turn his back on them. You talk to him, John, and you'll see he'll listen to reason.

John   I'll see he will – take my word for it.

Mrs O'Hara (*quickly*)   Now, John, don't be using any force or threats to him. The quiet way is the best. And anyhow, he can stiffen his back too as good as anyone, and then God knows what he might do. I know him through and through. He'd stop at nothing while the hot blood would be surging up in him (*Sadly.*) God help him, sure 'tis that same hot blood is leading him astray now.

John   Hot blood be damned.

James (*impressively*)   Well, now, I have faith in Maurice. 'Tis true they're a rotten lot, them Dunns. They're all that John says. But all the same, Maurice will come out of this all right. You'll see he will. When a man is clean and honest all the devils in hell couldn't do him any harm. Look at Saint Anthony.

John (*sarcastically*)   Yes, look at Saint Anthony. (*Raising his voice.*) But we're talking about ordinary people, man.

Mrs O'Hara (*reflectively*)   Maybe you're right, James.

James (*brightly*)   I am, I feel sure I am. She's a light woman but –

John   The jade.

Mrs O'Hara (*sadly*)   But when a woman like that marks a man down, he goes down like a flower before the scythe, God help him.

James   No, Mary, no. There's twenty-nine years of decent, orderly living behind him, and that holds him to what he was, like the roots of that old tree out there holds it in the soil. It would take a mighty strong wind to blow up that tree, I'm telling you.

John (*his anger going; emphatically*)   He has no right to be going next or near that house at all.

Mrs O'Hara   Sure he has the simple heart of a child that takes everyone at their face value; and they're got round him.

James (*thoughtfully*)   John is right. He shouldn't be going there at all; they're a godless lot. But no harm will come to Maurice, you'll see it won't. The O'Hara and the Deasy blood is in his veins, and that will speak out; you'll see it will. It will speak out – when – when – things are put plain to him. When John speaks to him everything will be all right.

Mrs O'Hara (*sadly*)   Things are very simple to you, James; but with some people they are a life-and-death struggle.

John (*to himself*)   A pack of dirty cadgers that won't leave a decent man alone.

James (*sententiously*)   There's just the one straight road in life, Mary, and one should follow that without turning either to the right or to the left.

Mrs O'Hara (*standing up, passionately*)   Arra, shut up, man, you don't know what you're talking about. It isn't the one road for an old nag jogging along and for a racehorse tearing up a hill. You don't know what way he feels. But I know it, I know it. Can't I see him before my two eyes – my own son – wasting away – and all the joy going out of him – (*Tearfully.*) – he that used to be as lively as a young colt.

John (*angry – to hide his softness*)   The divil mend him. Couldn't he mind his own business? Why should he go trucking with the likes of that one? (*Changing tone.*) Where is he now?

Mrs O'Hara (*drying her eyes*)   I don't know; he went out there a little while back. Maybe 'tis up the fields he is. He likes to go up there sometimes in the quiet of the evening – since the trouble came on him – kind of moping, standing, staring in front of him, as if –

John (*angry again*)   Standing. Staring. Moping. My God, to think a son of mine would be such a damned fool! Moping? Moping? And all the work there's to be done.

Mrs O'Hara (*at once on the defensive*)   Well, a person must take their ease sometime.

John (*emphatically*)   There's no taking your ease on a farm. And no one should want ease. Moping? And a fine bullock lying sick on us.

Mrs O'Hara   Well, isn't the bullock getting better? And anyhow it wasn't Maurice made him sick.

John (*roughly*)   Ah, shut up, woman.

James (*brightly*)   I think he's pulling up fine, John; he'll be as good as ever in a week; plenty of nourishment now is all he wants.

John (*moving to the door; more gently*)   I'll go around and have a look at him.

He goes out.

James (*following him out*)   I'll go with you. (*His voice is heard trailing.*) Sure 'tis a grand thing –

Mrs O'Hara *removes one or two things from the table to the dresser. She does it slowly and thoughtfully. She then puts the kettle on the fire. At this moment* **Kitty Doyle** *puts her head in over the half-door, smiling. She is a strongly made girl, vigorous in voice and gesture.*

Kitty   God save all here.

Mrs O'Hara (*looks round, hesitates a moment, and then in a tone of pleasant surprise*)   'Tis Kitty Doyle surely?

Kitty   'Tis myself, and no one else.

Mrs O'Hara (*going over to greet her*)   Come in, come in. You're as welcome as the flowers of May. My, isn't it grand you look, and more lovely than ever. (*Leading her to the armchair by the fire.*) Dublin didn't take the roses off your cheeks, Kitty.

Kitty (*laughing*)   Indeed no! Even Dublin couldn't turn me into a grand pale-faced lady. I'll always be a country girl, Mrs O'Hara.

Mrs O'Hara (*warmly*)   You're lovely, just lovely, child.

Kitty (*opening a parcel*)   Just wait till I show you something nice I've brought you from Dublin. (*Standing up and showing a dainty apron.*) Look, isn't that nice?

Mrs O'Hara   Oh Kitty. Well now, that's too good of you. (*Taking and admiring it.*) My, what a masher I'll be. Wait till himself sees me. (*Earnestly.*) 'Tis the good kind heart you have, Kitty Doyle, to be thinking of me like that. A thousand thanks to you.

Kitty   You have a good kind heart yourself, Mrs O'Hara.

Mrs O'Hara (*pushing her into armchair*)   Sit down, sit down, and tell me all about yourself. But wait till I put my grand apron away – maybe 'twould get soiled here. (*Talking all the time, she takes apron into parlour and comes back to stool near fire.*) Well, isn't it grand to see you again. I'm sure your mother is delighted. And when did you come home, Kitty? Strange, I never heard you were coming.

Kitty   I came last night. (*With energy.*) And to tell you the truth, Mrs O'Hara, I'm glad to be home again.

Mrs O'Hara (*wondering*)   Indeed? But sure Dublin is a grand place – all fine houses and shops – and everything?

Kitty   Yes, that's true. But somehow I could never make my own of it all the same.

Mrs O'Hara   Isn't that strange? And the long time you've gone. When did you go away – let me see – when was it?

Kitty   Four years ago.

Mrs O'Hara Four years? Are you as long gone as that? It must have been so about the time that Maurice married; he's married now this four years come Shrove.

Kitty (*her voice softening*) Poor Maurice. It's a short spell of happiness he had in his married life.

Mrs O'Hara (*sighing*) Ay. But God's will be done.

Kitty (*sympathetically*) Amen. One must be satisfied with God's will – but it is often hard. (*Reflectively.*) Poor Maurice. And his two little orphan children.

Mrs O'Hara There was another – but it lived only two months.

Kitty Yes. I heard that. I used to hear all the news. Maybe it was a good thing the little one to go, now that the mother is not here. Poor Maurice! His burden is hard enough as it is.

Mrs O'Hara (*emphatically*) You may well say that. In more ways than one.

Kitty (*with deep feeling*) I was terrible sorry when I heard of his trouble – I can't tell you how sorry. Oh, it is terrible. Poor, poor Maurice.

Mrs O'Hara (*looking at her shrewdly, empathetically*) You are a good girl, Kitty. A good, kind girl. Better than a good many that's going.

Kitty Not at all, Mrs O'Hara. Surely 'tis only neighbourly to feel for a neighbour's trouble.

Mrs O'Hara (*standing up*) You'll take a cup of tea, won't you?

Kitty Now don't go to any trouble.

Mrs O'Hara (*busy during the following conversation, arranging things on table, making tea etc.*) It's no trouble at all – the kettle is just boiling. Anyhow I'd like a drop myself too – although we're only just after it. And sure Maurice ought to be in any moment now, and he'd like to see you.

Kitty (*thoughtfully*) I suppose he's changed a lot, Mrs O'Hara – with the trouble – and everything?

Mrs O'Hara He is – changed. He's a different man altogether – no more play-acting and joking, but silent and dark in himself – always looking in and brooding. I wish a nice good girl would take him in hands – a loving good girl. Whoever she'd be, she'd have my blessing. (*A slight pause. Pouring out tea.*) Sit in now, child.

Kitty (*sitting on left of table*) Thanks, ma'am. (**Mrs O'Hara** *sits on right.*) Now you shouldn't have gone to all this bother. (*Testing tea.*) Well, 'tis just lovely – 'tis the cream, I suppose.

Mrs O'Hara Ah, sure tea is no good at all without a drop of cream. And indeed cakes too – I always put cream in my baking.

Kitty (*eating with relish*) That's what makes cake so nice – I don't know when I tasted anything like it.

Mrs O'Hara   That's right – I like to see a person enjoying their food. (*Changing tone.*) I suppose now, Kitty, you'll soon be going back to Dublin again?

Kitty (*emphatically*)   Indeed I won't. Home I've come and here I'm going to stop. Wild horses wouldn't drag me back to Dublin again.

Mrs O'Hara   You haven't lost your heart to anyone there then?

Kitty (*laughing*)   You may be sure not. Them Jackeens³ aren't my kind at all. Arra, I'd only break my sides laughing to have one of them little hop-o'-my-thumbs for a husband. (*She laughs gaily.*)

Mrs O'Hara (*smiling*)   I'm afraid, Kitty, you're too hard to be pleased. It's a pity a nice pleasant girl like you not to be settling down.

Kitty (*continuing her own train of thought*)   Well, they haven't a bit of sense – them Jackeens. (*Laughing.*) Looking for something to carry they do be – they can't go out without a stick – or something – in their hand.

Mrs O'Hara   Rheumatics, I suppose?

Kitty (*laughing*)   Arra, no. Just to be carrying something – a little case – or something. And there they go, with the little case in one hand, and a pair of gloves in the other – like this. (*She stands up, takes the jug in her right hand and a spoon in the left, and struts up and down the stage with a very grim face.* **Mrs O'Hara** *laughs. Going back to her seat.*) Oh, they'd make you die laughing! And themselves as serious as a judge!

Kitty *eats with great relish during the whole of the following.*

Mrs O'Hara   And why don't they put on their gloves?

Kitty   Why – I don't know. Something to carry they want: to give their hands a bit of exercise maybe.

Mrs O'Hara (*wondering*)   They must be kind of childish.

Kitty (*nodding vigorously*)   Childish – that's just it! And you should see their little hands. Child's hands. (*Laughing.*)

Mrs O'Hara (*wondering*)   How do they do their work, in the name of goodness?

Kitty (*scornfully*)   'Tisn't men's work at all they do – just writing – and things.

Mrs O'Hara (*surprised*)   All day?

Kitty (*eating heartily and nodding*)   All day. Well, do you know what I said to myself coming down in the train?

Mrs O'Hara   What?

---

3   Jackeen (little Jack) is a long-standing nickname for Dubliners. It perhaps mocks the supposed Anglicization of Dublin, by using the common English name John or Jack and the diminutive 'een' meaning 'little'.

Kitty   Thanks be to God, I'll see fine big fists again. (*Doubling up her fists and shaking them merrily.*) For if there's one thing I like better than another – 'tis to see a good, big fist on a man.

Mrs O'Hara (*teasing*)   Indeed? And nothing would do you four years ago but to be running away from the men with the big fists. Nothing would do you but Dublin – Dublin, my dear! And all the poor countryboys breaking their hearts after you.

Kitty (*gaily*)   'Tisn't so easy as that to break countryboys' hearts. Girls with money they break their hearts after.

Mrs O'Hara (*seriously*)   All the same, there's a good many were fond of you – a good many.

Kitty (*gaily*)   To pass the time of day with maybe.

Mrs O'Hara (*emphatically*)   Well, isn't it your own fault? You don't give a man a chance.

Kitty (*seriously*)   In what way?

Mrs O'Hara   You're too – independent. You shouldn't hold off so much. (*Briskly.*) Make up to a man – make much of him – joke with him – tease him – look him in the eyes – get him to notice you – and – and to run after you.

Kitty (*in mock horror*)   Mrs O'Hara, shame on you to be teaching me how to flirt!

Mrs O'Hara (*impatiently*)   Ah, you make me mad, so you do! (*Turning away to herself.*)

Kitty (*very seriously*)   A man that I could get like that, I'd be kicking him out of my way all the day of my life – if I married him. (*Lightly.*) I'd rather have a Dublin Jackeen. He'd make me laugh anyhow.

Mrs O'Hara (*giving a look out to see if* **Maurice** *is coming*)   You're too clever with your tongue – that's what's wrong with you.

Kitty (*lightly*)   To get a husband, is it? First, I'm too independent – and now, I'm too clever – so the kind of woman a man wants for a wife is to be –

Mrs O'Hara (*turning round: sarcastically*)   I suppose smart talk like that is what you learned in Dublin?

Kitty (*with feeling*)   I learned a lot in Dublin – thanks be to God.

Mrs O'Hara   What?

Kitty (*enigmatically*)   Well – independence maybe. (*She rises.*)

Mrs O'Hara   Another cup, Kitty?

Kitty   Not another drop, and that was lovely.

Mrs O'Hara   It isn't much use to be making tea for you, if that's all you are going to take.

Kitty *sits in the armchair near the fire.* **Mrs O'Hara** *goes to the door and looks out anxiously.*

Mrs O'Hara   'Tis strange that Maurice isn't coming in. (*Coming back to the fire.*) He ought to be in any moment. (*Sitting on stool.*) Ah, well!

A short pause. They are both thoughtful.

Mrs O'Hara (*confidently*)   Wouldn't you like to be married?

Kitty (*quietly*)   As things are – no.

Mrs O'Hara   It isn't the will of God a person to remain single.

Kitty   Sure aren't there flowers in the fields without mates, so it must be God's way with people too.

Mrs O'Hara (*with heat*)   All the same, I think it's a shame for you, Kitty Doyle, to be letting brazen hussies capture decent men, when 'tis a good godly girl like you they ought to have. You make me mad, so you do.

Kitty (*surprised*)   But why, Mrs O'Hara? I'm quite happy as I am.

Mrs O'Hara   No woman is happy without the love of a man.

Kitty (*in a low voice*)   Ah – love!

Mrs O'Hara   You laughing and sunny as a flower, you were made for love – if ever woman was.

Kitty (*lightly*)   I hope so.

Mrs O'Hara (*shaking her head*)   Ah, well, well. (*Setting her knitting: speaking casually.*) And to think it's four years since you went to Dublin! Were you here when Maurice married?

Kitty (*a little nervously*)   No, I was gone then – a little before that – not long though – I wasn't here at the time. (*Brightly.*) It was a great wedding, wasn't it?

Mrs O'Hara   It was. (*A slight pause.*) It was his father was dead set on the match. She had a good fortune, and a big place like ours eats up money. She was a good girl too – a good, hard-working girl – no one could say a word against her. But I think, all the same, if Maurice could pick and choose, 'tis another girl – but there's no use talking now. (*She continues her knitting, and looking at the fire speaks dreamily.*) Isn't it strange now, I always thought that Maurice rather fancied yourself.

Kitty (*earnestly*)   Oh no! no! Don't talk of that, Mrs O'Hara. You are quite wrong – indeed you are. No, no! Don't talk of that at all.

Mrs O'Hara   Why not, child? Now, listen to me, Kitty. You are fond of Maurice – I know you are.

Kitty (*turning away*)   No, no!

Mrs O'Hara   Now, listen to me. I am an old woman – older than your mother – and I know the world. There you are – and the warm heart of you crying out for a man – and you tormenting yourself trying to crush it down – and that same man – a poor broken man – in agony – bleeding in his soul – suffering torture – oh, Kitty, Kitty – and you'll stand by and do nothing to save him?

Kitty   What can I do? Oh, no, no, no.

Mrs O'Hara   And you'll have God's own blessing down on you. Listen to me, Kitty. You are young, you are beautiful, you are loving – just the woman to make a man happy. (*As* **Kitty** *stands up.*) You can save Maurice – you are the only one –

Kitty (*turning away: facing audience*)   No, no, you don't know what you are saying. Don't speak of it – it was a shameful thing for me. But it is all over and done with now. No, no, no – I have suffered too much – I couldn't face it again.

Mrs O'Hara   For God's sake, child – for the sake of Christ, Mary's own Blessed Son – listen to me. There's a terrible thing happening to him – I can't tell you what it is – it is terrible – the devil's hand is in it – and you can save him – you are the only one. I wouldn't ask you if I could do anything myself. But what am I? A poor old grey woman. It isn't the likes of me a ripe young man wants – it's not a mother he wants at his age – it's a wife – young and ripe for love like yourself.

Kitty (*sadly*)   He doesn't want me.

Mrs O'Hara   He does, he does. You can ask him, if you try.

Kitty (*facing her, speaking passionately*)   And if I try and can't make him, what then? Is my heart a stick or a stone? Have you no thought for me? (*Sadly.*) I have suffered enough, God knows, during those four long years – crushing out my pain among strangers – learning to master myself – learning to find happiness inside in myself – and not to be depending on anyone else.

Mrs O'Hara   Have pity on a poor old mother!

Kitty (*letting herself go*)   A poor old mother indeed. A mother? Why, there's nothing more terrible on God's earth than a mother foraging for her child. There's nothing can beat her – there's nothing can down her. She'd walk on her knees round the world – she'd cringe – she'd beg – she'd rob – she'd steal – and that same to be the last crust in the wallet of an old bacach.[4] 'Tis little pity she'd have for anyone. You'd sooner get pity from the wild beast of the field and he mad with hunger – or the mountain torrent tumbling down over Sliavgorm and you to fall into it in the winter. And what change would I have against you? Let me go home. (*She rushes to the door.*)

Mrs O'Hara   All right. Go away. Maybe you're right.

Mrs O'Hara *sits down on the stool near the fire and buries her face in her hands.* **Kitty** *stops at the door to control her emotion. Her body is shaken with suppressed sobs. She looks back at* **Mrs O'Hara**, *uncertain what to do, then she comes back, all anger gone, and kneels down by her side.*

Kitty   Forgive me, Mrs O'Hara. I am sorry. Sure I love him too.

Mrs O'Hara *takes* **Kitty**'s *face in her hands and kisses her. They look at the fire. A fairly long pause.*

---

4   This Irish word means a lame person or a beggar.

Kitty   I think I'll be going now. I told my mother I wouldn't be long.

Mrs O'Hara (*standing up*)   Wait till I get a dozen eggs for your mother.

Kitty (*standing up*)   Now don't bother. Sure she has lots of eggs herself.

Mrs O'Hara (*going to door*)   Well, you mustn't go away empty-handed. (*Turning at door.*) Wait there – I won't be long. (**Maurice** *appears.*) Oh come in, Maurice. (*She keeps talking all the time.* **Maurice** *pushes in the half-door and comes in. He is very like his father but has his mother's gentle eyes and mouth. He stands for a moment, uncertain.*) You'd never guess who's here? Look at her. Isn't she the lovely girl! Back from Dublin – and to stay home too.

Maurice (*surprised*)   Kitty! (*Advances and shakes hands.*) I am glad to see you, Kitty.

Kitty   Thanks, Maurice. How are you yourself?

Mrs O'Hara   Sit down near the fire and be talking to her, while I get a few eggs.

She goes out. They sit down. **Kitty** *on stool.* **Maurice** *in armchair. A pause.*

Maurice   I suppose you had a great time in Dublin?

Kitty   The years slipped by without taking count.

A pause.

Kitty   I was sorry when I heard of your great trouble, Maurice.

Maurice   I know that, Kitty.

A pause.

Kitty (*gently*)   With some people it is how the whole of their life seems heaped into a few years – joys and sorrows together. Well, you have joys too – there's the children.

Maurice   Ay, surely.

Kitty   It's great to have them. What would you do without them!

Maurice   I wouldn't care then what I'd do.

Kitty   They fill a person's heart, don't they?

Maurice   They are dearer to me than my heart's blood.

Their tones are low and earnest. **Mrs O'Hara** *appears at door with the eggs. She looks in, and is about to go away again when* **Kitty** *sees her.*

Kitty (*stands up and goes towards door,* **Mrs O'Hara** *comes in*)   You shouldn't really have bothered, Mrs O'Hara. (*Taking basket.*) Thanks ever so much. Goodness, look at the size of them; everything is extra big and fine in this house, I'm thinking. Well, my mother will be delighted. Thanks, Mrs O'Hara.

Mrs O'Hara   Not at all – you're welcome, child. But what hurry are you in? Now that Maurice is here, I'm sure you'll have a lot to say to each other.

Kitty   Really I must be running.

Mrs O'Hara *makes an attempt to keep her. Both are talking together.* **John** *and* **James** *come in.*

Mrs O'Hara   Oh, wait a bit – sure you are in a neighbour's house.

Kitty   I'll come again soon – I will really.

John   Who is this we have here? Kitty Doyle – by all that's holy. (*Boisterously shaking hands.*) And how are you.

Kitty   I'm very well indeed, sir, thanks. I hope I find you the same? But I needn't ask you how you are – I never saw you look better.

John   And you are looking grand yourself. (*At last he lets go her hand.*)

James (*shaking hands*)   Welcome home, Kitty.

Kitty   Thanks, James. (*Looking at* **John**, *emphatically.*) Indeed 'tis glad I am to be at home again. There's no place like the old spot after all.

Mrs O'Hara *and* **James**   That is so.

John   I'm glad to hear you say that, Kitty. (*Moving towards the fire.*) Sit down and take a cup of tea. We want to hear all about the grand city. (*They sit down.* **Kitty** *on settle.* **John** *remains standing in front of fire.*) I suppose there's a power of money up there?

Kitty   There is so. But I don't know if people are much better off all the same.

John   How better off?

Kitty   Well – happier and that. They seem to wear themselves out – always running after something. (*Laughing.*) The first time I was going through O'Connell Street, I thought they were all running for a train. Such a crowd! More even than you'd see at last Mass on a Sunday. And they all looking straight in front of them – kind of frowning – and not wishful at all to say good-day to anyone. (*Laughing heartily.*) Begor, I thought they might be late for the train – they looked so sour.

They all laugh.

James   And where were they running to?

Kitty   Oh, nowhere in particular. Home maybe – or to their work.

John   And why don't they go like honest people? What put the fright on them?

Kitty   There's no fright at all on them – that's just their way of walking.

Mrs O'Hara   Glory be to God. No wonder you came home out of a place like that, child.

John (*thoughtfully*)   All the same, 'tis a great thing to have a power of money – never you fear – Kitty Doyle. (*Pointing to a chair near table.*) Sit over here and take a cup of tea.

Kitty   Thanks, sir, but I'm only just after it.

John   Well, come over here near the fire then, and tell me more about them queer people in Dublin, with all the money and – my God! – not knowing how to get the good out of it.

Kitty (*standing up*)   I'll come again, but I must be going now, my mother is waiting for me.

Mrs O'Hara   Maurice will go down a bit of the road with you. Come again soon, won't you?

Kitty   Indeed I will, Mrs O'Hara. And thanks again, a thousand times. Good-bye all. (*She goes out, followed by* **Maurice**.)

All   Good-bye, good-bye, good-bye, Kitty.

Mrs O'Hara *removes some things from table to dresser. She is busy during all the conversation.* **John** *takes out his pipe and cleans it.*

John (*thoughtfully*)   Well, and to think Kitty Doyle is home again. I suppose Patsy will be fixing up a match for her one of these days.

James   Well, she's a fine-looking girl anyway, and that oughtn't to be hard.

Mrs O'Hara   (*enthusiastically*)   She is so – a fine-looking girl.

John (*filling his pipe*)   Arra, fine looks won't make the pot boil. I think them Doyles do be putting up for too much altogether, more than their betters maybe, cocking themselves up with fine clothes and that; and, believe you me, if Patsy Doyle has a hundred pounds to his name, 'tis as much as he has. (*He kneels down and lights his pipe.*)

James   Well, she's a nice, pleasant-spoken girl anyway.

Mrs O'Hara   And they are good neighbourly people with the kind heart and the open hand for everyone in need.

John (*to* **Mrs O'Hara**)   Have you any eggs to spare?

Mrs O'Hara   To be sure I have. How many do you want?

John   Half a dozen will do. (*He smokes for a few minutes.*) And – heat a drop of milk too. (**Mrs O'Hara** *pours milk into saucepan, he watching.*) That's enough. (*She puts it on fire. He moves towards the door.*) Don't let it boil. (*Going out.*) Call me when 'tis ready.

Mrs O'Hara (*putting eggs on table*)   How's the bullock, James?

James   Arra, he's getting on all right. My God, you'd think it was a Christian, the way himself is going on.

Mrs O'Hara   That's his nature I suppose – to be fussing about them animals.

James   But when there's no need.

A pause.

Mrs O'Hara (*going to fire and watching milk; reflectively*)   Well, maybe 'twas God sent her home. (*Turning her head.*) Wouldn't they make a lovely pair, James?

James   Just what myself was thinking. She'd make a good, wholesome wife.

Mrs O'Hara   May God and his blessed Mother grant it.

James   I'm thinking though himself would be against it – he'll be looking for money – always bettering the place.

Mrs O'Hara (*with heat*)   Surely to God the place isn't more to him than his own son?

James (*dubiously*)   N-n-o-o; but the place and his son are the same thing in his mind.

Mrs O'Hara   Arra, shut up, James – or talk sense. (*Moving saucepan aside and standing up.*) Where is he now? – the milk is ready.

James (*going to door*)   Are you there, John?

John (*from outside*)   Yes, I'm coming. (*He comes in.*)

Mrs O'Hara   The milk is ready.

He goes over to the fire, takes the saucepan in his hand and puts his finger in.

John   It's a bit hot. (*As she pours some more milk in.*) Easy, easy. What a heavy hand you have. (*He feels the milk again and seems satisfied. He then goes to the table and puts the eggs carefully into his pocket.*)

James   Here, let me carry the milk.

James *takes the saucepan, and as they are going out* **Maurice** *meets them at the door.* **Mrs O'Hara** *gets her knitting and sits in armchair.*

Maurice (*eagerly*)   Is it to the bullock you're taking it, father?

James   Yes.

Maurice   How is he this evening? He looked nice and –

He is talking as the three move off from the door together.

Mrs O'Hara (*calling*)   Maurice. Maurice.

Maurice (*running in*)   What is it, mother? Did they forget something?

Mrs O'Hara   Yeh, no. What do three of you want up to give a drink to a calf? Sit down there and draw your breath.

Maurice   But I'm not tired, mother.

Mrs O'Hara (*in a half-scolding tone*)   Well – you ought to be. Look at the state you were in at dinner-time – with the sweat pouring down off you. Glory be to God, you'd think it was out of the river you walked.

Maurice (*eagerly*)   Ah, it was great, mother – up there in the meadow.

Mrs O'Hara   Yes, but there's no need to be working yourself into oil all the same. Did you change your shirt as I told you?

Maurice   I did.

Mrs O'Hara   Aren't you going to sit down? (*As he is still doubtful.*) Of course there's time for everything but there's no time for a word with your poor mother.

Maurice   All the same I'd like to see how the calf is.

Mrs O'Hara   Arra, he's getting on all right. It's your father's way of going on. He's the deftest man about them animals. Glory be to God, if only one of them left a sneeze out of him, he'd be dosing him with medicine.

Maurice (*proudly*)   Father is a great farmer all the same. Look at the fine stock we have, and sure we hardly ever lose one.

Mrs O'Hara (*impatiently*)   Ah, I know, I know. But I want to be talking to you here by ourselves. (*Changing tone.*) The baby slept like a top after her milk. 'Tis just her teeth are plaguing her, the poor little lamb.

Maurice   Is she asleep now, mother?

Mrs O'Hara (*nodding*)   She is.

Maurice (*rising*)   I'll go up and have a peep at her.

Mrs O'Hara (*decisively*)   You can't. Sit down and keep quiet. The two of them are asleep. (**Maurice** *sits down again.*) Oweneen does be played out – going all day from the time he gets up in the morning. Just like what yourself used to be.

Maurice (*anxiously*)   Do you think the baby is thriving, mother? She seems to me terrible small and thin.

Mrs O'Hara   Of course she's thriving. What nonsense you're talking. She's small, but she's hardy.

Maurice   Oweneen used to be a lot fatter at her age.

Mrs O'Hara   Ah well, that's only natural. She misses the mother, the poor little crathereen.[5] But I wouldn't mind about that. 'Tis many a fine child I've seen reared on the bottle. (*A slight pause. Changing tone.*) But tell me, Maurice, weren't you very surprised to see Kitty Doyle here before you this evening?

Maurice   I was then.

Mrs O'Hara (*with animation*)   And we were the first one of the neighbours she came to see. What do you think of that. 'Twas last night she came home – so she

---

5   Little creature. The 'een' suffix indicates a diminutive of creature, and the spelling (crather) gives the local pronunciation. The word carries connotations of pity and sympathy for the infant.

didn't waste much time. Wait till I show you the nice apron she bought me from Dublin. (*She gets up briskly and goes into the parlour.* **Maurice** *looks at the fire. She comes back exhibiting apron.*) Look at it, Maurice. Isn't it grand? And won't your mother be the masher? (*He smiles and nods.*) Well, what I always said was that Kitty Doyle was the best girl in the parish – a kind, hard-working, pleasant, comely, honest girl, that any man would be proud to have. (*Folding up apron.*) And God's own blessing she'd bring into any home, for a good graceful girl she is that is at her Holy Communion every Sunday morning, come rain or hail. (*Taking apron back to room.*) Oh, she's a grand girl, a jewel of a girl. (*She comes back again and kneeling down to poke fire says casually.*) I suppose she was telling you all about Dublin going down the road?

Maurice   She was not then – we were talking about ourselves.

Mrs O'Hara (*looking up at him – surprised*)   Yourselves?

Maurice   Yes then – ourselves. She's a kind of girl you can tell things to, she's so –

Noise of footsteps heard outside. The **Murnanes** *come to the door. They are strong, thick-set young men.* **Jer** *is the elder. He has a habitual smile of self-assurance and cunning.* **Tim** *is flushed and angry.*

Mrs O'Hara (*intuitively scenting trouble*)   Come in, boys, come in.

They come in but stand near the door. In advancing to meet them she is standing between them and **Maurice**.

Jer   'Tis himself we want.

Mrs O'Hara   He's gone out to the cattle-shed, but he'll be in shortly. A sick bullock he's tending but won't you sit down? Sit down, boys. (*They sit on settle.*) Isn't it lively weather we're having, thanks be to God? (*She comes back to her chair. They see* **Maurice**.*)

Tim (*springing up and shouting*)   So there you are, is it? What's this story we hear about your carrying on?

Maurice   Talk plain, man. What carrying on?

Tim   What carrying on? What carrying on? And he the talk of the whole country. What carrying on?

Jer (*with ironical good humour*)   Maybe you'd tell us, if it wouldn't disoblige you too much, what's taking you up the mountain every Sunday after dinner? Picking heather, I suppose? Or taking a walk for your indigestion maybe? Good mountain air – and plenty of exercise – five miles going – and five miles coming.

Maurice (*raising his voice*)   It's my own business where I go, mountain or no mountain.

Jer (*in his slow, self-assured, ironical voice; enjoying having* **Maurice** *in his power*)   Just stretch your mind a little bit – a small, little, weeshy bit – and maybe you'll see 'tis a little bit of our business too. (*With great sarcasm.*) Me fine buck.

Tim (*shaking his fist*)   Answer me this, Maurice O'Hara – what takes you up the mountain? Answer me, or by heaven, I'll strangle you with my own two fists.

Mrs O'Hara (*rushing over to* **Tim**)   Oh for God's sake, for God's sake, keep quiet. He'll answer you, he'll answer you, only keep quiet. (*She gently pushes him back on settle and sits beside him.* **Tim** *is in the middle.*) Sure aren't we all neighbours?

Maurice (*standing up and speaking with concentrated anger*)   Tim Murnane, you're in my house and you have the advantage of me, but I tell you this, keep a civil tongue in your head, or – (*Pointing to the door.*) there's the broad road outside, and if 'tis fighting you want, I promise you plenty of it. (*He takes a chair from left of table, and moving it forward noisily and defiantly, sits down.*) Is your business here with me?

Tim (*somewhat cowed*)   It is.

Jer (*still very sure of himself*)   Well – I'd say – it is partly with you – and partly – with your father. There's nothing like being precise and – business-like. (*Turning to* **Mrs O'Hara**.) Is there, ma'am?

Mrs O'Hara   No, Jer, no.

Jer (*giving a side look at* **Maurice's** *stern face*)   And I want you all to know, that I'm here as a businessman – and want to treat this as a business matter – pure and simple. Isn't that right, ma'am?

Mrs O'Hara   'Tis, Jer, 'tis.

Jer (*feeling his way; as* **Maurice** *doesn't relax*)   Tim here is different – he's no businessman. Feelings are alright – but they shouldn't interfere with business. That's my motto. I'm not against feelings – oh no – but, keep them in their right place. Isn't that so, ma'am?

Mrs O'Hara   'Tis, Jer, 'tis.

Tim   Well – I'm not ashamed of my feelings. Anyhow. (*Jumping up again.*) 'Tis enough to make your blood boil.

Mrs O'Hara (*pushing him back on the settle*)   Now, Tim, you're spoiling everything. Let us keep nice and friendly, and talk over our business like good neighbours – as Jer says.

Jer (*pleased at being so successful*)   Quite right, ma'am, quite right. Give me the hand there. (*He stretches across* **Tim** *and shakes hands with her.*) You're a woman after my own heart. (*Looking at* **Maurice**.) And what does himself think?

Maurice (*angrily*)   That 'tis taking you a damn long time to say what you have to say.

Jer (*to* **Mrs O'Hara**) His father's son, ma'am. (*To* **Maurice**.) I see you're a businessman – like myself. Very well, then. (*Changing tone; more respectfully.*) You married our sister?

Maurice   I did.

Jer   We gave her a fortune of five hundred pounds – a big sum. We drained ourselves dry to give it to her – never mind that, we will keep to business. She brought in here five hundred pounds – a big sum – but we gave it willingly – we wanted to see her settled in a comfortable place – but never mind that either, we'll keep to business. She died six months ago, God rest her soul –

Mrs O'Hara (*piously*)   And all the souls of the dead.

Jer And now we're after hearing that you're thinking of putting another woman in her place –

Tim (*springing to his feet*)   But, by heaven, if you do, we'll take her body up out of the grave – we'll bring her back to her own people – we will, we will – the name of O'Hara would stink her in her coffin –

John *and* **James** *come in.*

John   Oho, what's all the noise about? We heard it coming in the haggart.

Tim (*sitting down, subdued*)   Ask your son there – he'll tell you.

John (*looking at* **Maurice**)   What is it?

Maurice *does not answer.*

Jer (*with affected frankness*)   I'll tell you, John O'Hara, without any beating about the bush – I know you're a plain, straight man – like myself. It is this: we want to know if there's a young woman coming in here in our sister's place.

John (*his big voice rolling*)   Young woman? What young woman? I know of no young woman.

He goes to the fire and stands in front of it, facing them. **James** *sits on chair, right of table.*

Jer   Maybe you do, and maybe you don't – that's not our business. But we heard tell that your son does be going up the mountain very often, and that 'tis a wife he's after. (**Tim** *springs up.*) Be easy, Tim. (**Tim** *sits down again.*) Very well – John O'Hara – business is business – there's five hundred pounds of our money stuck in this place – and 'tisn't to feather the nest of another woman we handed that over to you. No, by God.

Tim (*aggressively*)   And we pinching and screwing – and doing without our rights – to put together five hundred pounds, and cock him up with a new slated house, and twenty head of cattle, and fine cattle sheds – and now he can go gallivanting – gallivanting –

John (*his anger rising*)   Easy, man, easy – not quite so fast. The O'Haras weren't waiting for your money to set them on their feet. Begor, they weren't. They were well there before they ever saw a penny of your money, and any girl – any girl – would be glad to come in here. Not that I have anything to say against your sister – she was a good girl and –

Tim   'Tisn't much of a life she got here anyway – working like a galley slave from morning to night – and giving him a child every year – but we'll look after her rights, we will – we'll see that not one penny of her money goes astray, we will – she'll always be alive for us – alive, and in this house – and no one will ever supplant her – by heaven, no – no one will put a slur on her memory, while there's a puff of life in us.

John (*trying to restrain his anger*)   There is no one putting any slur on your sister. Keep cool, man. Now, about this house, and as to who comes in or goes out here – well, I am master – and I can tell you that I have enough brains in my own head to be able to manage my own business. And (*Letting his anger escape.*) surely to God, I take enough of interest in my own house to see that no undesirable person comes in here.

Tim (*springing up and pointing to* **Maurice**)   Ask him, though – ask him. He's saying nothing.

John (*arrogantly*)   What has he to say? I am master.

Jer (*standing up and speaking quietly*)   If any woman comes in here – desirable or not – remember, John O'Hara, there's a question of money with us.

He goes towards the door, followed by **Tim**.

Tim   Love-making! And his wife still warm in her grave.

Jer (*turns; out the door*)   And remember one other thing: Jer Murnane is no fool. Goodnight.

Mrs O'Hara and **James** (*relieved*)   Goodnight. Goodnight.

John (*sternly*)   Stop! Jer Murnane – and you too, Tim Murnane – you are always welcome in this house as friends and neighbours, but when I want your advice about how to manage my house, and how to spend my money – I'll send for you. Do you hear? I'll send for ye. Now, ye can go home.

They go away. Silence for a few moments. **John** *is controlling his anger. He walks to and fro, and then stands on the right, well front.*

John (*quietly*)   James, you close the door. (**James** *closes the big door and then sits on settle.*) Mary, light the lamp.

Mrs O'Hara (*nervously, as she lights the lamp*)   I didn't notice the dark coming on. (*She then sits on the stool near the fire.*)

John (*in a rather friendly tone*)   Now, Maurice, I want this matter cleared up, and 'tis just as well to do it now. I wouldn't talk of it in front of the Murnanes – it has nothing to do with them or anyone else. 'Tis for me to settle what goes on in my own family. Now, listen here, my lad, your visits to that house must stop.

Maurice (*quietly*)   And if I refuse, father?

John   Refuse? What do you mean – refuse?

Maurice   Well – just refuse; that's all.

John (*flaring up*)   Then out you go, bag and baggage, out of this.

Mrs O'Hara   Oh, for God's sake, for God's sake – what are you saying, John O'Hara? Would you turn your own son out on the roadside?

John   Keep your mouth shut, woman – you'd exasperate any man. Refuse? I'm master here – I'll let them see I'm master here. (*Turning to* **Maurice**.) Out you go – out – you go – do you hear?

Maurice (*quietly*)   Yes, father – I hear.

John (*quivering with anger*)   I'm not excited – there's no use in getting excited – but, out – you – go – on the roadside.

Maurice (*quietly*)   You are right, father, there's no use in getting excited. I am cool; and knowing well what I'm saying, I tell you (*With great firmness.*) that I'd rather be out on the side of the road with that woman – begging for a crust of bread – than to go on living without her.

John (*laughing harshly*)   Words, my boy, words! You can't bend me with your fine talk.

Maurice   I'm not thinking of the like.

John   And what are you thinking of?

Maurice   Her – only her. (*Firmly.*) And I'm going to have her even if the whole forces of hell and heaven are up against me.

John   Well – have her – and be damned to you.

Mrs O'Hara   Easy John, easy. Leave him alone – you'll spoil everything. (*Moving her stool over to* **Maurice** *and patting his hand.*) We'll have a nice quiet chat by-and-by, and he'll listen to his poor old mother.

Maurice (*sadly*)   It would be no use, mother. I must go on with this now – no matter what it costs me.

Mrs O'Hara   And what do you mean to do, son?

Maurice   I don't know, mother – I haven't thought of that yet – I haven't thought of anything. I don't know yet – but I suppose we'll manage to live – somehow.

John (*gruffly, but not unkindly*)   Haven't you a good home here?

Maurice   I have, father.

John   What more do you want?

Maurice *does not answer.*

James   And your father and mother, lad? Aren't they a good father and mother?

Maurice   They are – couldn't be better.

James   And will you go against them, and break your mother's heart?

Maurice (*passionately*)   But I must live, I must. I have my rights too. I am no longer a child, having things arranged for me by others. I am a man! and I will live the life of a man, deep, deep, and full! No matter what it costs me!

James   If it is a wife you want, there is many a nice girl –

Maurice   No, no!

John (*quietly*)   It's too soon to think of that yet – say in another six months – then we can get a woman who –

Maurice (*his voice vibrating*)   I have my woman, the one woman in all the world for me.

John (*impatiently*)   For God's sake, man, talk sense. The one woman in all the world. (*Raising his voice, baffled.*) Aren't all women the same? Haven't they all eyes, and ears, and – and tongues, and – and – (*He makes a gesture with his two arms.*)

James (*sententiously*)   Well, John, there's good ones, and bad ones.

John (*to James: fiercely*)   And he's choosing a damn bad one.

Maurice (*quietly*)   I'm not choosing her, father – she was made for me from the beginning of the world.

John (*in desperation*)   Oh, my God, listen to that. And he's a son of mine.

James   And what about your home and land, Maurice? Have you no love at all for the land, boy?

Maurice   I have, uncle. I love the land as good as anyone ever loved it.

John (*gently*)   And yet you talk of leaving it?

Maurice *is silent.* **John** *goes over to the chair on the right of the table, sits down, and with his elbows resting on the table, addresses* **Maurice** *plaintively. His voice sometimes breaks.*

John   Listen here, son. The land – our land – don't play a dirty trick on it. For a dirty trick it would be to turn your back on the land for the sake of a woman. The land that the men who went before us watered with their sweat! The land that is more to you than a mother – that stands by you from cradle to grave – that feeds you – and puts a roof over your head – and a coat to your back. The darling land – always with a welcome for you – and you digging the potatoes out of her! And her fields of ripe yellow corn! And she always so fresh – and clean – and – and – why, man, just like God Almighty Himself! (**John** *covers his face with his hands. They are all touched. Silence for a few moments. Brokenly.*) And you are thinking of leaving all that.

Maurice (*sadly*)   A greater love has come to me, father.

John (*angry and mortified*)   Bah! You are no son of mine.

A short pause.

Mrs O'Hara (*very gently*)   And your poor little children?

Maurice (*becomes rigid: silence for a minute or two; then in a low harsh voice*)   I have no children.

Mrs O'Hara (*waving her arms*)   He's mad, he's mad. No children? He said he had no children. John – James – did you hear? Gone out of his mind he is. My poor boy, my poor boy. (*She stands up and gently pushes back the hair from his forehead. Then, with a scream.*) God! His forehead is scorching! A fever is on him! My God, my God! No children. He said he had no children. (*Soothingly.*) Go to bed, my son. Lie down, and rest yourself. (*She lights a candle.*) 'Tis tired out he is – jaded tired – and don't know what he's saying. (*Putting the candle into his hand.*) Take a long sleep, son, and don't get up in the morning if you're feeling tired. (*Caressing his hair.*) Is the pain very bad, here?

Maurice   It is, mother. There, and everywhere.

Mrs O'Hara   Everywhere, son?

Maurice (*standing up*)   Yes, mother, everywhere – in every drop of my blood.

Mrs O'Hara (*as he moves towards bedroom on left, front; soothingly*)   You'll be better in the morning – after the night's rest. You will indeed.

Maurice (*his hand on the handle of the door*)   I'll never be better again.

He goes in. **John** *slowly leaves the chair at the table, comes over to the fire, and sits in armchair. He takes out his pipe and fills it. The three are despondent.*

John   It is bad, James, bad.

James   It is so, John – very bad.

John *smokes for a while.* **Mrs O'Hara** *pushes her stool over near fire.*

Mrs O'Hara (*reflectively*)   Well, she's a good hard-working girl, anyway.

John (*flaring up*)   Don't talk of it, woman. Don't talk of it, I say. It is out of the question.

Mrs O'Hara (*getting her knitting*)   Well, I was only saying that she's a good hard-working girl – (*Firmly.*) and so she is. Isn't she, James?

James   She is, I suppose.

Mrs O'Hara (*knitting*)   Late and early she was kept at the work, ever since she was so high. (*Indicating height with hand.*) I used to feel sorry for her – and she a little slip of a thing going past in the grey morning with her basket of eggs to the village yonder. And I remember one time coming across her – I don't remember rightly what took me up their way, maybe 'twas hunting for Maurice I was, for he was always fond of climbing the hills when he was a young lad – but anyway, I came on her, kind of sudden. Peeping from behind a furze bush she was, shy as a fawn. And the great black eyes of her staring – staring! I declare to God, I got a bit of a start, thinking that maybe it was no human child at all, but a fairy, she was so –

John (*roughly*)   Ah, shut up, woman! A fairy!

A pause.

James (*to* **John**)   I don't think the mother had much love for the child; she takes after her father too much.

John (*to* James)   And her gypsy grandmother.

James   And 'tis little schooling she gave her either.

Mrs O'Hara   Well, if she can say her prayers, sure –

John   Prayers! (*Very scornfully.*) A lot of prayers are troubling the likes of that wan.

James   Arra, where would she be got? That father of hers never went near the house of God.

John   And her grandmother to drown herself, God bless us.

Mrs O'Hara   Well, the girl is a hard worker anyway; and maybe she is what she is, because of the bad example around her.

A pause. **John** *smokes noisily.*

John (*impatiently, as if dismissing an unpleasant thought*)   Ah! They're a mean lot, all the same.

Mrs O'Hara   They are – 'tis true. (*A pause.*) But there's Maurice to be thought of. (*A pause.*) And there's one thing to be said for her: she wouldn't neglect the work.

James (*sternly*)   She's a light woman, Mary.

Mrs O'Hara   She's airy – but she's young – and she'd settle down in time.

A pause.

John (*thoughtfully*)   The money is there too.

Mrs O'Hara   If it comes to the worst, well –

John (*impatiently*)   Ah, they're a mean lot, all the same.

Mrs O'Hara (*plaintively*)   His heart is breaking – and he's our only child.

John (*wistfully*)   Do you think, Mary, he was in earnest when he said – you know? – about the land, and – and – leaving us?

Mrs O'Hara (*sadly but firmly*)   He's desperate, John, desperate – he's capable of anything.

A pause.

John (*gently*)   No, Mary, no – I don't like the idea at all.

Mrs O'Hara (*fervently*)   Sure I don't either – God knows, I don't – but if everything else fails –

John (*with determination*)   We won't leave any stone unturned.

Mrs O'Hara (*fervently*)   We won't, John, we won't – but if the worst comes to the worst – then, in God's name, let her come in here.

James (*standing up; he speaks very sternly during the whole of the following*)   Shame on you, Mary Deasy, to talk of letting a light woman into your house.

Mrs O'Hara (*somewhat annoyed*)   Oh, shut up James; what do you know about it? Sure you're half a monk anyway.

James (*sententiously*)   I know that right is right, and wrong is wrong.

Mrs O'Hara   She'll settle down when she has a husband.

James   She can't wipe out what she was before. I don't care about anything else – let her be a poor orphan girl without a brown penny to her name – let her be blind, or lame, or deaf – but let her be an honest woman in the sight of God, Mary Deasy.

Mrs O'Hara   She's honest all right – she's only a bit airy.

James   She's not honest, I say; how can you call a woman honest who does be wilfully taking a man's love, and then not marrying him, and look at all the men she's after doing that to. (*Emphatically.*) I tell you this: if that woman comes in here, out – I'll – go –

John (*sarcastically, to hide his pain*)   On the side of the road, I suppose?

James (*firmly*)   Yes, on the side of the road.

John (*annoyed and baffled*)   Begor, 'tis the queer sudden desire ye are all getting for (*Very emphatically.*) 'the side of the road'. (*Turning to* **Mrs O'Hara**.) I suppose you'll be the next one to talk about going on 'the side of the road'?

Mrs O'Hara (*very meekly*)   No, John, I won't.

John (*to* **James**; *raising his powerful voice*)   Haven't you a good home here, James Deasy?

James (*quietly*)   I have, John.

John   Then what more do you want? (*As* **James** *is silent.*) Ah, sit down, man, and for goodness sake let me hear no more talk about 'the side of the road'.

James (*firmly*)   I have my conscience, John.

Mrs O'Hara   You won't be to blame surely?

James (*sternly*)   I'd be to blame for staying here, countenancing what is wrong and sinful.

Mrs O'Hara (*tearfully*)   But the boy is fretting himself to death – he will get into consumption and die.

James   Let him die – he won't be afraid to meet his God!

Mrs O'Hara (*raising her voice; firmly*)   You're a hard man, James Deasy, and that, because you are laying down a law about a thing outside your knowledge.

James   There are two little innocent children in this house – think of them, woman.

Mrs O'Hara (*passionately*)   I think of no one but my son.

The latch is lifted, the door pushed in, and a young man – a stranger to them – is seen. They look at him curiously.

Come in, friend. Come in.

He comes in. He is tall and thin, and is comfortable dressed in a dark frieze overcoat and a soft dark hat pulled well down over his eyes. He is very dark, with well-cut regular features, healthy yellowish-brown skin and deep-set serious eyes. He stands, dazed a little by the light and puts his hand to his forehead.

Mrs O'Hara   Sit down, sir, and rest yourself.

James *slightly moves the chair right of table – an invitation to sit down. The* **Stranger** *staggers a little and sits down slowly.* **James** *closes the door.* **Mrs O'Hara** *pulls out a glass of milk and puts it on the table near him. He takes no notice.*

Mrs O'Hara   Maybe you'd like to sit over near the fire and warm yourself?

Stranger (*in a dull, lifeless voice*)   I am not cold.

A pause.

John   You have travelled far, friend?

Stranger   More than ten miles – without stopping.

A pause.

John   From Kilbride side?

Stranger   No – from Sliavnavar.

John   A hard, mountainy road.

Mrs O'Hara   No wonder he looks dead beat! (*To* **Stranger**.) You'll stop the night, I suppose?

He makes no answer. **Mrs O'Hara** *goes back to the fire and puts on the kettle. Then she sits down and blows the fire with a bellows.*

Mrs O'Hara (*turning*)   I'll make a cup of tea for you – you don't seem to like the milk.

Stranger   No, good woman, no. I'm not tired – or hungry. It isn't that at all. There is something I want to say.

A pause. The three look at him curiously. **Mrs O'Hara** *stops blowing. The* **Stranger** *pulls himself together and speaks in a voice with a certain amount of force.*

Stranger   Is this the house of the O'Haras?

John   It is, friend. I am John O'Hara – the man of the house.

Stranger   It is a young man – Maurice O'Hara – I want.

John   That's my son. What do you want to say to him?

Stranger   I'll say it to himself – face to face.

John (*to* **Mrs O'Hara**)   Mary, call him.

Mrs O'Hara *goes to the door of* **Maurice**'s *room and knocks gently.*

Mrs O'Hara   Maurice, are you asleep?

Maurice (*voice from within*)   Yes, mother? What is it?

Mrs O'Hara   Come down, lad, for a couple of minutes. Hurry.

She comes back again to her seat. **Maurice** *comes in half-dressed and in his bare feet. The* **Stranger** *becomes alert and stands up. He advances towards* **Maurice**. *The two men stand in the middle of the stage and look at each other steadily for a few minutes.*

Stranger (*in a low, clear, tense voice*)   Give me back the woman you stole from me.

Maurice (*catching the* **Stranger**'s *tone*)   Who are you?

Stranger   She was mine first – till you came. Pouring lies into her ears about your rich lands and fat cattle.

Maurice   'Tis me she wants.

Stranger   I am worth a dozen of you – you poor soft man from the plains.

Maurice   She has turned her back on you.

Stranger   I don't care. I would take her – even if she was to be spitting at me all the days of my life.

Maurice (*gently*)   Is it like that with you – too?

Stranger (*plaintively*)   Give her back to me.

Maurice   You – too? Then, God help you, friend.

Stranger   Give her back to me. She was mine – first.

Maurice (*firmly*)   She is mine now, and no one can take her from me.

Stranger (*with impotent rage*)   She will bring a curse on you. She will bring a curse on any man who looks into the black fire of her eyes. Oh, God! Her eyes! You will never have a minute's peace by her side. She is a woman of flame. She will blight you. She will suck the youth out of you. You will be older than your father when she's finished with you. And she will finish with you soon – and another man will be drinking in her kisses of fire – another man –

Maurice (*springing at him with a cry of rage*)   You lie, you lie.

Stranger   Didn't she leave me for you?

Maurice *lets go. A pause.*

Maurice (*passionately*)   If the red jaws of hell were open before me – the red flames licking up around them – I would lep into them – holding her in my arms! (*He* *stumbles blindly to the door, and nervously raises the latch. Then he turns, and speaks defiantly, almost tearfully.*) Holding her in my arms. (*And with a cry which is half a sob, he rushes out into the night.*)

Mrs O'Hara (*to* **James**)   For God's sake, run, run, James. There he is without a bit of the coat – and in his bare feet – and his head burning with fever. (**James** *hurries out.* **Mrs O'Hara** *turns and sees the* **Stranger** *sitting again at table, dazed as before. She goes to him and speaks very gently.*) Come, drink a little drop, my poor man. (*As he takes no notice.*) God help us all. 'Tis many a trouble a foolish woman brings with her. (*She goes back to the fire and looking at the* **Stranger** *says to herself.*) Maybe a cup of tea would warm him. (*A pause.*)

Stranger (*standing up firmly*)   I must be going now, I have a long way to travel.

John (*looking at the fire; quietly*)   There's a bed here for you – if you want it.

Stranger (*going out*)   I have a long way to travel.

Curtain

Act Two

A small, drab, poorly furnished kitchen. At left, a small table, chair, door leading into bedroom. At back, door opening on farm-yard, a window, a large table, two chairs, one at each end of the table. At right, an open fireplace, two low chairs, one at each side of the fire.

Evening. **Mrs Dunn** *is busy drying dishes at the back. She is of medium height, thin and wiry. She holds herself erect, and moves with a free, independent, almost masculine gait. Her features are sharp and intelligent but mask-like in their impassivity. Her stiff, dark hair is drawn tight back. Her eyes are small and shrewd. Her voice is hard, resonant and decisive.*

William *is sitting at the fire, left, smoking. He too is thin, dark and wiry; but in no other way does he resemble his mother. He is shrunken, nervous, irritable, weak in every way: in fact it would seem that his mother had gained her surplus amount of mental and physical independence by draining him of all his. He is in the early twenties, but at first glance one would take him to be much older.*

William   I'm told there's great friendship for Kitty Doyle at the O'Haras. She's in and out there like one of themselves. (*A pause.*) It isn't like that it used to be. (*A pause.*) The old man's pride must be falling – and 'tis about time – the pompous old blackguard!

Mrs Dunn   I doubt that.

William (*looking at her*)   Do you? Why?

Mrs Dunn   The O'Haras are stronger than ever they were.

William (*meditatively*)   They are, blast them. And old John as stiff-necked as ever, very likely. And the young buck – oh, his father all over – when he wants to. Riding roughshod over people. A domineering, stinking lot. (*Looking at* **Mrs Dunn**.) All the same, I wonder what's the game about Kitty Doyle? 'Tis Jer Murnane was telling me – and Jer can't be wrong. (*Admiringly.*) There isn't a stir that goes on in the O'Haras that Jer don't know of. Himself and Tim do be always watching the place.

Mrs Dunn   A thorn in their side it is.

William   Well, small wonder. Isn't their money stuck in the place.

Mrs Dunn   They didn't give it for nothing.

William (*doubtfully*)   No – they did not. (*With assurance.*) You may be sure they did not. (*Admiringly.*) Jer Murnane is no fool. He didn't give his hard-earned money for nothing. (*Meditatively.*) If the sister lived – well – they'd be in with the big man – one of the family, as the saying goes – and getting many a leg-up in this way and that. (*To his mother.*) Jer Murnane is no fool, and if John O'Hara is thinking for the son, there'll be trouble with the Murnanes.

Mrs Dunn   Arra, a lot John O'Hara would care. What would a dog care about a couple of fleas.

A pause.

William   Do you think – now – John O'Hara would be thinking of Kitty Doyle for the boyo?

Mrs Dunn   No.

William   He'd be looking for bigger game, I suppose?

Mrs Dunn   Aye.

William (*pensively*)   But the old woman? (*Getting angry.*) It would be like that old one to be wanting Kitty Doyle. Birds of a feather. Church-going and craw-thumping the pair of them. Not to mention Jameseen – the old hypocrite. They're well met – and then turning up the whites of their eyes – (*Emphatically.*) praying. (*With great scorn.*) Oh – them. That sort – makes me – sick.

Mrs Dunn   Arra, don't be wasting your spit on them. They don't count in that house.

William (*with satisfaction*)   No – they do not. Spiders' webs their little plans are. (*Changing tone, shrewdly.*) But 'tis well to watch everything – and if there's anything to be made out of his coming here – the sighing lover – (*He nods slowly.*)

Mrs Dunn   Ay.

William (*meditatively*)   'Tisn't a match old John will want – and what he won't want – he won't have. (*A pause.*) And Maurice won't have the guts to hold out against the father. Anyhow he's only an empty man. 'Tis the old man we must think of. If only we could put the screw on him?

Mrs Dunn   We can.

William (*turning and looking at her*)   How?

Mrs Dunn   He's a great man for the law and justice – a great proud man – he won't face the law-court.

William (*looks long interrogatively, then slowly*)   A breach of promise.

Mrs Dunn   Aye.

William (*admiringly*)   Well, you're a deep man, and no mistake. The divil himself couldn't beat you. (*With animation.*) We'll put the screw on tight, never fear. The pack of bloated hypocrites. They riding in their traps, and we having to walk the roads. We'll squeeze them though – we will – we will.

Mrs Dunn (*happening to look out*)   Here's the pair of them coming up the road, so they'll be here soon. And mind, be civil.

William (*goes to the window and looks out*)   Oh – the sighing lover. Good luck to you, girl, lead him on. That's right – stand and look into his eyes. Good girl, good girl. (*Almost hissing.*) Blast him, how I hate him. If I too could be living well, and riding horses, I'd be every bit as big and as fine to look at as that – whelp.

Mrs Dunn   Here, 'tisn't with sour looks we can snare our cock-sparrow. Here, get out of this, and leave things to me.

William   Where will I go? If I go out, he'll see me – and I don't want to meet him, the rotten cur.

Mrs Dunn   Go down in the room then. (*As he goes.*) And keep your ears open.

Maurice *and* **Ellen** *come in.* **Maurice** *is grave and sad.* **Ellen** *is small and dark like her mother and brother. Her face is sensitive and delicate, and under her heavy mass of dark hair looks almost elf-like. She is very agile, and moves with quick, rhythmic, feline grace. When at bay, she elongates her neck and throws up her head in a manner which suggests a beautiful untameable bird. Her voice is flexible, vibrating and extremely sensitive to all her varying moods. She comes in carrying an armful of mountain flowers and rowan berries. She arranges these in a jam-crock on the small table, and stands back every now and then to examine the effect. She is busy during the conversation between her mother and* **Maurice**, *apparently dead to what they are saying.*

Mrs Dunn (*advancing*)   Oh, welcome, welcome, Maurice. (*Leading him by the hand to the chair on the left of the fire.*) Come and sit down here. It's a cure for sore eyes to see you after a long week. (*Half kneeling, she arranges the fire and talks in a low confidential tone.*) It's Ellen herself now will be satisfied. Every day it was the same story with her: 'I wonder will Maurice come today, mother, do you think?' And every five minutes she'd be looking out the door and down the road. It's lonesome she does be for you. (*Playfully.*) But I suppose she does be telling you that herself? Ah, well, well. (*Changing tone.*) How are they all at home, Maurice?

Maurice   They are all well, thank God.

Mrs Dunn   The health is a great thing surely. And if you searched high and low you couldn't get a stronger, healthier family than your own. The last time I saw your mother, what I said to myself was: 'It's finer and fresher and younger-looking that decent woman is getting every day.' And sure, more luck to her. (*She stands up, pauses as if uncertain what to do, and turns to* **Ellen** *with a smile.*) Did you see the goats on your way up?

Ellen (*looking at the flowers, listlessly*)   I did not.

Mrs Dunn (*angrily*)   No – you'd rather be fooling with them berries. (*In a different tone to* **Maurice**.) She's a terrible girl for flowers and faldals,[6] Maurice. But she's a good girl for work too, and can turn her hand to anything. A well-handed wife is the best thing any man can have. Is fear bean na spre,[7] is what I always say. Well now. (*Going to table and taking a basin.*) I must go out to milk the goats. (*Turning round.*) Tell me, Maurice, is there any truth in the rumour that there's a match being talked of for Jer Murnane?

---

6   Faldals meaning trivial or nonsensical fuss, or trivial items.
7   A woman is better than fun.

Maurice   I didn't hear anything about it.

Mrs Dunn   Ay, a match with Kitty Doyle, I heard. But I don't suppose there's anything in it. Who'd be wanting that poor thing for a wife, without money – or looks or anything.

Maurice (*warmly*)   She's a very good girl, Mrs Dunn.

Mrs Dunn   Oh, she's that – she is indeed. I'm not saying anything against her. But somehow I'm sorry for Patsy Doyle to have a daughter that 'tis so hard to get matched. But maybe she'll have luck this time. I hope she will – she's a good girl, as you say. (*Brightly.*) Wait there now, Maurice, and I'll be back soon with the milk for a nice cup of tea. Yourself and Ellen will have a lot to be saying to each other. (*She nods playfully, and goes out.*)

Maurice *looks at the fire sadly.* **Ellen** *continues with the flowers. Silence for a few minutes.*

Ellen (*eagerly*)   Look, Maurice, aren't they nice?

Maurice   What? Oh yes, of course – very nice.

Ellen   Don't you love them, Maurice?

Maurice   Oh yes – of course I do.

Ellen (*imitating*)   'Oh yes – of course I do.' (*Emphatically.*) No, you do not. (*Pouting.*) You don't even look at them. (*Soothingly to flowers: low, almost singing.*) There's nobody – loves you – but me. (*Kneeling down and putting her arms round them.*) You poor little – poor little – red berries. (*Springing up and running over to* **Maurice**, *still half singing.*) Poor little, poor little Maurice. (*She sits on his knees, catches his head in her hands and looks steadily into his eyes. He smiles gently at her.*)

Ellen (*putting her cheek against his*)   Tell me, Maurice, do you love me?

Maurice (*very earnestly*)   You know I do.

Ellen (*naively*)   How much do you love me?

Maurice (*with deep feeling*)   There is nothing in the world big enough to measure my love.

Ellen   Do you love me more than everything you have?

Maurice   I do.

Ellen   More than your father, and mother, and house, and lands, and cattle, and money, and everything?

Maurice   Yes.

Ellen (*pouting*)   But tell me that yourself.

Maurice   I love you more than my father and mother and house and lands and everything. (*Smiling.*) Now are you satisfied?

Ellen (*thoughtfully*)   I don't know. I wonder do you love me that much? (*Confidentially.*) I want an awful lot of love, Maurice, so much that there'll never be any end to it. I am always looking for love, and I never get enough of it. (*Nestling to him.*) Tell me again that you love me.

Maurice   I love you.

Ellen (*disappointed*)   That's not enough. Say how much.

Maurice (*earnestly*)   I love you more than all I have in the world, more than all the world holds. If I were to get all the riches of the world without you, I would be poor. If I was to have nothing at all only you, I would be rich.

Ellen (*eagerly*)   Yes, yes.

Maurice (*with vibrating voice*)   If it was a cold day in winter, and we two going the roads with no shelter at all in the bushes – and the sleet cutting into our bones – I would be warm, and thankful to God for the great happiness of having you beside me.

Ellen (*fretfully*)   But I don't like the cold roads, Maurice. (*Childishly.*) Tell me about summer, and us two waking up in the morning, and all the larks in the world singing to us, and the bog water soft and warm, and we dipping our hands in it.

Maurice (*catching her tone, then warming*)   And sitting down in the middle of the day, and the hot sun shining on us, and we looking at the bawn – a wonder to the world with daisies and buttercups.

Ellen   And meadows waving, and big red poppies.

Maurice   And we sitting under a honeysuckle bush – sitting close up against each other.

Ellen (*still with childish delight*)   And butterflies in the sun.

Maurice   And bees buzzing. And our eyelids growing heavy with sleep.

A fairly long pause.

Ellen   Maurice.

Maurice   Yes, Ellen?

Ellen   Let us go away now.

Maurice   Where, Ellen?

Ellen (*dreamily*)   To the lovely country where all the sun is. (*Passionately.*) I hate this dirty hole, and I hate the mountains, they are so bare and hard, and so cold. (*She shivers.*) With the mist creeping up on them, and then creeping down again. (*Simply.*) Sometimes the mountains do be nice, when there's a clear blue sky and the sun shining on the heather and bracken, but that does be seldom. (*Tearfully.*) Take me away out of this dirty hole of a house, where the floor does be so cold when it is raining outside, and the wind whistling under the door, and my mother and William always fighting, and telling lies. Take me away, Maurice.

Maurice   Where will we go?

Ellen   Very far away.

Maurice   To Cork?

Ellen   That's not far enough.

Maurice   To Dublin?

Ellen   Farther even than that. (*Eagerly.*) Let us go away in the big ship to America. (*Dreamily.*) And we will be sailing over the water! And it will be blue! And soft too like the water in the bog holes when you'd want to be dipping your feet in them. And maybe as soft and as still as the black water of Poulgorm where my grandmother drownded herself. It would be lovely to be standing in Poulgorm if it was warm, and the feel of the water on you and it up to your neck. (*A pause.*) Maurice.

Maurice   Yes, Ellen?

Ellen   Won't it be grand for us two to be together out in America?

Maurice (*sadly*)   Will you always love me – out there, Ellen?

Ellen   Of course – that's part of the picture.

Maurice (*sadly*)   Maybe you'll tire of me?

Ellen (*tearfully*)   Now you are spoiling it all.

Maurice (*in a low voice*)   You tired of other men.

Ellen (*confidentially*)   But they were ugly. I found them out – one after the other – and they were all ugly and small – and then I couldn't bear them anymore. (*Quickly.*) But don't talk of them – they spoil everything. (*Harshly.*) I hate them – they are all liars. (*A pause. Then wistfully.*) Let me look into your eyes. (*She catches his head and looks steadily.*) I want to see the love in your eyes. (*Kissing each eye slowly.*) Oh, yes, it is there. (*To herself.*) While I see that love I am satisfied – at least, I think I am. (*Getting up and moving away.*) But I don't know. (*Her voice swells.*) I have a terrible thirst for love – a terrible thirst – bigger than if I was without a drink for a year of days. A terrible thirst. And I have no peace night or day. (*Passionately.*) It's not fair, it's not fair. (*She swings round, rushes over to* **Maurice** *and falls on her knees, then tearfully.*) Oh, Maurice, I can't bear it, I can't bear it. 'Tis killing me. I want love. I want beautiful things. I want to go to America (*Dreamily.*) to be watching the grand ladies dressed in red and purple, and they driving in their beautiful carriages. (*Closing her eyes.*) It will be lovely out there. The sun will be always shining, and it won't ever be cold. And the water will be blue. (*Quietly, with closed eyes.*) We will go away, Maurice?

Maurice   Yes, we will go away.

Ellen (*dreamily*)   Out there no one will be talking about buying – or selling – or money – or prices of things. Out there we will be always talking of love. (*Still with closed eyes.*) We will go away there now?

Maurice   We can't go now.

Ellen (*opening her eyes*)   You don't love me. (*With a cry of grief.*) You are like the others – you don't love me. (*With scorn.*) You are a small man after all.

Maurice (*earnestly*)   Indeed I do love you. We will go soon.

Ellen   How soon?

Maurice (*sadly*)   In a week – just a week.

Ellen (*brightly*)   And we will meet each other at the bend of the road by the hawthorn bush.

Maurice (*sadly*)   By the hawthorn bush.

Ellen   In the evening time after the cows are milked.

Maurice   Yes, in the evening time we will go away together.

Ellen   That will be grand. (*Dreamily.*) And it will be quiet, and your arms around me will be as soft as the dark water of Poulgorm. (*A pause: then anxiously.*) You will be sure to come, Maurice?

Maurice (*sadly*)   Quite sure.

Ellen (*eagerly*)   Let me look into your eyes again. (*She looks: then sadly.*) I am afraid of you. Maybe you will fail me.

Maurice   But I love you, my Ellen – I cannot be happy without you.

Ellen (*sadly*)   While I am here you feel like that.

Maurice   Indeed no, Ellen. I love you always.

She springs to her feet, and moving a little distance away, faces him, her body poised like an animal about to spring.

Ellen   Look here, Maurice O'Hara, if you fail me, if 'tis lies you're telling me, I will go to your house, I will ferret you out, and – and – spit in your eyes.

He buries his face in his hands. She looks at him a moment, then goes to him slowly, her anger gone, and kneeling beside him puts her head against his shoulder.

Ellen (*in the tone of a tired child*)   Don't be hurt, Maurice. Don't be angry with me. It is this dirty hole is driving me mad. Forgive me. (*She takes his hand and kisses it.*) Maurice, look at me. (*He looks at her.*) Let me look in your eyes. (*She looked steadily, then sadly.*) You don't want to go to America?

Maurice   I do, Ellen.

Ellen   Then why do you look so sorrowful? What's grieving you?

Maurice   Everything. The ties that are holding me.

Ellen   Your father and mother?

Maurice   Ay – and more than that.

Ellen   Your old home?

Maurice   More than that.

Ellen   Your dead wife?

Maurice   More than that.

Ellen   What then? Tell me, Maurice?

Maurice   The hands of my little children.

Ellen (*dropping his hands: to herself; wistfully*)   The hands of little children. (*Getting up and moving away.*) The hands of little children. The hands of little children. (*Swinging round, with fierce scorn.*) Then stick to your little children. Catch their hands and play with them – you poor tame man, and no lover at all. (*With wild tearful laughter.*) He loves me more than anything in the world.

She makes to run out. He rushes to her and catches her.

Maurice   Ellen. Ellen. For God's sake, listen to me. I love my home and my children, but I love you more. I am ready to go with you. I will leave everything for you.

With a sob she breaks away and he follows her out of the house. **William** *comes in from the room. He goes to the door and looks after them for a few moments. Then he goes to the fire and sits on chair, left. He looks at the fire thoughtfully. After a short time* **Mrs Dunn** *comes to door looking pleased, but when she sees only* **William** *her face takes on its natural sharp expression. She comes in and puts the basin of milk on the table.*

Mrs Dunn (*without turning*)   Where are they?

William (*apologetically*)   I don't know.

Mrs Dunn (*turning angrily*)   You don't know? And why don't you know? You idiot. Didn't I tell you to keep a close watch on them? (*She sees* **Ellen***'s flowers, goes over and throws them out contemptuously. Turns at door.*) I suppose 'tis asleep you were up in the room.

William (*defending himself*)   Indeed then it wasn't. I was listening with all my might. And a cramp in the small of my back bending down with my ear to the keyhole, fearful lest I'd miss a word.

Mrs Dunn (*comes back and sits on the chair right of fire: more gently*)   What did you hear?

William (*pleased, and anxious to please*)   They were talking a lot about catching[8] butterflies.

---

8   'catching' is inserted by hand on the typed manuscript.

Mrs Dunn   You can skip that – that's *her* romance.

William   And then they were saying something about going the roads – and sleeping under the bushes.

Mrs Dunn   More romancing. (*Bitterly.*) 'Tis only people with a warm bed to lie on do be always talking about the joy of going the roads and lying on the hedges. And she'd be the great one for that surely – she that does be shrivelled up in the raw winter mornings like a stray leaf on a windy November day. (*A pause. Then thoughtfully.*) Tell me, did they say anything about marriage?

William   The word was never mentioned – but he was talking a lot about love – and she drinking it in like a fish.

Mrs Dunn (*half to herself*)   That was the time to catch him.

William (*contemptuously*)   But she'll never have any sense. It's my opinion that it never enters her crazy head how to get a pound, or even a shilling.

Mrs Dunn (*bitterly*)   Her father's fool daughter.

William (*anxious to please*)   Making little of his fine farm she was, and without a thought at all of how to get in there. Just love – love – love. Nothing else. Always harping on the one string. (*Imitating.*) 'Tell me, Maurice, do you love me?' God, it was terrible having to listen to that, and I cramped up with the pain in my back, and afraid to stir in case they'd hear me.

Mrs Dunn (*thoughtfully*)   And he said nothing at all about marriage – are you sure of that?

William   Certain.

Mrs Dunn (*disappointed*)   Did they talk any sense at all?

William   Let me see now. (*Pondering.*) She was saying something about America, and wanting to go there.

Mrs Dunn (*looking at him intently*)   America?

William (*nodding*)   Ay, America.

Mrs Dunn (*to herself*)   Her wild father breaking out in her again.

William (*anxious to please*)   But, by the hokey, she had so much full talk about grand ladies driving in carriages, and something about being thirsty and looking in his eyes, and lepping up and down like a wild cat, that it would take the ould boy himself to follow all the twists of her, and make any sense at all out of what she was saying.

Mrs Dunn   Did he say he is go with her to America?

William   He did. She wanted to go there and then, but he said to wait for a week.

Mrs Dunn   A week? Did he say the day?

William (*nodding*)   Ay – this day week.

Mrs Dunn (*angrily*)   And why didn't you tell me that at the beginning, instead of wasting my time with your fool nonsense? (*She gets up and moves away in deep thought. Low to herself.*) If the bird escapes we can whistle for our money.

William   Hold the female!

Mrs Dunn (*angrily*)   Hold the wind. (*Waspishly.*) Why didn't you hold her the other night when she threw the bucket of water over you and sent you flying out the door?

A pause.

William (*subdued*)   She's a bad lot. It would be a good thing for us all if she cleared off to America, for you can't get her to lead nor drive, and she raising hell all the time.

Steps are heard approaching. **Mrs O'Hara** *looking very tired comes to the door.*

Mrs O'Hara   God save all here.

Mrs Dunn *and* **William**   And you too.

Mrs Dunn (*with affected pleasure*)   Well, if it isn't Mrs O'Hara. Come in, ma'am, come in. (**Mrs O'Hara** *comes in, staggering a little and panting.*) Sit down, ma'am – over here near the fire. (**William** *gets up from his chair, and* **Mrs Dunn** *leads* **Mrs O'Hara** *to it, speaking as gently as she can.*) You look dead bate, ma'am. But 'tis a long hard road you've come. (*Bringing over the basin of milk.*) Here, take a drop of this milk. (**Mrs O'Hara** *drinks some of it, pausing a few times to take breath.*) There now, that will do you good. Don't talk a while. Rest yourself. (*A pause.*) Now you are beginning to look better.

Mrs O'Hara *smiles and hands back the basin. In this house there is an atmosphere of great dignity about her.*

Mrs O'Hara   Thanks, Mrs Dunn. That's a terrible road, and mounting all the time takes the breath out of the body.

Mrs Dunn (*sitting down on chair right of fire*)   That is so, ma'am, indeed – especially when you are not used to long distances – going on foot. Will you be going much farther, ma'am?

Mrs O'Hara   No, I came to see you, Mrs Dunn. I have something to say to you.

Mrs Dunn   In that case, ma'am, maybe you'd be taking your hat and coat off?

Mrs O'Hara   No, thanks, Mrs Dunn. It won't take me very long what I've come to say.

Awkward silence. **Mrs Dunn** *and* **William**, *who is sitting on the chair near the small table, wait, wondering.* **Mrs O'Hara** *looks at the fire. She raises her head, makes one or two attempts to speak, then remarks.*

Mrs O'Hara   Anyhow, the evening will be soon falling, and I have the same road before me again.

William (*pushing to be agreeable*)   It won't be so bad – you'll be going down the hill on your way home.

Mrs O'Hara   That is so, but it isn't young I'm getting, and the body is a terrible drag when the years are on a person.

She looks again at the fire. Again silence. Finally, still looking at the fire, she speaks gently and evenly. During the following conversation the contrast between the two women is very marked. **Mrs O'Hara** *seems softer than usual, and* **Mrs Dunn** *harder.*

Mrs O'Hara   I suppose you know, Mrs Dunn, that my son is friendly with your daughter?

Mrs Dunn   I do, ma'am.

Mrs O'Hara   I'm afraid it will bring sorrow into our home if it goes on.

Mrs Dunn (*combatively*)   What's wrong with my girl, ma'am? Isn't she good enough for him?

Mrs O'Hara   It isn't that, Mrs Dunn – but you see his wife is not long dead, and 'tisn't of another woman he should be thinking so soon.

Mrs Dunn   There's no mad hurry. Waiting a bit won't kill them.

Mrs O'Hara   Then he has two little children, and they're enough for any man surely.

Mrs Dunn   That's for himself to judge.

Mrs O'Hara (*very sadly*)   I'm afraid it isn't, Mrs Dunn. His father is dead against it, and it will bring bad blood between father and son.

Mrs Dunn   I am sorry his father is so hard, ma'am.

Mrs O'Hara (*turning round; somewhat eagerly*)   But, Mrs Dunn, couldn't we do something? The two of us – we are both mothers – and – and – they are our children.

Mrs Dunn   That is so, ma'am – and I am thinking of my child. Her heart is stuck on Maurice.

Mrs O'Hara   But she wouldn't be happy marrying him without his father's blessing – (*Rather tearfully.*) – no blessing at all – but a black and bitter curse?

Mrs Dunn   But what about her, ma'am? Is it fair to a young girl to have a young man coming after her, and then leaving her lone and lonesome in her mother's house?

Mrs O'Hara   There's many a man would be glad to wed her – a young beautiful girl, and a great worker, as she is.

Mrs Dunn   Then why not, Maurice, ma'am?

Mrs O'Hara (*firmly*)   I have told you – it would break up the peace of our home.

Mrs Dunn (*stiffly*)   They are drawn to each other, ma'am, and they will have each other, come weal come woe.

Mrs O'Hara (*with animation*)   But how are they going to live, Mrs Dunn? Maurice will have to clear out of the place if he goes against his father – leave his home, and his father and mother, and his two children. (*She wipes her eyes and rocks herself.*) A poor boy, well-reared, going round as a beggar man, or a hired man with his little bit of weekly wages, and that same not certain.

Mrs Dunn (*very decisively*)   John O'Hara wouldn't do that.

Mrs O'Hara (*shaking her head sadly*)   You don't know him.

Mrs Dunn   And what would people think of him?

Mrs O'Hara (*with feeling*)   A lot he'd care. If he wouldn't care for his own child, do you think he'd care about other people or what they'd say?

A pause.

Mrs Dunn   And who'll get the place?

Mrs O'Hara   There's the children.

Mrs Dunn (*raising her voice*)   But the law, ma'am, the law?

Mrs O'Hara (*firmly*)   Every man can do what he likes with his own: that's the law.

Mrs Dunn (*in a loud voice*)   And what about my girl, ma'am? What's the law about her? (**Mrs O'Hara** *is silent. A pause.*) Is it fair or just law that a young man can ask a girl to wed him, and then at his father's beck to be leaving her, a by-word to be mocked at by every penny-boy in the whole country? (*More gently.*) I ask you that, ma'am, as woman to woman? (*Still no answer, then meditatively.*) A poor girl, ma'am, but might perhaps be wishful to go to America where her story wouldn't be known.

Mrs O'Hara (*eagerly*)   Would she be wishful for that?

Mrs Dunn (*cautiously*)   I don't know, ma'am, I'm sure. But how could she go there anyway? It would take a purse of money; and 'tis hardly enough to eat we can draw out of the rocky land, not to be talking at all of a handful of money.

Mrs O'Hara (*eagerly*)   Listen, Mrs Dunn. I have some money – if Ellen is wishful to go to America – 'tis some money of my own, made out of the fowl and eggs – all my married life I was putting it by, not knowing when I might want it – and now – thank God, that I have it – and 'tis about that same I made my journey here today – take it, ma'am, take it, keep it, give it to Ellen, do what you like with it – and – and may God bless you.

William (*eagerly*)   How much is it, ma'am?

Mrs O'Hara (*turning to him*)   A hundred and eighty pounds.

William   Have you it with you?

Mrs O'Hara   I have the eighty. The other hundred is still in the Savings Bank, but I will give it to you as soon as everything is settled.

William (*approaching*)   The money you have, halve it between my mother and me, and we will give the other hundred to Ellen.

Mrs O'Hara   What do you say, Mrs Dunn?

Mrs Dunn (*scornfully*)   What is a hundred and eighty pounds. Nothing at all, ma'am. And John O'Hara the big rich man he is.

Mrs O'Hara (*rising*)   I am sorry then my journey is for nothing. I am giving you all I have, and if I had more I'd give it too. But John O'Hara's money is his own, and I have nothing to do with it.

Mrs Dunn (*eagerly*)   Sure I know, ma'am, you have a good, kind heart and I'm saying nothing against you at all.

William (*with emphasis*)   No, nothing at all, at all.

Mrs Dunn   Sit down again, ma'am. (**Mrs O'Hara** *sits down.*) Indeed I would go a long way to meet you trying to prevent bad blood between father and son.

William (*effusively*)   That's true, ma'am.

Mrs Dunn (*quietly*)   And I'm sure 'tis his father would be glad to have his son beside him working away the best of friends, as they always were.

Mrs O'Hara   You may well say that, ma'am. Himself would be a happy man if all this trouble was over.

Mrs Dunn   And I'm sure 'tis a happy man he was too today seeing you off on your journey – and a hard journey it was for a woman by herself.

Mrs O'Hara (*confidentially*)   He didn't know it at all, Mrs Dunn. I had to slip out unbeknownst. He'd be raging mad if he knew.

Mrs Dunn (*thoughtfully*)   Indeed. (*A pause. Then rising.*) Now, I'll make you a cup of tea, and then we'll slip down a bit of the road together and it will shorten the way for you.

She is busy preparing the tea during all the following. **William** *sits down in his mother's place.*

William (*to* **Mrs O'Hara**)   Have you the money now, ma'am, and I'll be counting it – half to my mother and half to me.

Mrs O'Hara (*opening her purse*)   It is easy to count it, William. (*Taking it out.*) There it is, eight ten-pound notes – one, two, three, four, five, six, seven, eight.

She gives four to **William** *who examines them with delight, and four to* **Mrs Dunn** *who takes them impassively and puts them in the bosom of her dress.*

William (*eagerly*)   I'm going to help in this too, ma'am – and my mother and me will go halves – and maybe we could fix up a match between Ellen and a man back North that wants to wed her – and then there will be no loophole at all for Maurice, ma'am, and (*Smiling and nodding.*) that will please you greatly, I'm thinking.

Mrs O'Hara (*eagerly*)   Yes, yes. Is that the man from back yonder in Sliavnavar?

Mrs Dunn (*suspiciously*)   What do you know about him?

Mrs O'Hara (*indifferently*)   Oh nothing, nothing. I just heard tell of him.

Mrs Dunn   What did you hear?

Mrs O'Hara   That he was after Ellen – that is all.

Mrs Dunn   And might it be any harm to ask who told you?

Mrs O'Hara (*evasively*)   Well now, I disremember. Someone of the neighbours, or maybe a strolling beggar. (*Changing tone.*) But anyhow coming back to our own business, I will hand you over the other hundred pounds, as soon as the match is fixed up for Ellen.

Mrs Dunn   Or she goes to America?

Mrs O'Hara (*nodding*)   Or she goes to America. (*A pause, then with a happy sigh.*) That's settled now, thank God. And 'tis glad I am to have the bit of money saved.

Mrs Dunn   There's the kettle boiling now. Maybe you'd like an egg, ma'am? We have them nice and fresh.

At this moment, **Ellen** *pushes in the half-door with a jerk. She wears a sulky face. When she sees* **Mrs O'Hara** *she stops short, stares questioningly, but says nothing.*

Mrs O'Hara (*gently*)   Good evening, Ellen.

Ellen (*in a hard, aggressive voice*)   Good evening. (*She sits on the chair near the little table.*)

Mrs O'Hara (*addressing* **Ellen**)   Isn't it nice weather we're having?

Ellen *doesn't reply. She sits staring in front of her.*

William (*effusively*)   It is so, ma'am, grand weather, thanks be to God.

Mrs Dunn (*on her knee at the fire*)   Do you like the eggs well boiled, ma'am?

Mrs O'Hara   Middling, thank you. It takes all the good out of them to have them too hard.

Mrs Dunn   That is so.

Mrs O'Hara   The way I like an egg is to have a milky top, and to drink down the milk before you put your spoon in the egg at all.

Mrs Dunn (*at table: pouring out the tea*)   Sit over now, ma'am, you must be famished with the hunger.

Mrs O'Hara (*sitting on chair, right of table, pleasantly*)   Well, I am a bit hungry. There's nothing like the mountain air for giving you an appetite. (*To* **Ellen**.) Maybe you'd like a cup too, Ellen?

Mrs Dunn (*to* **Ellen**)   Sit over and keep company with Mrs O'Hara.

Ellen *takes no notice.*

Mrs O'Hara   Do, come over, my girl. I want to be talking to you.

Ellen (*fiercely*)   I don't want none of your 'my girl'. What's bringing you here anyway? What brought you here this evening?

Mrs O'Hara (*timidly*)   I came, my girl, as a –

Ellen (*jumping up: angrily*)   There it is again. Say what you have to say straight and honest without any trimmings. My girl, my girl. (*Bitterly.*) I know you and your likes. It isn't the joy of climbing the stony road or lepping over the locks of water that drove you up here this evening. Nor 'tisn't for love that you're getting tea and boiled eggs from my mother. What's your game? (*Her anger grows.*) What divil's plot are ye hatching? 'Tis about me. I know by ye'r rotten, oily, foxy faces, that 'tis about me. I know ye – I know ye all. I have damn good reason to know ye – and I tell ye this – (*Looking round fiercely.*) – all of ye – and you above all, Maurice O'Hara's mother – that if you think you can stop me – if you think you can rob me of my rights – if you think you can bend me to ye'r rotten stingy level – ye're making the greatest mistake of ye're life. (*Defiantly.*) Do ye'r worst. Go on, if ye like. I'm not afraid of ye – or a thousand like you – but ye're only wasting yer melt – and I'll best ye in the end.

She sits again, her sulkiness gone, and a glow of exultation in her face.

Mrs Dunn (*sharply*)   Keep a civil tongue in your head, Ellen Dunn, and don't insult a decent woman under your own roof. She came here as a good friend to you and yours.

Mrs O'Hara   I did, Ellen. I came out of kindness to help you.

Ellen (*defiantly*)   I want no help from no one. You can keep your nose out of my business. And as for kindness? (*She laughs harshly.*) Kindness? Kindness? I am too old a bird to be caught by that kind of lime. (*Springing up again and pointing threateningly at* **Mrs O'Hara**.) I tell you this, Maurice O'Hara's mother, that your son belongs to me – me – and me only – and a thousand mothers or a thousand Kitty Doyles can't take him from me. (*Speaking like an oracle.*) He belongs to me – I hold him body and soul – and all his life long he'll be aching for me.

Mrs O'Hara (*sadly*)   Then he'll never have any happiness at all.

Ellen *turns her back on them all. She comes well forward, left. She speaks in low, dull tones.* **Mrs O'Hara** *in low, sad tones. They are both quiet, looking into the future, for the moment passive, feeling perhaps their powerlessness.*

Ellen   I know he won't.

Mrs O'Hara   You will bring discord where there's peace.

Ellen   I don't care.

Mrs O'Hara   You will divide father from son.

Ellen   I don't care.

Mrs O'Hara   You will bring a mother to the grave before her time.

Ellen   I don't care.

Mrs O'Hara   You will rob little helpless orphans of their father.

Ellen   I don't care.

Mrs O'Hara   Then you are a ravenous wild beast!

Ellen   A wild beast must live.

Mrs O'Hara (*with animation: putting up a fight again*)   You wouldn't rob the orphans surely?

Ellen (*decisively: answering the challenge*)   I would!

Mrs O'Hara (*standing up and speaking passionately*) Oh, woman, have you no heart at all? Are you the devil himself hiding in woman's shape going round with his hungry maw seeking them he may devour?

Ellen (*turns: with a bitter, mocking laugh*)   Maybe I am!

Mrs O'Hara (*seriously and quietly*)   Take care, Ellen Dunn. There's a good God over us all and no one can fly in His Blessed Face for nothing. I will go away now. I will leave my son in the hands of God, and I will pray night and day without stopping. The good God will protect him.

Mrs O'Hara *moves towards the door to go out.* **Ellen** *is standing turned towards the audience. She mumbles something, and then swinging round towards* **Mrs O'Hara** *cries with a sob.*

Ellen   It's a lie you're telling. A damned lie. Why didn't He protect me then – a little helpless child? (*Fiercely.*) I hate your good God – I hate you – I hate everyone – I hate the whole world.

Mrs O'Hara (*with compassion*)   You poor child. May God help you – for it is you are the most to be pitied.

Ellen (*moving quickly, right, and screaming wildly*)   Pitied? Pitied? Did you say pitied? Blast you, who wants your pity? Get out o' this house. Get out – before I throw you out. Get out, you hypocrite – you rotten, comfortable preacher – and (*And with a broken cry, she sinks on the chair at the table, right, and burying her face in her arms, bursts into passionate sobbing.*)

Mrs O'Hara *turns, looks distressed, comes back a step or two, then stops, uncertain what to do.*

Mrs Dunn (*harder than usual*)   Arra, don't mind that one at all, ma'am. She does be always going on like that with her tantrums. We tried to beat it out of her when she was young, but we might as well be idle. She has our hearts scalded. Don't heed her at all, ma'am. (*Getting her shawl.*) I'll be going down a bit of the road with you.

Ellen *stops quite suddenly, raises her head, stares in front of her and then speaks in a quiet tone.*

Ellen   You are a good woman.

Mrs O'Hara (*thoughtfully: more to herself than to* **Ellen**)   I am a woman – that had a child.

Ellen (*gently*)   Go away home out o' this.

William (*going over to* **Mrs O'Hara**)   Don't mind her at all, ma'am. We're not turning you out. You know our feelings towards you. (*As* **Mrs O'Hara** *goes out.*) Goodnight, goodnight. And thanks.

Mrs O'Hara *and* **Mrs Dunn** *go out.* **William** *stands a moment looking after them.* **Ellen** *sits staring.*

William (*turns; irritably*)   That's a nice way you carried on. Nearly spoiled everything. Couldn't you keep your temper before that old one.

Ellen (*still staring*)   Get out o' this.

William   I'll get out when I want to.

She springs up, catches a cup and makes to throw it at him.

Ellen   Get out.

William (*gruffly*)   I'm going out. Put down that cup. You can't frighten me like that. (*Taking a bucket.*) I have to feed the cows anyhow.

He goes out. She sits down again and stares. After a few moments **Jer Murnane** *comes to door and looks in. He sees* **Ellen** *and an evil look comes into his face. He cranes his neck and looks all round the kitchen. He pushes the half-door and comes in. She takes no notice.*

Jer (*rubbing his hands with pleasure*)   Well, isn't it grand to find the darling little girl all by herself.

Ellen (*jumping up and facing him*)   What do you want here, Jer Murnane?

Jer (*ingratiatingly*)   Well, I came to see William, but sure he can wait. (*Opening his arms and going towards her.*) Well, isn't she a beauty. (*She springs near the fire, her lips quivering.*) Just wan little kiss? My, what a temper she's in. My beauty.

He moves towards her again. She snatches the poker and raises it.

Ellen (*in a low, tense voice*)   Jer Murnane, if you come a step nearer I'll brain you.

Jer (*getting angry*)   Begor, 'tis a different tune you were singing some little time ago. Then you were glad enough to be giving me your kisses, and without much coaxing either. Oho, Jer Murnane isn't good enough for you now, since you have the young Buck with the big place at your heels. But take care, take care, my lady. There's many a slip twixt the cup and the lip, and – you're not married to him yet. (*Spitefully.*) Maybe 'tis left in the lurch you'll be, and 'tis glad you be to turn to Jer Murnane again – but I tell you this – (*Raising his voice.*) I wouldn't have you – no – not if you were to come begging on your bended knees. Taking a man up one day and throwing him down the next. What do you take me for? A fool, I suppose? (*His self-esteem growing.*) Aha, Jer Murnane is no fool. He is not going to let anyone make little of him. And if anyone thinks they can insult him, they're up against the wrong man. Aha, he's the boy for them. He sees through every little move, and anyone that stands in his way against him, let them look out (*Very emphatically.*) for he'll crush them – like you'd crush a beetle under your boot. Do you hear? A little – dirty – black – beetle. (*Bending towards her.*) And when you'll come crawling back to me – (*Opening his hand wide and then closing it slowly.*) – crushed – like a little dirty black beetle. (*A pause. He turns away: then gruffly.*) Where's William?

Ellen (*gruffly*)   I don't know.

He goes to the door, and is about to open it when **William** *appears.* **Ellen** *puts down the poker.*

William   That you, Jer.

Jer   I was just going out to look for you.

William (*dryly*)   Well, you're saved the trouble now I'm here. Sit over there near the fire.

Jer *sits on chair left of fire. He takes out his pipe and begins to fill it.* **William** *comes in with a hare on his arm. He goes to table, takes a bit of bread and pours a little milk into a saucer. He sits on chair right of fire, and feeds the hare with these. They take no notice of* **Ellen** *who is standing at the window looking out. After a few moments she goes out slowly. The tension is at once relieved.*

Jer (*jocosely*)   In the name of God, where did you get the hare?

William   I found her – with her leg broken.

Jer And you mended it?

William   Ay. With a bit of cipin[9] as splinter.

Jer   Begor, William, you're wasting your time here. 'Tis a doctor you should be.

William (*with animation*)   See how tame she is, Jer. All the wildness gone out of her.

Jer   Yes, my lad, a doctor. An animal doctor. And setting up a menagerie with all the maimed animals you do be finding and curing. Begor, William, if you got a sixpence for all the birds and beasts you doctored, you'd have a fortune now. The last time 'twas a sparrow.

William   No, 'twas a finch.

Jer   And she flew away, I suppose – like all them female creatures when they don't want you.

William   No, she died. (*Getting up and going out with the hare.*) I'll be back in a second.

---

9   A little stick.

Jer *continues smoking. In a few seconds* **William** *returns.*

William (*putting saucer back on table*)   How's the world using you, Jer?

Jer (*thoughtfully, smoking*)   Ah – all right?

William (*sitting on chair, right of fire*)   Any news down your way?

Jer (*knowingly*)   You have news yourself, my bucko.

William *looks at him questioningly.*

Jer (*nodding and winking*)   What brought a certain old woman trudging up here today?

William (*just to say something*)   John O'Hara's wife.

Jer (*nodding, slowly*)   Ay. John – O'Hara's wife.

William   I suppose you followed her?

Jer   That's neither here nor there. What brought her – that's the point.

William (*indifferently*)   Something about hens – I don't remember rightly – 'twas to my mother she was talking.

Jer (*his habitual smile broadening*)   Oh – hens?

William   Ay.

Jer   And nothing about chickens?

William   Well now, to tell the truth, I didn't take much notice.

Jer (*taking out his pipe and bending over confidentially*)   Maybe it was about *a* hen – and – that – hen – *Ellen*?

William (*emphatically*)   Jer, you can take my oath on it, Ellen's name wasn't mentioned from beginning to end.

A pause, they both look at the fire. **Jer** *smokes.*

Jer (*pensively*)   Well, that's a great come-down for old John. (*A pause.*) To be sending his wife as a kind of – (*Emphatically.*) – ambassador. (*A fairly long pause: then turning suddenly to* **William**.) I suppose she offered a couple of hundred?

William (*taken off his guard*)   She did not then, only – (*Suddenly remembering.*) – nothing at all.

Jer (*good-humouredly*)   And how the devil did she get round your mother with nothing at all?

William (*making the best of his slip: with would-be humour*)   Oh, the usual holy-Job stuff: discord in homes – hearts broken – father and son separated – mothers and orphans crying. You know. That kind of thing.

Jer (*laughing*)   I know it all right.

William (*confidentially*)   Well, Jer, if there's anything that sticks in my gullet, it's them chapel-going wans. My God, they would make you throw up what you never ate.

Jer (*enjoying himself*)   Well, no one can call you a chapel-goer, William. Not even your worst enemy.

William (*combatively*)   Well, I'm as good as them that are maybe.

Jer (*agreeably*)   Ay, that's true. (*A pause. Then with cordiality.*) You're a man after my own heart, William. Put the hand there. (*They shake hands.*) A man after my own heart. (*A pause. Both are pleased. Then* **Jer** *takes out his pipe and, looking at* **William** *with a friendly open smile, says with hearty good-humour.*) Well, glory be to God, isn't it a great change in the world to see your mother and herself going down the road together as thick as thieves.

William (*cautiously*)   Ay.

Jer   As thick as thieves, as all true Christians should be.

William   Ay.

Jer   And seeing each other home too like all true, loving Christians.

William (*quickly*)   Ah no, she's only going down a bit of the road with her.

Jer (*with friendly contempt*)   You're an innocent man, William Dunn, God help you.

William   Why so?

Jer (*emphatically*)   Your mother is going down to John O'Hara's house – take whatever meaning you like out of that.

William (*cautiously*)   How do you know?

Jer (*with a knowing nod*)   I heard it.

William (*bewildered*)   Where?

Jer (*confidentially*)   Myself and Tim were inside a hedge, and just as they were passing I heard her saying it with my own two ears.

William (*standing up slowly and moving away: to himself*)   The old fox. Oh, the mangy old fox. (*Raising his voice, and striking his hand with his fist.*) I knew it. I knew she'd do me. She always done me. The old fox. (*Bitterly.*) Although, God knows, I ought to be up to all her tricks and turns by now.

Jer (*standing up: encouragingly*)   What is it, man? Out with it.

William (*turning: in a burst of confidence*)   It is how Mrs O'Hara offered us a hundred and eighty pounds to stop Ellen going with Maurice.

Jer   Yes, yes.

William   She gave us eighty, half to my mother and half to me, and – and – we were to get the other hundred when everything was settled. And now I'm thinking –

Jer   Yes, yes?

William   That maybe I'll be done out of my share of the hundred. If that old fox goes down with her to the house – my God, man, wherever she'd smell money she'd worm it out. She's the divil. (*Raising his voice.*) I knew she'd do me. She always –

Jer   Whisht. (*They listen. Footsteps are heard.*) There's someone coming.

William (*joyfully*)   Maybe 'tis herself.

Tim *comes in quickly. He looks at* **Jer** *questioningly.*

Jer (*self-satisfied*)   'Tis all right, Tim, speak out. William is with us.

Tim   They're saying goodbye at the bend of the road – a good mile down. I ran up a short cut to let you know.

Jer (*to* **Tim**)   Good. The old woman was here to prevent the match. She offered a hundred and eighty. She gave the eighty, and the rest will come later. (*To* **William***: with hearty geniality.*) Put the hand there, William. (*They shake hands.*) We'll help you in this. We'll watch the O'Haras' house for you, and if we see your mother putting her nose near the place one of us will butt in at her elbow and – (*Winking broadly.*) – talk about the weather, you know – and the other one of us will come in hot haste to warn you.

William (*eagerly*)   And I'll be on her traces too, following her down the road.

Jer   Right you are, my son. You're a man after my own heart. Put the hand there. (*They shake hands. Then confidentially.*) And remember, my lad, 'tis fifty per cent for the service, you know.

William (*letting his hand go; dubiously*)   It's a lot you're asking.

Jer (*very sure of himself*)   Business is business. What do you say, Tim?

Tim   I don't mind about the money at all. I'm satisfied if no one goes into that house in my sister's place.

Jer (*with good humour*)   Never mind, Tim – he's no businessman. Well, William, is it agreed or not? Do you want our help or not? Quick, man, before your mother comes. Quick, I think I hear footsteps.

William (*grudgingly*)   You're the divil, Jer.

Jer *laughs as they shake hands again.*

Jer   Agreed then?

William   Agreed.

Jer   Fifty per cent of forty pounds – that's twenty pounds.[10]

---

10 This line to the end of the act is inserted by hand on the typed manuscript.

William   Twenty pounds.

Jer (*holding out his hand*)   Quick man before your mother gets back.

William (*grudgingly getting out the money*)   You're the divil.

As he counts the money the curtain falls.

Act Three

Scene the same as Act One, except that the table is cleared. Evening. Rays of setting sun are seen through window. **Maurice** *is sitting on chair, left of table. His face is stiff and set, and he is staring in front of him.* **Mrs O'Hara** *comes in from room on left, back.*

Mrs O'Hara   Well, I thought I'd never get her to sleep. But she's off at last, thanks be to God. (*Going over to fix fire.*) It's them old teeth that are at her. It's terrible to see a little crathereen[11] like that suffering, and not to be able to do anything for her. (*Sighing.*) But sure it's the way of the world to be suffering, and we must be satisfied; only 'tis hard on little infant children that have no understanding. (*Standing up and looking at clock.*) Indeed it is time for Oweneen to be in now, and going to his bed. The little rascal would stay for ever out romping about. I'd better be going to look for him. (*She goes to door and turns.*) Indeed it was just the same with – (*She looks at* **Maurice** *and stops. Anxiously.*) What's wrong with you, avic?[12] You're as white as a ghost. (*Coming back and speaking very gently.*) Tell your mother, won't you? Whatever trouble is weighing you down.

Maurice (*quietly*)   It's nothing at all, mother. A bad pain in my head I have. (*Standing up firmly.*) I'll look for Oweneen – you stay here.

Mrs O'Hara (*decisively*)   Indeed I won't – I know his haunts better than you. (*Going to door.*) Around the yard somewhere he is. (*Turning, at door.*) And if the baby cries, call me – I won't be far.

Maurice *stands up, panting.*

Maurice   By the hawthorn bush at the bend of the road now for a full hour, and a point in her wild, black eyes looking for me!

He rushes to the dresser, snatches a black felt hat hanging up on the side, puts it on, and is about to rush out when the half-door is pushed in, and **Kitty Doyle** *with the sleeping child in her arms comes in.*

Kitty (*in a whisper*)   Fast asleep he is, Maurice. Look at him. He is worn out. (*As* **Maurice** *puts out his arms to take the child.*) No, no! – you'd wake him may be. (*Looking round.*) Where's herself?

Maurice   Just this minute she went out looking for him.

Kitty (*pondering a moment*)   Ah, sure I'll put him to bed myself. (*With sweet tenderness.*) The poor little lost lamb. Sit over there near the fire, Maurice, and hold him. (**Maurice** *sits on stool and takes the child in his arms.*) So – let his little head rest against you. So. Now I'll run up and ready his bed for him. You could be taking off his boots and stockings there near the fire.

---

11 Little creature, as before.
12 Son. Avic is an Anglicized spelling of *a mhic*, meaning son.

She goes into room on left, back. **Maurice** *opens the lace of the child's boot with his disengaged right hand.* **Kitty** *comes back in a moment with a white garment in her hand.*

Kitty   That's his little night shirt. I'll put it here to air for him.

She puts it on the back of the armchair. She goes back again to room. **Maurice** *stops unlacing the boot. He holds his child in his two arms and bends his head low down on the face of the sleeping child. His face is hidden. After a short time* **Kitty** *returns.*

Kitty (*brightly but softly*)   Everything is ready now.

She looks at the pair for a moment, then comes over quietly, kneels down and takes off the child's boots and stockings.

Kitty (*standing up*)   Now, Maurice, give him to me – everything is ready.

Maurice (*standing up*)   I'll put him to bed myself. (*As she shakes her head.*) You needn't be afraid, I won't wake him. I'm accustomed to the children.

She feels the shirt to see if it is warm and then hands it to him. He goes into the room with his head still bent over the sleeping child. **Kitty** *picks up the child's stockings, feels them to see if they are damp and hangs them on the line over the fire. She picks up the boots, feels the insides, and puts them in the chimney-corner to dry. She then puts the armchair back in its place.*

Mrs O'Hara (*putting her head in over the half-door; anxiously*)   Did Oweneen come in? I can't find a trace of him anywhere.

Kitty   He did, Mrs O'Hara.

Mrs O'Hara *looks relieved and comes in.*

Mrs O'Hara   Good evening, Kitty. That little rascal gave me a bit of a start. I couldn't find him high nor low. Where is he?

Kitty   Maurice is putting him to bed. (*Reflectively.*) He's as tender as a woman with a child – and he such a big, powerful man.

Mrs O'Hara (*wondering*)   And where was Oweneen at all?

Kitty   Going down to my house he was to see the pups. Fan has a fine litter – and yesterday I was telling him about the little weeshy pups, so he must have got it into his head to go and see them, for where should I find him but down near Foley's corner, sitting on the side of the road and crying his eyes out. The poor little lamb must have lost his way and got frightened. It would go through a stone to see him.

Mrs O'Hara (*a little angry*)   The little devil to be straying away like that. We won't be able to hold him at all soon!

Kitty (*admiringly*)   Isn't he the grand little man to have so much courage! (*Quickly.*) But I must be off. Looking for the geese I was when I seen him, but sure I left geese and everything to bring him home. (*Pensively.*) I declare he'd make your heart bleed to see him there crying, just like a little lost lamb bleating for his mother! (*Quickly.*)

But I must be running – my mother will be wondering what's keeping me. (*Hurrying out.*) Goodbye, Mrs O'Hara.

Mrs O'Hara   Goodbye, and God bless you! (*Going to door and calling after her.*) Come up again soon!

Maurice *comes in, closing the door gently.*

Maurice   Kitty is gone, is she?

Mrs O'Hara (*turning*)   She is – she was in a hurry.

Maurice   She found Oweneen. (*As his mother goes towards the children's room.*) 'Tis all right – I put him to bed.

Mrs O'Hara (*at children's door; in a whisper*)   And you didn't wake the baby?

Maurice   No: the two of them are asleep.

Mrs O'Hara   I'll just take a peep at them.

She opens the room door very carefully and goes in on tip-toe. **Maurice** *sits on the chair, left of table. He stares in front of him with a stern, rigid face. After a short time* **Mrs O'Hara** *comes back, a happy glow on her face.*

Mrs O'Hara   So quiet and peaceful. And kind of smiling! (*Taking her knitting out of a work-basket on the window-sill and talking to herself.*) It is how the angels themselves do be sheltering them with their wings when they are asleep – the poor little motherless orphans!

She sits on stool at fire and knits. There is a comfortable, placid, restful air about her – in sharp contrast to **Maurice**.

Mrs O'Hara   It's a great taking way Kitty Doyle has with children – she that never had a child. I declare to goodness, Oweneen couldn't be fonder of his own mother – if the Lord had spared her. Don't you think so, Maurice?

Maurice (*abstractedly*)   Oh yes, I do.

Mrs O'Hara   And she's so bright and pleasant in her manner that 'tis like a ray of sunshine to see her face at the door. And then, she's not the kind that does be up one day and down the next; or the kind that would be flying out into a temper that you wouldn't have a minute's peace nor ease wondering what they were going to say or do next. Oh no, she's not that kind at all. But sure where there's the grace of God it is always the same. There's always peace and happiness and contentment. (*A pause.*) Going to see the pups down at Doyles the little lad was when he lost himself. And there he was, sitting crying on the side of the road without father or mother. It would go through a stone, she said, to hear him. (*With animation.*) Sure a little orphan child without a mother – and he not to be crying at all – would go through a heart of flint. (*Putting down her knitting; thoughtfully.*) I don't think there's anyone in the whole wide world so bad, as to do wrong to an orphan, or to bring one tear of sorrow to –

Maurice (*starting up*)   For God's sake, mother, shut up! You'll drive me mad!

Mrs O'Hara (*looks up at him surprised*)   What is it? What am I doing to you? Ah sure, I forgot – your poor head.

He goes quickly to the door and then stops dead short. His face and body are rigid. She looks at him anxiously and then goes on knitting. A fairly long pause.

Mrs O'Hara (*very gently*)   My old talk is maybe making your head worse?

He doesn't answer for a little while. Then turning, he walks gently back to his seat.

Maurice (*sadly*)   No – it isn't that, mother. It isn't anything at all. (*Looking at her fondly.*) Go on talking, mother. I like listening to your voice, and to the sound of the knitting, and to be looking at you there, sitting warm near the fire. (*Wistfully.*) It's a good thing to have a warm fire to sit at, isn't it, mother?

Mrs O'Hara (*fervently*)   It is so, lad. And a warm roof over your head, and a warm meal to eat, and a warm bed to lie on. Sure we ought never to be done thanking the good God who gave us that same when there are so many without them. (*A pause. Looking at clock.*) 'Tis a wonder your father and James aren't coming in. But sure your father would stick out with them animals from dawn till dark and would never think of giving himself a bite nor a sup so long as they were all right. (*Shaking her head.*) That's all very well but 'tisn't younger he's getting. (*Putting down her knitting.*) And somehow, I was noticing lately that he's aging a lot – a kind of dhreeng[13] is coming on him.

Maurice (*anxiously*)   You don't think father is failing? Do you, mother?

Mrs O'Hara (*not heeding him, proudly*)   And glory be to God, the fine straight back he used to have in his young days!

Maurice   But he's not failing, mother?

Mrs O'Hara (*knitting again*)   Well, child, we can't be young always. Remember he's going on for seventy. (*Proudly.*) And isn't he the grand man for that! There's many another at that age crippled up with rheumatism. And himself is out late and early, and he working as good as the best. But all the same, lad, I'm thinking 'tis time for him to ease off a bit. And thank God, there's a fine young strong man to take his place – (*Solemnly.*) – just as Oweneen will be helping you too when the day comes that you are feeling the weight of the years.

Maurice (*quietly*)   Yes, mother.

Mrs O'Hara (*putting down her knitting; in a deep dreamy voice*)   And a fine strapping man Oweneen will grow up to be too, just like you and your father. A great breed of men all the O'Haras. Tall and strong, with their heads high, and their long swinging legs. And they sticking into the work and enjoying every minute of the day! God, the love John O'Hara has for that land!

---

13 The meaning of this word is unclear, but from the context it seems to mean a shadow, or an age-related weakness.

Maurice (*earnestly*)   And isn't it a grand and a great thing to love?

Mrs O'Hara   And he loving the feel of the red soil on his hands!

Maurice (*beginning to glow*)   Ay, ay – the feel of the soil!

Mrs O'Hara   Sweet to the blood the feel of it is, he says.

Maurice (*intensely*)   Ay – sweeter than the touch of a woman's hair!

A pause.

Mrs O'Hara (*knitting again; brightly*)   And why wouldn't he love the land? Sure weren't his people always on it for generations!

Maurice (*with animation*)   Yes, mother. There's the gravestone over in Kilnagluck – and there was an O'Hara here – (*Slowly and proudly.*) – two hundred and fifty years ago.

Mrs O'Hara   Ay, and longer than that maybe. And all that time going partners with God Almighty in His work. Tilling the fields and rearing grand families – all big men and women!

Maurice (*catching the proud ring in her voice*)   Without guile, without trickery, without blemish.

Mrs O'Hara (*putting down her knitting; intensely*)   And in the bad black times when the red stranger came from over the seas, and turned the O'Haras out on the side of the road –

Maurice (*proudly*)   But they weren't downed, mother. They held out!

During the following, **Mrs O'Hara** *speaks intensely, as if she had lived through what she is saying.* **Maurice**'s *emotion is happier: his imagination dwells only on the contest and the final victory. His voice expresses exhilaration, pride, exultation.*

Mrs O'Hara   And they filling their bellies with wild haws maybe!

Maurice   But they clung to the land of their fathers!

Mrs O'Hara   Ay – with tooth and nail!

Maurice   With beak and claw!

Mrs O'Hara   They were never ousted!

Maurice   There was always an O'Hara there!

Mrs O'Hara   Even though 'twas born under the bare black bush he was!

Maurice   They held out, they held out – from father to son!

Mrs O'Hara   With black Death and pale Hunger stalking them down!

Maurice (*triumphantly*)   But they bate them two old Trojans!

Mrs O'Hara (*taking up his shout of triumph*)   And the red stranger too!

They pause breathless, their faces aglow. **Mrs O'Hara** *takes up her knitting again and continues quietly.*

Mrs O'Hara   And now they are living again in their home as they should be, their own masters, in their warm house, milking the cows, and tilling the land.

Maurice (*quietly*)   And what better could anyone want?

Mrs O'Hara   Nothing better – nothing at all. There's God's joy when a man is young, and God's peace in his old age.

A pause. Both are calm and peaceful-looking.

Maurice (*eagerly*)   And the Deasys, mother? Your people, what about them?

Mrs O'Hara (*pensively*)   Well now, they were different.

Maurice (*as above*)   They loved the land too?

Mrs O'Hara (*as above*)   Not in the same way. You see, they hadn't the bone and sinew like the O'Haras, and they couldn't enjoy the hard work the same way. (*Proudly.*) Why, 'tis better than a fist of gold to John O'Hara to have the beads of sweat standing out on his forehead, and they shining in the sun! (*She stops.*)

Maurice (*very eagerly*)   But the Deasys, mother? Tell me about them.

Mrs O'Hara (*quietly*)   Small men the Deasys were, and given more to reading books. Some of them were schoolmasters, and there was a priest here and there in the line. (*Proudly.*) In the Penal Times there were three of the Deasys priests. Three brothers' sons they were, little wisps of men all of the them, like James there, that wouldn't say booh to a goose. And there they were –

Maurice (*breathless*)   With the gallows hanging over them!

Mrs O'Hara (*quietly*)   And they going about doing God's work.

Maurice (*proudly*)   Without fear or tremble!

A pause.

Mrs O'Hara (*very quietly*)   One of them three was hanged.

Maurice (*proudly*)   But there was no fear in his heart – and they putting the noose around his neck.

Mrs O'Hara (*pensively*)   The poor little maneen – like James there – that would step out of the way from a mouse. (*A pause.*) Ah yes, small men they were, with not much to say except when the visions came to them, and then they would spend hours saying off the beautiful ranna[14] made by the grand poets of the olden times. (*Putting down her knitting and looking into space. It is growing dark.*) I remember my

---

14 Stanzas of poetry.

grandfather used to be like that. And when the Great Famine was there, and we with nothing to eat but the yellow meal, for the potatoes were all rotted, there would he be telling us – and he warm in the telling, and we forgetting our hunger – telling us of the beautiful women of olden times, and their golden hair sweeping the ground, and the long white arms of them, and they living forever in the Land of the Young, where there is no sorrow or pain. (*Her voice trails off to a whisper.*)

Maurice (*dreamily*)   And the white – warm – arms of them!

Mrs O'Hara   And their – golden – hair – sweeping – the ground.

It is now dark. Silence for a few moments. Then **James** *pushes in the half-door excitedly.*

James   Mary, Mary, the two loveliest twin calves! In the name of goodness, why are you sitting in the dark? Hurry and light the lamp.

Maurice (*starting up*)   The darling little red cow! The little darling.

Maurice *runs out.* **Mrs O'Hara** *lights the lamp.*

James   Two beauties. And the mother as proud as punch.

Mrs O'Hara   Glory be to God. Two of them!

James   And they so beautiful and strong.

Mrs O'Hara   Thanks be to God.

James   Give me a fistful of salt, hurry.

Mrs O'Hara (*gives him some salt out of a box hanging on the wall near the fire*)   Well, isn't she the great little cow!

James   Great is no name for her, she's trem-end-ous!

James *hurries out.* **Mrs O'Hara** *sees the child's stockings and feels them. She goes to the children's room door, listens for a moment, and then comes back to her seat at the fire. She takes up her knitting, knits a few stitches, puts it down again and thinks. Steps are heard. She starts knitting again.* **Ellen** *puts her head in. She looks round and, seeing only* **Mrs O'Hara**, *pushes the half-door and comes in.*

Ellen (*a little shyly*)   Good evening, ma'am.

Mrs O'Hara (*wondering*)   Good evening, Ellen. (*A shade of awkwardness. A slight pause.*) Maybe you'd like to sit down for a bit and rest yourself?

Ellen *sits on chair right of table. She stares in front of her abstractedly.*

Mrs O'Hara   I hope you left your mother and brother well, Ellen?

Ellen (*dully*)   They're all right. (*A fairly long pause.*)

Mrs O'Hara (*brightly*)   One of our calves is just after calving – two beautiful calves they're telling me. (**Ellen** *takes no notice.*) Oweneen was lost this evening. (*Still no* *notice.*) Going to see the pups down at Doyles he was, but 'tis a long road for a little gorsoon[15] and –

Ellen *has pulled herself together and is looking around critically.*

Ellen   'Tis a fine warm house ye have here. And all the doors painted. I suppose them are all rooms? (*She goes over quickly to door on right, front, and opens it; then a cry of pleasure.*) My, what a lovely parlour! And carpet on the floor! (*She stoops and touches it.*) Isn't it grand to be walking on that. (*Turning to* **Mrs O'Hara** *and speaking fiercely.*) But I don't want yer house anyhow, and it could be ten times as good for all I care! (*She half turns, faces audience, gazes into space, smiles a little, goes over rather slowly to her chair and sits down. Then in a quiet friendly voice.*) I'm going away.

Mrs O'Hara (*starting*)   You're going away?

Ellen (*nods slowly*)   Yes.

Mrs O'Hara   To America, Ellen?

Ellen (*half to herself*)   I'm going away – to a far-off country.

Mrs O'Hara (*with pleasure*)   Well, now. Isn't that grand? But it will take a bit of time of course – there's such a lot of things – a big trunk – and new dresses – and papers to be signed. And then there'll be the ticket – ah, there's no show but the things you'll have to do before starting on that long journey. When my own sister went, it took near three months before she was ready – and when she got there, it was how she had to buy a lot more. I'm thinking there must be a powerful lot of money out in America – the foolish way they spend it. So you're going to America? Arra, you'll do well out there – a fine active girl like you! I suppose tis by Cove you're going?

Ellen (*still gazing into space*)   To a far-away country I'm going – a grand beautiful country – where the sun does be always shining, and where there's no rain or cold.

Mrs O'Hara (*thoughtfully*)   Well, alanna,[16] I don't know all about that. 'Tis a mistake to be expecting too much. Of course people do be always talking about the grand life they have out in America – but I don't know – far-away cows wear long horns. And sure they do be cracking up places like that to make people go out there, for 'tisn't likely anyone would want to leave their own kith and kin to be going out to a strange land. I don't know. Maybe 'tis all they say, and maybe it isn't. But I wouldn't be building any fairy castles about it, and then you won't be disappointed. It strikes me there's good and bad in every place. Sure the good God when He made the world knew that we must have our trials to get to Heaven and He knew too that we must have our little bits of joy to keep us going. But there's no getting away from the trials, alanna. And maybe, though there's the big houses out in America, and the lashings of money, maybe 'tis how the people are there like what they are in Dublin:

---

15 A boy.
16 Child, used as a term of endearment.

running all day long without giving themselves time to draw their breath, just as if the devil was at their heels all the time.

Ellen (*in a deep, low voice*)   I am going away to a far-off country, and I am going alone, for there is no one brave enough to come with me. (*Fiercely.*) Lies they do be telling, all of them! (*Quietly.*) And now I'm going alone.

Mrs O'Hara (*soothingly*)   I wouldn't mind that, alanna. There was my sister Kate, and sure didn't she go off to America without a soul with her that she knew – that is, on the journey I mean – but she went to friends – a first cousin of ours that was out in Boston –

Ellen (*not heeding; with a cry of happiness*)   My, aren't them the lovely shiny candlesticks!

She jumps up, walks quickly towards the fire, looks at the articles on the mantlepiece with admiration, takes down one of the candlesticks and examines it critically. All the time **Mrs O'Hara** *is talking in her comfortable way.*

Mrs O'Hara   They are so. They are in the O'Hara family for generations. 'Tis in them the blessed candles do be put when one of the O'Haras do be waked. (*Piously.*) May the Lord grant it be a long time before they're used!

Ellen (*putting back the candlestick*)   I suppose it is you do be shining them?

Mrs O'Hara   It is, alanna.

Ellen *sits in armchair, left of fire, and looks at* **Mrs O'Hara** *pensively for a few minutes.* **Mrs O'Hara** *continues knitting and takes no notice.*

Ellen (*thoughtfully*)   Tell me, do you never get tired of shining candlesticks, and knitting stockings, and things like that?

Mrs O'Hara   Wisha then, I don't, while the Lord leaves me my health.

Ellen (*wondering*)   And were you always like that – always?

Mrs O'Hara (*good humouredly*)   Well, when I was a young girl I used to be a bit fidgety – like all young girls – wanting love, and romance, and all sorts of foolish things. But sure I learned sense with the years.

Ellen (*earnestly*)   What was that?

Mrs O'Hara   That love is just feeding your man well, and keeping a warm shirt to his back.

Ellen (*wondering*)   Love is just eating and drinking and being warm. (*She springs up and away from* **Mrs O'Hara** *with a sharp cry.*) No, no, no, no! (*She moves her hand across her forehead. Then her face brightens. Triumphantly.*) Your man broke you. (*Proudly.*) But no man will ever break me in.

Mrs O'Hara (*stops knitting; pensively*)   No – 'twasn't my man – it was things – everything – the child maybe.

Ellen (*turning to her*)   The child?

Mrs O'Hara (*thinking hard; then with conviction*)   It was God – that's what it was.

Ellen (*wondering*)   God?

Mrs O'Hara (*knitting again*)   And when God breaks you in – somehow you never want to be free again. (*Brightly.*) It is then you see the real meaning of everything.

Ellen (*comes back and kneels near* **Mrs O'Hara**. *Very earnestly*)   How? Tell me.

Mrs O'Hara (*putting down her knitting*)   Well now – let me see – it is hard to explain. You let go of yourself – and you get knitted in with everyone around you – and God too – altogether – in one swim – and you lose yourself – for the others. (*Knitting again: brightly.*) And there is such a lot of them to be taking care of: there's himself, and there's James – that's my brother – and there's Maurice – and then there's the children.

Ellen (*to herself*)   Ah – the children! The hands of little children. (*To* **Mrs O'Hara**.) Where are the children now?

Mrs O'Hara (*nodding towards door*)   They're within there, alanna, asleep in their bed. (*As* **Ellen** *springs up and goes hurriedly towards the door.*) No, no, alanna, you'd wake them. (**Ellen** *stops.*) And the little one does be cross.

Ellen (*rushing over and kneeling at her side; beseechingly*)   No, I won't wake them at all – I'll only look at them – and touch their hands.

Mrs O'Hara   But their hands will be under the clothes, and if you tried to pull them out –

Ellen   No, no, I won't. I'll only look at them – I won't touch them at all. (*Confidentially.*) I have never seen a baby – close. I will only sit down – and look at them – look at them breathing. That's all.

Mrs O'Hara (*smiling*)   Very well then.

Ellen *goes quietly to the door, carefully opens it, goes in and closes it behind her.*

Mrs O'Hara (*with a pensive smile*)   Wisha, I think after all, you're just a child yourself.

She gets up, fills the kettle with water and puts it on the fire. She looks at the clock and then sits down again and knits. **Mrs Dunn** *comes to the door. She is dressed in a hood cloak, with the hood down.*

Mrs Dunn (*quietly*)   Good evening to you, ma'am.

Mrs O'Hara (*with pleasure*)   Oh, is it yourself that's in it? Come in, come in! (*She stands up and goes to meet* **Mrs Dunn**, *gesticulating towards the bedroom door. Then in a confidential whisper.*) Isn't it great? I know all about it! (*Admiringly.*) Well, it took yourself to manage it!

Mrs Dunn (*mystified, but asking no explanation*)   About that business –

Mrs O'Hara (*leading her to armchair*)   I know, I know! (*Taking money out of cloth purse around her neck.*) I have the money here with me. I drew it out of the post office to have it ready. (*Handing money to her.*) Here it is: a hundred pounds; and may God bless you!

Mrs Dunn *takes it without saying anything. Steps are heard outside. She quietly hides it in the bosom of her dress.* **Jer Murnane** *puts his head in over the half-door.*

Jer (*in a loud, cheery voice*)   God save all here.

Mrs O'Hara   And you too, Jer.

Jer (*coming in and looking round*)   Is himself here?

Mrs O'Hara   Well, no, then. He's out with a cow that's after calving.

Jer (*sitting on settle*)   Oh, then I'll wait for him. I suppose he'll be soon in anyway. (*A pause. Agreeably.*) Well now, isn't it grand weather we're having, thanks be to God.

Mrs O'Hara   It is so, but I find it a bit chilly this evening. The nights are beginning to get cold, I think.

Jer (*with energetic friendliness*)   And the mornings too, ma'am. This morning the air was as sharp as a razor, and – my God! – it would cut you right into the bone. (*To* **Mrs Dunn**.) But sure it must be worse than that up the hills, ma'am?

Mrs Dunn (*drily*)   We don't take any notice of the cold. We're used to it.

A pause.

Mrs O'Hara   Wouldn't you come over here near the fire, Jer?

Jer   Oh, I'm all right here, ma'am – thanks all the same. (*A pause.*) Which of the cows is it, ma'am?

Mrs O'Hara   The little red cow with the white forehead – and two lovely calves!

Jer (*surprised*)   Two? (*With a touch of jealousy.*) Begor, everything fine comes on the double to this house. John O'Hara was born under a lucky star – as the poets would say.

Mrs O'Hara   Well, God has been very good to us, glory be to His Holy Name. (*A slight pause.*) Maybe you'd like to go out and have a look at the twins, Jer? The men are outside.

Jer (*smiling roguishly*)   Well now, one would think that you wanted to get rid of me.

Mrs O'Hara   Not at all, not at all, Jer. Only I'm thinking 'tis dull company for you to be here with two women.

Jer (*amusing himself*)   Oh, I'm fond of the ladies too, ma'am. I'm a bit of a ladies' man – in my own small way.

Mrs O'Hara *smiles. A pause.*

Jer (*to* **Mrs Dunn**, *with a knowing smile*)   It's a long walk you had down here this evening, ma'am. And a bad, rough road!

Mrs Dunn (*shortly*)   I'm not complaining.

Jer (*with sly humour*)   You don't ever complain, ma'am, do you? You're blissful and serene – as the poet would say. (*A pause.*) Oh, 'tis a grand thing to have a light heart. Then the roads are not long, nor the nights not cold. No, you don't feel nothing, ma'am. A light, merry heart you have, ma'am, lepping inside in your bosom. (*He laughs and winks slowly.*)

Mrs Dunn (*drily to* **Mrs O'Hara**)   John Jameson is talking.

Mrs O'Hara (*in the same tone to* **Mrs Dunn**)   Without a doubt in the world.

Jer (*enjoying himself immensely*)   But 'tis all right, ma'am, I'll not say a word. (*Winking.*) Jer Murnane is no fool. He knows when to talk and when to keep his gob shut, when to open his eyes and when to shut them. Open your eyes and close your mouth and you'll see what God will send you: that's my motto. (*He winks again and nods.*) We understand each other, ma'am. We do indeed – better than you think. (*Genially.*) But we're all friends, all neighbours, and I'm not the one to –

John *and* **James** *come in.*

John (*in high spirits*)   God bless the company. Good evening to ye all.

James   Good evening to all. (*He sits quietly on settle.*)

Mrs Dunn   Good evening, John O'Hara.

Jer   Good evening, good evening. (*Running to* **John** *and shaking his hand.*) And so it is an increase you're having? Well, may God bless and multiply your store every time!

John   And yours too, Jer.

Jer (*still shaking his hand*)   For you're an honest and deserving man, John O'Hara.

Maurice *excitedly rushes in, his face aglow.*

Maurice   They're lovely, mother, lov –

He then sees the strangers and stops. At this moment, there are three sets of actions going on: the first, that of **John**, **James** *and* **Jer**; *the second, that of* **Maurice** *and* **Ellen**; *the third, that of* **Mrs O'Hara** *and* **Mrs Dunn**. *In the first,* **Jer** *goes back to the settle and sits down beside* **James**. **John**, *who is in his shirtsleeves, latches the door and then puts on a coat hanging on the back of it.* **Jer** *and* **James** *are watching him. He acts slowly, and is probably making low ejaculations of self-satisfaction. In the second,* **Maurice** *is facing the children's bedroom door. Looking in that direction, when he stops speaking, he sees the door ajar, and* **Ellen** *standing in the shadow, the door handle in her hand. He stares, amazed. It is only when she begins to move that he speaks. In the third, the following conversation takes place.*

Mrs Dunn (*starting on seeing* **Maurice**)   Maurice O'Hara? In the name of God, what makes you be here?

Mrs O'Hara (*answering* **Mrs Dunn**)   And where else would he be, ma'am, but in his own house?

Mrs Dunn (*not listening to* **Mrs O'Hara**, *looking at* **Maurice**, *and speaking her thoughts aloud*)   And where then is Ellen?

Maurice (*with a glad cry*)   Ellen! (*He takes a step towards her.*)

Ellen (*advancing slowly – her light, firm, rhythmic movement from the hips expressing power and cruelty*)   Stand back from me, Maurice O'Hara! Stand back, I say! So here you are, is it? – you poor little farthing man! – so here you are, minding your calves and your cows, and without any thought at all of the grand words you were saying to me a week ago today. (*Her scorn increasing.*) Then stick to your cows and your horses, Maurice O'Hara; live in your fenced-in little fields; eat and drink and grow fat and contented; but with all that you have made a fools bargain; for never again will you speak grand words (*Losing herself in her vision; her voice swells.*) – never again will you see in your mind the grand country where the sun does be always shining and the birds always singing. But I am going away into that country, and I am going alone, for there is no one brave enough to come with me.

Maurice (*earnestly*)   I will go with you.

Ellen (*coming back to reality; rather sadly*)   What would you be doing with me, Maurice O'Hara, and the biggest half of you yearning for your home and your stock? Looking back over your shoulder you'd be at every step you'd take, and not listening at all (*With vibrating voice.*) – with the larks rising up in the bogs in the morning and filling the world with joy.

Maurice (*moving near her earnestly*)   I will go with you.

Jer (*with angry sarcasm*)   You're welcome to her: my lavings.

Maurice (*his earnestness increasing*)   There would be no sense at all in the larks singing if the two of us weren't together.

Ellen (*unheeding*)   And 'tis I can take my fill now of everything, for there will be no hurry on me at all to be coming home milking the cows and churning the butter. I'll be lying in the sun by the hawthorn bush and it all in blossom –

Maurice (*with animation*)   Yes, yes, Ellen: the hawthorn blossom; when I do be kissing your cheek.

Ellen (*unheeding*)   And the brown thrush himself will be singing to me, telling me of the grand country that lies beyond in America; where there's always a blue sky, and green lawns, and red flowers; and a beautiful man giving me his love –

Maurice (*with deep feeling*)   'Tis me, Ellen, 'tis me: giving you every drop of my heart's love.

Ellen (*unheeding*)   The most beautiful man in all the world he will be: a prince maybe: the son of the King of Spain himself –

Mrs Dunn (*standing up; to* **Ellen** *gruffly*)   Come home out of this and put a stop to your raimeis.[17]

John (*bewildered*)   A prince!

Jer (*with great satisfaction*)   Aha! So she's laving himself in the lurch too!

John   Oh, she's mad – crazy mad!

Mrs Dunn (*to* **John***; apologetically*)   Arra, don't mind her at all: she does be often like that.

Mrs O'Hara (*standing up*)   God help her, the poor innocent girl; 'tis queer in her mind she's going surely.

Tim *and* **William** *burst in breathless. They leave the door open.*

Ellen (*turning towards the door*)   Away my own road I'm going.

Maurice (*gently*)   The two of us, Ellen.

Ellen (*quietly*)   By myself.

Mrs O'Hara (*holding her*)   Don't go away like that.

Ellen   No one can stop me now.

Mrs O'Hara   I'm afraid – you're talking so queer – something might happen to you. (*As if humouring a child.*) Wait till morning and then you can see your way better.

Ellen   I am going now.

Maurice   And me with you.

Ellen   By myself I'm going.

Mrs O'Hara (*anxiously*)   But where, child?

Ellen   To a far-off, beautiful country.

Mrs O'Hara   But you have no money.

Ellen   I don't want any money.

Mrs O'Hara   Indeed you do. How will you get your ticket? (*Soothingly.*) Wait a while, and your mother here will give you the money. You'll have lots of things to buy – oh, lots of things. Your mother here has a hundred pounds for you, and you'll want it all.

Mrs Dunn (*challengingly*)   What hundred pounds?

Mrs O'Hara   The hundred I'm after giving you.

---

17 Nonsensical talk.

Mrs Dunn (*raising her voice*)   Is it taking leave of your senses you are, ma'am? You gave no hundred pounds.

William (*dully*)   The old fox. She bate us after all; and sure I might have known it!

John (*in a loud voice*)   What hundred pounds? (*To his wife.*) What's this talk about a hundred pounds, Mary Deasy? Whose pounds? What pounds?

Mrs O'Hara (*firmly*)   It's my own hundred and eighty pounds that I made with my own two hands; and I can do what I like with it.

John   But where is it, where is it? Am I your husband at all, woman?

Mrs O'Hara (*quietly*)   I gave it away.

John   Gave it away? A hundred and eighty? In the name of God, for what?

Mrs O'Hara (*quietly*)   To save my son.

Ellen (*in a stinging voice*)   So they bought you, Maurice O'Hara, and they sold me.

Maurice (*nettled*)   Mother, you have no right to be interfering with me; I can look after myself; I don't want your interfering.

John (*bewildered; to himself*)   A hundred and eighty pounds.

Mrs O'Hara (*hurt*)   But your happiness, Maurice – 'twas of your happiness I was thinking – for your whole life long.

Maurice (*angrily*)   I can find my happiness myself without any help from you, or anyone else.

Mrs O'Hara (*deeply hurt*)   Maurice!

John (*still bewildered; to himself*)   A hundred and eighty pounds! My God, and I knowing nothing about it! (*To* **Mrs Dunn***; in a thundering voice.*) Give me back that money.

Mrs Dunn (*firmly*)   You'll get no money out of me.

William (*frightened*)   I only got twenty.

John (*turning and glaring at him*)   Twenty? Twenty? And where's the rest?

William (*almost whimpering*)   Jer here took the other twenty; sure no one gives me fair play.

John (*choking with anger*)   Jer? Jer? The whole country in it! Thieves and robbers all of ye!

Jer (*enjoying himself heartily*)   Well, if there's a little money going soft, I might as well have my whack off it as well as the rest; Jer Murnane has a good eye for business: take everything except kicks is my motto.

John (*shaking his fist*)   Every penny will be paid back? Ye thieving ruffians.

James   Easy, John, easy. Sure what harm about the money if –

John (*turning on him*)   What harm about the money? Isn't my money my own? Isn't everything I have my own? Isn't it all my belongings? And am I going to give away my belongings to every thieving blackguard that comes the way? No, by God! I'll cling to what is mine with tooth and nail.

James (*quietly*)   Well, if everything else is alright sure –

John (*contemptuously*)   Ah, shut up! You're a fool, James Deasy, and so are all belonging to you.

Tim (*fervently*)   I'm of your mind, James; I took none of the money.

John   Every penny of it! Every penny of it! I'll tear it out of ye!

Ellen (*in a ringing voice*)   Oh, tear each other's eyes out! Claw them out! Spit on each other, and vomit out the dirt on each other's faces!

Jer (*enjoying the fun*)   Aha!

John (*mortified*)   You crazy jade!

Ellen (*her scorn increasing*)   Gather the pennies and half-pennies! Smell them and count them and hoard them! With yer squinty eyes and grabbing claws! And ye going everyday more blind and deaf, and all of ye dead long years before ye go in the grave! And some of ye never alive at all! Ah, 'tis laughing at ye all I can be now, if I can spare the time to be thinking of ye. (*Dreamily.*) But 'tisn't of ye I'll be thinking when the big shiny stars will be standing out in the sky, and all the voices of the silent Knights will be whispering to me –

Maurice (*echoing her tone*)   And the two of us together, Ellen.

Ellen (*looking thoughtfully at him for a moment; then quietly*)   No, Maurice, not you any more.

Maurice (*wondering*)   Not me?

Ellen (*quietly*)   No.

Jer (*with a shout of satisfaction*)   Aha!

Maurice (*bewildered*)   You don't want me with you?

Ellen   Not any more.

Maurice (*dully*)   But you – but – you said you loved me?

Ellen (*thinking hard; drawing her hand across her forehead*)   It wasn't you at all.

Maurice   And who?

Ellen (*thoughtfully*)   My own man. (*Vibrating.*) A man brave and beautiful.

Maurice   Your own –? Another man?

Ellen (*vibrating*)   And 'tis hearing his grand words I'll be all the long nights and I lying down beside –

Maurice (*stung; letting himself go*)   Oh – you slut! You serpent with ten thousand fangs! You wolf! You abomination! You spawn of hell!

Ellen (*looking at him a moment; then quietly*)   And you? What are you? A poor little tom-tivy[18] man: living in your shell: sticking out your four horns frightened; and drawing them back again frightened.

Maurice (*hissing his pain and rage*)   False as hell!

Ellen   And able to do nothing braver than spit, and spit again. (*Her voice swells.*) Do you think I could be loving a man like that? A man who is afraid? I – I – who was never afraid?

Maurice (*turning away; to himself*)   False as hell! And as heartless!

From this to the end **Maurice** *stands with his back to the others, at the right, front. He is stiff, rigid, concentrated. All the others, except* **Mrs Dunn** *who is indifferent, watch* **Ellen***. They are fascinated and deeply impressed in spite of themselves.*

Ellen (*proudly*)   No one could ever make me afraid. No one could ever break me. And they all tried, and they never stopped trying. But I bested them. I won out against them all, against everything.

Jer   Begor, that's true.

Ellen   And now ye will leave me alone, and I will go my own way by myself. I don't want any of ye.

John (*gruffly*)   We're not wishing you any harm.

Mrs O'Hara   Indeed we are not, child. We wish you well in the country you're going to.

Ellen (*to* **Maurice** *who is turned away; rather kindly*)[19]   Goodbye, Maurice O'Hara, you won't see me again. Stop here; this is the place for you. They will get you another wife – a good wife like the last. (*With a touch of mockery.*) She will mend your stockings and boil your bacon and cabbage. She will milk the cows and churn the butter. Oh, she'll be the grand housekeeper, and you'll be the lucky man. With your fine farm, and house, and wife, and children!

John (*wondering*)   And what more could anyone want?

Ellen (*with swelling voice*)   But for all that, Maurice O'Hara, you won't forget me. And often in the night-time when you wake up out of your sleep, you'll turn your back to the good wife sleeping beside you, and every drop of your blood will cry out for me. There will be no hunger like that hunger, and no thirst like that thirst. You will be parched and burning, and your eyes will drop scalding tears. You won't forget me.

---

18 This appears to be a colloquial expression that is no longer in use. It carries connotations of pettiness and smallness.

19 The typed manuscript states 'sadly' but this is replaced with kindly, inserted by hand.

And Jer won't forget me. And no one will forget me! But away my own road I must be going now – (*Moving to the door.*) – find myself and not thinking at all of any of ye. (*Standing at the door, with a cry of gladness.*) My! There's a grand roundy moon sitting up in the sky! (*Softly.*) And 'tis grand and shiny the water in Poulgorm will be now, and so soft – (*Moving away into the night.*) – so soft!

Silence for a few moments.

Mrs Dunn (*matter-of-factly*)   It's about time for us all to be going.

Mrs O'Hara (*thoughtfully*)   God help her, 'tis a long journey she'll have looking for happiness, I'm thinking.

James (*thoughtfully*)   That woman will never know happiness nor peace.

Jer (*thoughtfully*)   Nor anyone that comes anear her. She leaves a scar on all of us.

Mrs O'Hara   'Tis her and her likes that the grand stories of the world are about, like Helen the Beautiful and Deirdre of the Sorrows.

John   The woman that brings destruction!

James   And she herself thinking only of the moonlight on Poulgorm!

Maurice (*suddenly starting*)   Poulgorm? – where her grandmother was drowned! (*He dashes for the door.*)

Curtain

Youth's the Season – ?

Mary Manning

Premiered at the Gate Theatre, Dublin, on 8 December, 1931. The script included here is a revised version that was performed in 1932 and published in *Plays of Changing Ireland* (Macmillan, 1936).

Mrs Millington	Florence Morrison
Desmond	Micheál Mac Liammóir
Deirdre	Meriel Moore
Constance	Coralie Carmichael
Toots Ellerslie	Betty Chancellor
Terence Killigrew	Hilton Edwards
Horace Egosmith	Rodney Homer
Harry Middleton	Lionel Dymoke
Gerald Parr, M.B.	Harry Laing
Willie Sullivan	Rex Mackey
Pearl Harris	Hazel Ellis
Mary	Diana Vernon
Director & Lighting	Hilton Edwards
Set	Micheál Mac Liammóir

Mary Manning (1906–99) was born in Dublin and attended Alexandra College, where she was taught English by Dorothy Macardle. Before embarking on her playwrighting career, Manning studied acting with Sara Allgood and performed in both Abbey Theatre and Dublin Drama League productions. She served as understudy for Ria Mooney during tours of the Irish Players. Manning was a theatre critic for the *Irish Independent*, as well as founder and editor of *Motley*, the Gate Theatre in-house magazine. Her first play, *Youth's the Season– ?* (1931), offers a searing critique of post-colonial Ireland through examination of the lives of a young, urban, educated and privileged set. She wrote two more plays, both of which were staged at the Gate: *Storm over Wicklow* (1933) and *Happy Family* (1934). *Youth's the Season – ?* was the most successful: it was revived at the Gate in 1933 (directed by Denis Johnston) and was produced at London's Westminster Theatre in 1937. Manning's talents extended to adapting literary works for the screen and she also produced short films. She moved to America in 1935, where her engagement with experimental art continued unabated in the post-war arts scene. During her time at The Poets' Theatre, Cambridge, Massachusetts, Manning introduced a generation of young writers to avant-garde work (see Reynolds 2016). *The Voice of Shem*, her theatrical adaptation of James Joyce's *Finnegans Wake*, premiered in 1955, under her direction. Samuel Beckett, a childhood friend of Manning's, granted her the rights to stage the American premiere of *All That Fall* in 1958.

Youth's the Season – ? offers the perspective of a generation who have come of age following the fight for Independence and the Civil War. The stark reality is that Free State Ireland offers 'no scope' for them. Societal expectations are stultifying and overwhelming; despair, depression and death permeate their lives. For the women, there are no options beyond a passive femininity and marriage, while the men are limited to restrictive notions of masculinity which incorporate 'the perfect city man' in bowler hat, an 'Empire Builder' and the rugged 'Hairy Man'. They are 'the Imitation Bright Young People', whose performances reveal the hollow masquerade of restrictive conceptions of gender, sexuality and Irishness. The 'mental and moral indigestion' of Dublin encumbers the lives of the central characters (Desmond, Toots and Terence). Desmond's desire to work as a designer in London is quashed as he is forced to carry on the patrilineal family tradition; he describes working in his father's office as 'death in life for me'. The 'shambling literary loafer', Terence, commits suicide in the devastating conclusion to the play, while Toots is left pleading for escape: 'Let me out.' Beneath the sparkling social comedy, the play is replete with violence and dead ends, supporting the questioning title which references the song lyrics, 'Youth's the season made for joy'. Manning's insertion of the question mark affirms Desmond's angry declaration that it is 'a bloody lie'.

The veneer of cosmopolitan energy and wit belies the dullness of lives moulded by conformity; yet the play offers a challenge to the Free State's coherence around gendered identity: 'If Catholicism and sober masculinity were identified as the key characteristics of Irishness, doubtful sexual orientation and failure to act out polarized gender roles spelt the destabilization of hegemonic national identity' (Leeney 2010: 137). Desmond states that, 'I *am* effeminate. It's my temperament. I was born that way'; a line amplified by the fact that openly gay actor Micheál Mac Liammóir played the role in the premiere production. Key to the destabilization of identity, and to exposure of the grotesque process of being 'buried alive', is Manning's use of theatrical expressionism as evidenced by the skilfully interwoven episodes of Act Two. In this act Desmond's birthday party is presented as a 'farewell to happiness' and an attempt to shock the audience out of complacency. Terence's belief that 'this house needs to be shaken to its bourgeois foundations' resonates with Manning's annihilation of the realist domestic setting with expressionist techniques. In the premiere production, Hilton Edwards' expertise in the application of expressionist techniques in both direction and lighting enabled him to augment the fast and fluid mise-en-scène which aided Irish audiences 'to confront and experience affectively the process of modernisation that the country was undergoing' (Walsh 2018: 41). In the same year as Manning's playwrighting debut, Sophie Treadwell's *Machinal* received its British premiere; a play which also draws on expressionist techniques to convey women's experiences of modernity. Leeney notes the influence of Noël Coward on Manning and asserts: 'Remarkably, what Coward achieves for barely five pages in *The Vortex*, Manning sustains over an entire act, and the accumulated impact unbalances the entire play' (2010: 152). Manning's skilful deployment of social comedy with a dark undercurrent of despair is heightened by expressionist techniques to reveal a crisis of possibility for the younger generation, while simultaneously exploring the stage as a space of resistance against normative identities in the independent State.

DUBLIN GATE THEATRE

THE DUBLIN GATE THEATRE COMPANY LTD.

*Directors :—Hilton Edwards, Micheál Mac Liammóir,
The Earl of Longford, Norman Reddin.*
Secretary : Mrs. Hughes. *Telephone 44045*

Present the first production of

YOUTH'S THE SEASON—?

A tragi-comedy of Dublin life in three acts
By MARY MANNING.

The play produced and the lighting devised by HILTON EDWARDS

Settings by MICHEÁL MAC LIAMMÓIR

Stage Manager—Art O Murnaghan.
„ Electrician—Martin Rabbitt.
„ Carpenter—Michael Lambert.
Wardrobe Mistress—Christina Keely

4 Programme cover, *Youth's the Season–?* by Mary Manning. Premiere: 8 December 1931.
Gate Theatre Digital Archive, Hardiman Library, NUI Galway.

Characters

Mrs Millington
Deirdre Millington, *her daughter, a medical student*
Constance Millington, *her other daughter*
Desmond Millington, *her son, an aspiring designer*
Toots Ellerslie, *friend of Desmond*
Terence Killigrew, *Constance's boyfriend, a writer*
Horace Egosmith, *Terence's friend*
Harry Middleton, *family friend, in love with Constance*
Dr Gerald Parr, *Deirdre's fiancé*
Willie Sullivan, *family friend*
Philip Pryce, *family friend and neighbour*
Priscilla Converse, *family friend*
Europa Wrench, *family friend*
Pearl Harris, *family friend*

'Boys and girls come out to play,
The moon is shining as bright as day,
Leave your supper and leave your sleep,
Come with your playfellows into the street.
Come with a whoop, and come with a call,
And come with a good will or not at all.'
Nursery rhyme

The action of the play takes place during an afternoon, the following evening and following afternoon of March 1932, in **Mrs Millington***'s house in Dublin.*

Act One

Scene: The **Millingtons***' drawing room.*

The time is late afternoon.

The **Millingtons***' drawing room: a beautiful, if faded, eighteenth-century room. There are two long windows at the back. The door is to the extreme left of the stage. The fireplace is also to the left, and a large sofa is drawn in front of it. There is a small writing table and chair between the windows. The telephone is on the writing table. There is a piano to the right piled with books and music. Two flimsy Louis Quinze chairs face each other in the centre of the room. There is a mirror above the mantelpiece. The whole room is full of flowers and magazines. Newspapers are scattered over the floor.*

Desmond *is sitting on the ground with a drawing-board balanced on his knees. The floor around him is strewn with paints and brushes.* **Deirdre***, his eldest sister, is seated at the writing table, working. She is mannishly dressed in sage green tweeds and wears large horn-rimmed glasses. She is taking a degree in natural science.* **Desmond** *is frail and appealing. He is yawning over his work. The clock on the mantelpiece strikes six.*

Deirdre (*briskly – she is always brisk*)   The other should be in. Where's Connie?

Desmond   At the pictures with her paramour . . .

Deirdre   Hardly the way to speak of your sister.

Desmond   Technically I may be wrong – 'at the flicks with her fella'.

The door is thrown open, and **Toots Ellerslie** *bounces in. She is an attractive young woman of two and twenty.*

Toots   May I come in, or do I interrupt the life's work?

Deirdre (*frowning portentously*)   Come in, Toots. Please forgive me if I don't talk, but there's such a tremendous amount of reading to be done.

Toots   Of course. I'll be as quiet as a little mouse. (*She tip-toes cautiously into the room and falls over some of* **Desmond***'s paints.*) Damn! Curse! Blast! My favourite corn! Sorry, Deirdre, – I wish you doctors could find a cure for corns. All God's chillun got corns! Where's our Connie?

Desmond   Darling, sit down. Connie will be in soon. She's at the cinema with a gentleman friend. Smoke?

Toots   Thanks. What are you working on now?

Desmond   Lampshades. Some maniac in Foxrock has ordered them.

Toots (*looking at them*)   Greek! How phallic!

Desmond   'Scatter ye fig-leaves while ye may!' Any gossip? Do say you have some gossip.

Deirdre (*rising and gathering up her books*)   I think I had better finish my reading upstairs. Forgive me, Toots, but I have Senior Fresh next month. Desmond, if Gerald rings up let me know. You might tidy up the room, Desmond, before Mother comes in. Why don't you work up in your studio?

Desmond   I can't. Nobody works in studios nowadays – they only give parties in them. Run along.

Deirdre   It's disgusting. (*She slams the door.*)

Toots   The wind's in the east!

Desmond   There you are: the higher education of women – nerves frayed, tempers soured, faces set in hard grim lines . . .

Toots   That's enough! Poor Deirdre. What is the matter with her anyway? (*She takes off her hat and examines her face in the glass.*)

Desmond   Now let's gossip. Let's be vilely libellous. Let's be salacious and treacherous. Let's stab our best friends in the back. Let's betray our relations; let's wash our dirty linen in the drawing-room. In other words – let's be *Dublin*.

Toots   Oh do, do, do! I feel like a murder party. (*She sits down facing him.*) Now is Deirdre going to be married soon? People are beginning to ask when? And why is she so moody?

Desmond   One question at a time, darling. She's moody because Gerald was two minutes late for an appointment. And she's going to be married when Gerald's in a position to marry –

Toots (*nodding*)   I see! One of those Five-year Plans! Well, she's certainly getting poor darling Gerald house-trained in good time. Gerald's rather a lamb, but *he's* full of ruthless medical efficiency too, and he's such a careful young man.

Desmond   He has to be. All rising young doctors have to be very careful. Very, very careful, dear.

Toots   I never could understand why he fell for Deirdre. All Gerald wants is a wee wifie just for breeding and laying out his slippers, but you could hardly describe Deirdre as a wee wifie.

Desmond   That's where you're wrong, Diana Ellerslie. Deirdre really is a wee wifie, underneath. It's her voluptuous bustle and bust appearance that captivated Gerald. It appealed to his latent Victorianism.

Toots   How strange it all is! (*At the window.*) Hallo! There's Philip Pryce arriving back from London. He *is* a dull little boy, isn't he? Why is it that frightfully rich people are invariably frightfully dull? Look at Philip's nice blue overcoat, his bowler hat, his neatly folded umbrella. I see him every morning going to his father's office just a minute before ten. On Saturday morning he gets a book out of the library, an interesting novel, recommended by the Book Society; and on Saturday afternoon he plays golf; in the evening he joins some nice little party of four – never two; – on Sunday he plays golf. And he drives a very nice little two-seater, and twice a year he goes to London and sees all the best plays, recommended by the best critics; and he has been known to go to the Winter Sports, and once he went to Paris. Soon he'll take unto himself a wife and they'll buy a house with a tennis-court at Carrickmines, Foxrock, or Killiney. Two years after they'll have a son and they'll call him Philip Pryce . . .

Desmond (*jumping up and tearing his hair*)   If you don't stop I'll go mad!

Toots (*relentlessly*)   . . . and he'll die and be buried in a well-kept grave, and when the Last Trump sounds, he'll arise with his umbrella neatly folded, and report himself for Judgment just a minute before ten.

Desmond   And why not? Isn't he normal and clean and healthy – the backbone of the nation? What would we do without Philip Pryce? O God, I'm so depressed!

Toots   So am I.

Desmond   I'm sick of everything, sick of myself, and unutterably sick of Dublin.

Toots   It's only a mood. It'll pass.

Desmond (*pacing wildly up and down*)   The umbrella – the symbolic umbrella. That's what I want to escape . . . Father's office, the bowler hat and the umbrella. Ah, don't laugh at me!

Toots   I'm not laughing. Go on.

Desmond   I won't give in. I *won't*. Listen Toots – this is serious. You know Derek Howard – well, he wants me to go over to London and take a job there as a designer. The pay would be small, at first, but if I can persuade Father to give me an allowance for the first year or two, until I get a rise, then everything would be all right. I'm not going to dabble in this duckpond any longer.

Toots   You're right! How I envy you! O boy, if only I had your courage.

Desmond (*bitterly*)   Courage! I've no courage. I haven't the guts to get out myself. It all depends on Father, and you know he's set his heart on my going into the office. But he might be made to understand – he might be . . .

Toots   Couldn't your mother persuade him?

Desmond   That's my only hope. I'm going to tell her this evening.

Toots   Oh Desmond, I do hope she does.

Desmond   I don't know why I feel so depressed today. I woke up this morning with the most awful feeling of apprehension . . .

Toots   It's the weather. March is always a hideously restless stormy kind of month. Spring in the blood . . .

Desmond   It's worse than that. I often have presentiments, and I have one now. Something is going to happen in this house, something evil and overwhelming . . .

Toots   *Don't*, Desmond! My nerves!

Desmond (*going over to the mirror*)   Don't take me seriously, darling. (*He combs his hair carefully.*) What are the wild waves saying? My hair is quite nice I think – don't you, Toots? I'll shoot myself when I go bald. You know I often think it would be amusing if our real selves, the inner man, or still small voice, or whatever it is, would suddenly take human form and confront us.

Toots   God forbid. I'd be embarrassed.

Desmond   We all cover up our real self under a dust-heap of trivialities; but occasionally it insists on being heard.

Toots   Well, don't let it get hold of you. Forget it. Oh how I envy you getting away from all this second-rate meandering. By the way, I really came to give Connie some good advice.

Desmond   You haven't a hope. Can't you see she's infatuated with that incorrigible waster, Terence Killigrew, who's never done anything in his life but scribble a few imitative bits of poetry and consume an inordinate quantity of alcohol?

Toots (*seating herself at the piano*)   Do you know anything about his people?

Desmond   They've a small place in Kerry, I believe. The mother died about ten years ago, leaving Terence just enough to keep him from starving. Papa has since cast him off. There is a brother, I believe, who's quite normal. I've seen him with Philip Pryce.

Toots   H'm. Terence won't marry anybody. Connie will just have to make up her mind to marry the worthy Harry Middleton, who's so obviously devoted. She can go out to Kenya with him, have a child and see the world. At least it is *reality*!

Desmond   Lord! Lord! I'm plumbing the depths. What's the use of anything? Better surrender gracefully to the inevitable.

Toots   Do you remember, Desmond, when we used to climb trees in the Square and bark our shins and make our governesses' lives a hell? At least I did.

Desmond   Golden syrup for tea.

Toots   And read Hans Andersen's fairy tales?

Desmond   And all those endless discussions on How Babies Come.

Toots   We were happy then. Why can't we be happy now?

Desmond   Because you're growing up my dear, because you're growing up.

Toots (*to the tune of 'Three Blind Mice'*)   And oh, how it hurts! Oh, how it hurts! Oh, how it hurts!

Desmond   None of us is quite broken in yet – that's the trouble. I thought your last love affair would have shocked you into accepting or refusing the conditions – it's queer how we all have to be shocked into a big change, isn't it? Something will have to shock me out of this, or chain me down forever – but perhaps you weren't really in love with Roger Coote . . .

Toots (*indignantly*)   I was, frightfully in love with him – you know I was. I only broke off the engagement when I saw how hopeless it was . . .

Desmond   It's a good thing you did; the last time I saw him he was being thrown out of somewhere or other for being drunk and disorderly.

Toots   Desmond, you are a *beast*!

Desmond   Sorry, Toots darling. Forgive me. Say you'll forgive me. (*He sits down beside her, strokes her hair.*) I know your little heart is broken; I know things can never be the same again; I know how hard it is to forget – *but* came Dawn, and with it a great big He-man, with a heavy golden moustache, who'll take you in his arms, and . . .

Toots (*tragically*)   You don't know what love is.

Desmond (*coaxing her*)   No, but I know what drink is. Uncle Alfred, Father's younger brother, used to have DTs in this very room – yes, my dear – and he shot himself in the end – in the head, I mean. It was all hushed up, but anyway Roger would have had DTs at least once a week so it's just as well you didn't marry him – the love of a pure woman can do anything *except* wean a man away from the bottle. But I know what I'll do; we'll have a party.

Toots   I hate parties.

Desmond   Not mine. I'm going to be twenty-one tomorrow, so I'll have a party tomorrow night in my studio, and we'll get very drunk, and forget . . .

Toots (*coming round*)   Is it your birthday?

Desmond   It is. Don't congratulate me, it is not an occasion for congratulation. No, when I've reached fifty and find myself safely anchored in an atmosphere of plush and prosperity, I shall *then* allow you to congratulate me.

Toots   Bitter pill, aren't you?

Desmond   This party tomorrow night is to celebrate the death of my childhood, and farewell to happiness. Rejoice, o young man in thy youth! Who said that? It's a stupid lie. I hate youth. The only happy people I know are doddering peacefully into the grave.

Toots   I'll get drunk tomorrow night. What is it like to get drunk, really drunk?

Desmond   Divine.

Toots   Now I know why so many spend their lives in an alcoholic haze.

Desmond   It will be a beautiful party; everyone will fight; we'll all be miserable – I *love* that!

Toots   Ring up the people tonight. There are some Americans arriving tomorrow from Poughkeepsie or somewhere. Mother and I are supposed to entertain them – I'll bring the daughter along.

Desmond   We'll go share on the drink.

Toots *suddenly starts playing and singing 'Youth's the Season Made for Joy'. She completes half the first verse, aided by* **Desmond**, *when* **Connie** *rushes into the room.* **Connie** *is a dark beautiful creature dressed rather after the manner of a third-rate musical comedy actress – with leanings towards bohemianism. The others stop singing and stare at her.*

Connie (*affectedly rushing to the mirror*)   Darling Toots, there you are. I'm so sorry I was late, but the film was so marvellous, I just had to stay and see it through twice – it was one of the new Russian films, all about a steam engine or something. Terence fell asleep. By the way, I brought him back with me for a drink. He's coming up now with some man he met on the way – I couldn't catch his name.

Desmond (*disgusted*)   Terence! Oh God!

Toots   What's his friend like? I hope he's sober?

Connie   Is sobriety really essential?

Toots   It is sometimes more convenient.

Connie (*with superiority*)   Calm your suburban fears. He is perfectly sober and perfectly inoffensive. One of those men you'd never notice under *any* circumstances.

Toots   How exciting!

Desmond (*contemptuously*)   Yes, you'll have to mind your virtue, Toots. (*Striking an attitude.*) Here he comes – the sham Prince of Darkness and attendant Devil.

Voices are heard outside.

Terence (*off*)   That's a good idea of yours, Egosmith. I'll try it some day.

Terence *enters first, followed by* **Horace Egosmith**. **Terence Killigrew** *is a young man of twenty-seven, who has cultivated his personality at the expense of his intelligence. He started off as a 'blood' and has gradually become a shambling literary loafer – untidy, dissipated and frowsy – but with a certain physical attraction. He wears a crumpled brown suit and an orange polo jumper, instead of a shirt, otherwise his clothes are fairly normal.* **Horace Egosmith** *might be any age up to thirty. He is a contrast to his companion as regards neatness and respectability. Indeed,* **Horace** *might be regarded as the model for the perfect young city man.*

Terence (*gaily*)   Do I intrude on a family party? Connie insisted on dragging us both along for a drink. Oh, by the way, may I introduce my friend Egosmith – Horace Egosmith?

He takes **Egosmith**'*s arm and pushes him to the front.* **Egosmith** *bows timidly to the room at large and rubs his hands nervously. There is a second's pause, then everyone talks at once.*

Desmond   How do you do? Sit down. Smoke?

Connie   This is my family, Mr Egosmith – all except Toots who lives next door.

Toots   How d'you do? Haven't I seen you somewhere before? I seem to know your face . . .

Terence (*seating himself in the centre of the room*)   Sit down, Egosmith, old man. Nobody's going to bite you. They're all tame. (**Egosmith** *sits beside him.*) Circus animals, you know – they go through a programme of tricks, most entertaining, but they *never* bite – bless you, no! They were born in captivity. No, Toots, you don't know Egosmith's face, because he and his face have only just arrived in Dublin.

Toots (*shortly*)   Sorry. My mistake. Perhaps he has a double (*Looking at* **Egosmith**.). Yes, he might easily have a double.

Terence   An interesting thought.

There is an awkward pause. **Desmond** *hands round cigarettes in a desultory manner.* **Terence** *appears to go asleep.* **Egosmith** *smiles vaguely round on everyone.*

Desmond (*trailing over to* **Connie**)   Harry Middleton rang up half an hour ago. He said he'd look in about six. He wants to see you, Connie. He'll be here any minute.

Connie   My dear, how terrible!

Toots   I like Harry Middleton.

Connie (*lighting a cigarette*)   Oh, he's awfully worthy. But his mind's a vacuum.

Desmond (*with a look at* **Terence**)   A change from the main drainage system anyway . . .

Terence (*fixing a hard stare on* **Desmond**, *who shifts uneasily*)   Come on, don't be priggish, Flossie. Middleton – Harry Middleton! I seem to know that name. Is he a clean-cut young man rather like a policeman?

Connie   Yes, that's Harry.

Terence   Undoubtedly the same. I've met him with my brother. Have you met my brother, Connie?

Connie   No, Terry. What's he like?

Terence   A pimply little bastard. Spends most of his time masochistically wallowing in rugby football. How exceedingly patronising he was this morning. D'you remember, Horace? (**Egosmith** *nods.*) How clean, how upstanding, and how sane! The very spirit of the English public school. 'Theirs is not to reason why . . .' And yet he's a very decent fellow. I'm really not as good as he is. I'm just a bood with a kink. Isn't that so, Egosmith? (**Egosmith** *laughs and* **Terence** *turns away from him irritably.*) I may as well face it. I hate to be patronised, but it's simply because I know that intellectually I'm not strong enough to despise it.

Toots   I hear you're writing a novel?

Terence (*yawning.* **Egosmith** *sits up alertly – his eyes wander restlessly seeking the reactions of each person to the next speech*)   Who *isn't* in Dublin? Thank God very few of them are ever published.

Toots   I suppose we are all in it?

Desmond   Oh yes, talking and analysing ourselves to destruction.

Terence   My dear Toots, people have almost ceased to interest me. Dancing, playing bridge, making love and writing novels are all equally fatuous occupations, and all have very much the same effect – intoxication. Sobriety is death to me. But to remain permanently intoxicated it is necessary to be everlastingly writing novels – or, better still, thinking about writing novels. Of course I've tried more commonplace methods – for example, playing with the thought of suicide. (**Egosmith** *starts, turns round and looks at him.* **Terence** *continues with his gaze fixed on* **Egosmith**.) But I've no faith, no capacity for work, no purpose, and to be born without continuity of purpose is to be born under sentence of death. I am foredoomed to failure, Connie. I wear the Order of the Skull and Crossbones – I've joined that worshipful company, the Brotherhood of Failure.

Connie   That's not true, Terence.

Terence (*he rises from his chair.* **Egosmith** *rises simultaneously.* **Terence** *takes his arm*)   Moods! Moods! This mood will pass. I will arise and go now, and sober up at Davey Byrne's, and a small bottle buy me there . . .

Connie   Don't be ridiculous, Terry. Desmond will take you downstairs and give you a drink.

Terence   You mean you don't want me to drink in pubs. How innately respectable you are, Connie . . .

Connie   I'm not.

Desmond   You are!

Toots   You are hopelessly suburban.

Terence   Where else am I to drink?

Connie   Well, there are hotels – and anyway why drink at all?

Terence   Come, come! You don't expect me to face life without my rose-coloured spectacles. That would be unendurable. I might see life as it really is. I might even see myself as I really am. D'you know, Connie, I promise you that the day I meet myself face to face I shall pull out my little gun and blow out my mediocre intelligence.

Desmond   Is that a promise?

Terence (*once more fixing a hard stare on him*)   Yes, brother – that's a promise.

Desmond *shudders and looks away from him.*

Connie (*very much on her dignity*)   Oh, isn't this all rather futile? Desmond, take Terence down for a drink.

Terence (*laughing*)   Dismissed with a caution. The prisoner left the court with a dark stain on his character.

Toots   Terence, I really believe you thoroughly enjoy imagining yourself some tragic figure in a Chekhov play.

Terence   My dear Toots, if I felt tragic I'd do the thing properly. I'd grow a black tangled beard and live on an island with three raging miles of sea between me and the mainland. An uncle of mind did that. They called him Timon of Aran. He died mad. No the truth is I'm a bloody farce. (*He points at* **Desmond***, who is fidgeting near the door.*) Portrait of a gentleman with the itch. There's real tragedy for you, Toots – Flossie won't die, he'll itch on and on. Courage brother, let me put you out of pain. (*He puts his hand in his pocket as if to draw out a gun.* **Desmond** *gasps.* **Terence** *withdraws his hand and grins maliciously.* **Desmond** *recovers himself.*) Misunderstood! But we must go ere PC Middleton comes on point duty. Isn't that so, Connie? (*He turns to meet* **Egosmith***'s deprecating smile.*)

Connie   Desmond, will you take Terence and Mr Egosmith down and give them a drink?

Desmond   Father's sure to be ramping around down there.

Connie   Nonsense, he isn't in yet.

Terence   Come, come, Flossie, don't show that nasty temper. (*He goes over to* **Connie***.* **Egosmith** *follows at a discreet distance.*) Farewell, Marie Vassilivitch! (*He kisses her hand.*)

Connie (*coldly*)   Goodbye, Terence.

Terence   Don't be too hard on the policeman.

Connie (*jerks away her hand and turns from him*)   Goodbye.

Terence *shrugs his shoulders and goes to the door.* **Egosmith** *takes his place before* **Connie**. *He smiles at her timidly, almost appealingly.* **Connie** *turns suddenly, unaware that* **Terence** *has gone.*

Connie (*there is a note of entreaty in her voice*)   Listen, Terence – (*She stops and looks at* **Egosmith**. *Her lips quiver, for a moment she might weep, and then she pulls herself together.*) Oh, Mr Egosmith – goodbye – I do hope you'll come again.

Egosmith *bows to her and to the rest of the room, then goes to the door and stands behind* **Terence**.

Terence   Lead, will-o'-the-wisp! (*He looms over* **Desmond**, *who shrinks from him nervously. He lisps.*) It's a shame to put this butterfly on the wheel. (*He grips* **Desmond**'s *shoulder.*) Come on, Horace! Goodbye, Toots; you should read Saint Teresa. Ask me why next time. *Adios.* (*They go out.*)

Toots (*after a pause*)   That man Egosmith is rather sinister.

Connie   He seems inoffensive – doesn't talk much.

Toots   That's just it; he's the only man I've ever met who listens – it's unnerved me. (*She sits fanning herself with one of* **Desmond**'s *lampshades.*)

Connie (*making up at the mirror*)   I got your mysterious 'phone message. What do you want to talk to me about?

Toots   Oh, before I forget – Desmond is planning a party, a birthday party tomorrow night in the studio. Just family and a few well-chosen 'butties'.

Connie   Marvellous! I must speak to him about this. Lend me a comb for God's sake.

Toots (*throwing her one*)   Here you are.

Connie (*combing her hair nervously*)   I look terrible – grey and old and shattered, and that awful Harry will be here at any moment. Now, Toots, what do you want to talk to me about?

Toots (*thoughtfully*)   When are you going to give up Terence?

Connie (*pausing*)   What do you mean?

Toots   You heard me, darling. When are you going to give up Terence and marry Harry Middleton?

Connie   How do you know I won't marry Terence?

Toots   Because – to be quite brutal – he won't marry you.

Connie   Thanks. And since you're so certain about everything what makes you think that Harry wants to marry me?

Toots   Snap out of it! The man is besotted. He exudes honourable intentions. He's probably asked you already, but you're so infatuated by this drunken egotistical loafer . . .

Connie (*swinging round*)   I won't allow you to speak about Terence like that. He's got genius. He's worth a hundred Harry Middletons.

Toots   We shall see. So you think you can reform Terence? Oh, Connie, take it from me, it can't be done.

Connie   Because you failed, it doesn't say I'll fail.

Toots   Ah, you're bound to fail. You haven't enough brains; you haven't enough guts; you're selfish and flabby; you'd never pull that job through. I couldn't, and I'm twice the man you are.

Connie   Go on, call me names – anything else?

Toots   Plenty. It would need a strong woman to pull Terence out of the morass he is in, and keep him out; you're not strong enough, my dear – no, you'll do very nicely behind mosquito nets in Kenya surrounded by pots of cold cream and all the latest novels from England.

Connie   Shut up! *Shut up*!

Toots   Terence is beyond hope. He's degenerate, decadent, effete and rotten. Leave him alone.

Connie (*almost shouting at her*)   I'll show you – I'll show you. I *can* pull him together – I *can* do it . . . I'll marry him.

Toots (*calmly*)   Has this man ever told you he loves you?

Connie (*hesitating*)   Not in so many words.

Toots   Only three are necessary.

Connie   But I know he does instinctively.

Toots   If you're so certain of Terence, why keep Harry hanging on?

Connie   Physically he's attractive enough – and he's useful . . .

Toots   As a whip to spur Terence on. Poor Connie, it won't work, not with that selfish egoist. Well I must be off . . .

Connie   No, don't go . . . oh Toots, I'm so miserable. (*She sits down on the sofa.*)

Toots   Of course you are. You simply won't look facts in the face. Even if Terence loved you . . .

Connie (*whimpering*)   He does love me – it's simply his financial position –

Toots   My dear girl, he hasn't got a financial position. He was obviously borrowing from his unfortunate pimply brother this morning; he'll never be able to marry.

Connie (*sobbing*)   He has a future, I know he has – he's writing a novel. Damn! Now I've gone and spoiled my make-up.

Toots   And so you think you're going to be his inspiration – his helpmate – Oh, Connie, if only you didn't imagine yourself an intellectual.

Connie (*sniffing*)   I *am* an intellectual (*Defiantly.*) I've read *Ulysses* through twice!

Toots   Only for the pornographic pickings.

Connie   You're horribly unsympathetic, and it's no use advising me. I want Terence, and I mean to have him. Do leave me – no, don't go. (*She sobs hysterically.*) Oh God, I don't know what to do – Oh, I'm so miserable, I don't know what to do . . .

Toots (*sternly*)   Now, Connie, I *am* sympathetic; I am really, it's only I can see the hell you're heading for . . .

There is a knock at the door.

Harry (*off*)   May I come in?

Connie (*springing up and rushing to the glass*)   It's Harry! My God! My face!

Toots   Don't fuss. (*Louder.*) Come in!

Harry Middleton *comes in like a mountain breeze. He has all the appearance of an amiable young policeman in plus fours.*

Harry (*rubbing his hands heartily*)   Hello, everybody! How are you, Toots?

Toots   Fine, thanks. (*She prepares to go.*)

Connie (*with her back to him, arranging her hair*)   Hello, Harry! Sit down and help yourself to a smoke. Don't go, Toots.

Harry   By the way, Connie, your young brother has just asked me to some show in his studio tomorrow night.

Connie   I'm so glad.

Harry   He came creeping out into the hall from the dining-room and absolutely hissed the invitation in my ear. There were two mysterious blokes like plumbers in the dining-room.

Toots   Plumbers! Oh, I see. (*She laughs.*) Well, I must be off.

Connie   Don't go. Stay and have some dinner.

Toots   Darling, I can't possibly. Have to take my poor old mother to the RDS[1] concert this evening. Duty first. See you both tomorrow night at Desmond's party. (*She goes to the door, slowly and thoughtfully.*) Oh Harry, do you know anything about Saint Teresa?

Harry   Good God, no! Why?

Toots (*she sighs*)   Nothing. It's all very difficult.

Harry (*opening the door for her*)   Mind the plumbers.

Toots   I'll never be a plumber's mate. (*She goes, laughing.*)

Harry *comes slowly back and sits on one of the chairs in the centre of the room.* **Connie** *sits bolt upright on the sofa.*

Harry (*breaking the silence*)   Nice little girl. Wasn't she engaged to Reggie Coote? Chap with side-whiskers?

---

1   Royal Dublin Society.

Connie   You mean Toots? Yes, she was – it was broken off some time ago.

Harry   I hear he was rather a rotter. Looked a bit of a Dago.[2] Went to London, didn't he?

Connie   Yes.

Harry   Damn good thing! Oh well, you know what I mean, better to find out your mistake, before getting tied up – don't you think so?

Connie   Yes, I suppose so.

Harry   I mean, marriage is such a hell of a toss-up and all that – it's better to be absolutely certain, if you see what I mean?

Connie (*yawning*)   Yes.

Harry   Am I boring you?

Connie (*mechanically*)   Yes. (*She pulls herself together.*) No, of course not, Harry darling. Indeed you're not.

Harry (*sitting beside her*)   I know I'm rather a boring sort of chap. I mean to say, I'm not highbrow or anything like that. And you're so damn clever . . .

Connie (*earnestly*)   I'm not clever, Harry. (*Viciously.*) And I hate highbrows.

Harry (*delighted*)   I can't stand those long-haired sort of poetic fellas either. Of course I do read a lot in my spare time. P. G. Wodehouse, Sapper and Edgar Wallace – good rousing yarns. I must confess I can't get round the highbrow stuff at all. A chap once lent me a poem by a man called Lawrence – something about a goat – pretty graphic. Did you ever read it?

Connie   No.

Harry   I'm glad to hear it. Extraordinarily unhealthy. Don't you think so?

Connie (*powdering her nose*)   Yes, Harry.

Harry   When are you going to come out with me, Connie?

Connie   You'll see me tomorrow night at Desmond's party.

Harry   Oh, you know what I mean – I want to see you alone. What about Friday night? We could dine somewhere.

Connie   Do you mind if I let you know tomorrow night? I'm not quite sure if I can manage Friday . . .

Harry   Oh, I say! Are you sure? I never seem to be able to get you alone, and I'll be going back to Kenya soon . . .

Connie   Very well, then – I'll have tea with you on Friday.

---

2   An offensive term for a person of Spanish, Portuguese or Italian heritage.

Harry   Fine. Where?

Connie   I hate tea in town. It's so suburban and provincial.

Harry   Well, I've got the car. We could take a run down to Glendalough.

Connie (*very tired*)   Oh Harry, please . . .

Harry (*rubbing his hands*)   Well, that's settled. Now I'd better be rolling along. I have to pick up the old man at the club. (*He gets up.*)

Connie   Goodbye, Harry.

Harry (*taking her hand*)   Goodbye, Connie. Connie – can't you love me a little? You know I want . . .

Connie (*impatiently*)   I've told you over and over again that it's no use. I'm not thinking of marriage at the moment.

Harry (*urgently*)   Couldn't you ever bring yourself to care for me? (*He takes her hand again.*) I'm mad about you. I can't stop thinking about you. (*He pulls her roughly to him and kisses her passionately.*)

Connie (*faintly*)   Leave me, Harry – please.

Terence *comes in swiftly and silently. He stands in the doorway smiling. The others fail to hear him.*

Harry (*releasing her*)   Forgive me, Connie. I'm an awful swine. Say you forgive me.

Connie   No, it was my fault. Please go.

Terence *coughs ostentatiously.*

Harry   Damn!

Terence (*gaily*)   Awfully sorry, Connie, but I left a book here somewhere. I just remembered it in time.

There is a tense silence. **Harry** *flutters the page of a magazine.*

Terence (*making a pretence of looking*)   Most extraordinary thing . . .

Connie (*suspiciously*)   I didn't notice you carrying it here. Perhaps you left it somewhere else. What's the name of it?

Terence   *The Lost Girl.* (*He turns to* **Harry**.) I think I've met you with my brother . . .

Harry (*stiffly*)   I'm afraid I didn't catch your name.

Connie   Sorry. Mr Killigrew – Mr Middleton. I forgot you didn't know each other.

Harry   Of course – your brother plays for Glenrock.

Terence (*vaguely hovering round the sofa*)   Yes. I believe he's hind-four, or centre-three, or something equally obscene.

Harry   He's one of the most useful backs we've got.

Terence   You're Colonial Service, aren't you? Going back soon?

Harry   Yes.

Terence   Good. (*He pulls a book from under the sofa cushions and thrusts it under his arm.* **Harry** *starts and looks at him suspiciously.*) Found. You must read this sometime, Connie.

Harry   Well, I must be moving off. Goodbye, Connie – I'll see you tomorrow night.

Connie (*effusively*)   And Friday. I won't forget Friday. Forgive me not coming down, Harry darling, but I feel so tired.

Harry   That's all right, dear. (*He glares at* **Terence**.) Oh, by the way, Killigrew, can I drop you anywhere? I've got the car here.

Terence   A kindly offer, a kindly offer. Which way are you going?

Harry   Anywhere round the south side.

Terence   Too bad. I've got to get to the north side.

Harry   Sure I can't leave you at the tram?

Terence   Don't worry about me, old man. I'll be all right. Don't let me keep you. Shut the door after you! There's a draught.

Harry   *Au revoir*, Connie. (*He bangs the door.*)

Terence (*provocatively*)   I was pained to find you in the arms of your policeman lover, Connie.

Connie (*angrily*)   He's not a policeman, and he's not my lover . . . at least, not yet.

Terence   He'll never be a lover – he's a born husband. I suppose he has already proposed to you?

Connie (*smiling*)   Frequently.

Terence (*shaking his head*)   This won't do. We must find something better for you. Something with intelligence and money.

Connie   You're very kind.

Terence   Not at all. I'd like to see you well married. If you had £500 a year I'd marry you myself.

Connie   This is too kind. How do you know I'd marry you?

Terence *suddenly kneels on the floor at her feet, and puts his arms around her.*

Terence   Because you love me.

Connie   I don't. I hate you. I despise you.

Terence (*leaning his head against her*)   You love me. Why can't we be happy?

Connie (*kissing his hair*)   Yes, I love you. Don't you love me? Don't you love me, Terence?

There is a short silence. He stays there for a moment, and then jumps up and walks into the middle of the room.

Terence   Have you ever read Catullus on kissing?
  'Kiss and score up wealthy sums
  On my lips, thus hardly sundered
  While you breathe . . .'

Connie (*confronting him*)   You haven't answered my question. Do you love me, Terence?

Terence (*dramatically*)   Connie, I love someone else.

Connie (*taken aback*)   Who?

Terence   Myself.

Connie (*turning away*)   You're intolerably cruel.

Terence   Yes, Connie, it has been going on for years. I love myself with a hopeless yearning passion. (**Egosmith** *appears in the doorway, followed by* **Desmond**.) Ah, Egosmith, I'm sorry to keep you waiting like this, old man, but I've had to search for my book. I'm ready now. (**Egosmith** *stands beside* **Terence**.) I've just been accused of cruelty, Egosmith. Would you accuse me of cruelty? (*They stare at one another for a second, and then* **Egosmith** *shrugs his shoulders and looks down deprecatingly.*)

Desmond   Mother's in, and Father's blazing away in the hall. We only just got out of the dining-room in time.

Terence   Boys, we must beat it.

Connie   Wait a minute. Hasn't Desmond asked you to his birthday party tomorrow night?

Terence   Birthday party! No. Flossie, this is a deliberate slight. Surely you wouldn't leave me out?

Desmond (*sulkily gathering up his paints*)   I'm not quite sure yet whether I'm having one.

Terence   Oh come, Flossie, you can't postpone your birthday like this, old man – it isn't done . . .

Connie   Nonsense! You've already asked Toots and Harry.

Terence   Flossie!

Connie   I hope you and Mr Egosmith will both come. Nine o'clock tomorrow night in Desmond's studio.

Desmond (*dropping his paints with a crash*)   Damn! Blast!

Terence   Dear! dear! We'd love to come, Flossie, we accept with pleasure. I answer for Egosmith. (*He takes* **Egosmith**'s *arm.*) Whither I go, he will go! (*They both laugh.*) Well, till tomorrow night. No, don't bother to show us out. I know the way. (*They go.*)

Desmond (*furiously*)   That's a pretty dirty trick you played on me!

Connie (*innocently*)   What trick?

Desmond   Asking Terence and that intolerable little blighter Egosmith to my party.

Mrs Millington *enters quietly. She is still dressed in her outdoor clothes. Her children are so busy quarrelling they fail to hear her. She drifts down to the back of the sofa, looking bewildered. A nice amiable, middle-class mother. There is a faded elegance, a certain vague elderly grace, about* **Mrs Millington**, *but she wears too many tulle scarves, bracelets, necklaces and bits and scraps to be really well-dressed.*

Connie   Well, I thought we needed at least one intelligent person at the party, so I asked Terence. I know he talks a little above your head . . .

Desmond   The fellow's a sham. He's never done anything but scatter a few drawing-room bombshells – as for his lousy shadow . . .

Mrs Millington   Desmond!

Connie   Lousy yourself! You're jealous.

Mrs Millington   Connie!

Desmond   Not of his looks anyway . . .

Connie   Cat!

Desmond   Bitch cat!

Mrs Millington (*mildly protesting*)   Connie! Desmond! I will not have this language in my drawing-room. Is it necessary to talk to each other like bargees?

Connie   Yes, Mother, it is. I'm tired to death of all this. I'm going up to my room till dinner. If anyone 'phones, say I'm dead or away for the week-end. (*She bangs the door.*)

Mrs Millington   I don't know what's happened to Connie lately – she's so nervous and irritable.

Desmond (*looking under the sofa*)   It's obvious – she's suffering from unrequited passion.

Mrs Millington   How horribly you put things, Desmond. What are you looking for?

Desmond   My library book. Did you see it, Mother?

Mrs Millington (*removing at least one scarf*)   No, dear.

Desmond   I can't keep anything in this house. (*He sits down.*) Connie is in love with Terence Killigrew – so there!

Mrs Millington (*removing her gloves slowly*)   I think Terence Killigrew is a most peculiar young man and not at all desirable. I'm afraid he's a little mad . . .

Desmond   I suppose all poets are slightly mad; even Shelley was a little mad.

Mrs Millington (*indignantly*)   Shelley was worse: he was immoral. That reminds me, I was at school with Terence Killigrew's mother. A perfectly charming woman, and now I come to think of it she was most unhappily married. She had dreadful chilblains at school. I think her husband was a little odd – he used to wear a kilt and ride a bicycle. I'm not quite sure now, but that it was Terence's uncle, Edward Killigrew, who wore the kilt and lived in the Blasket Islands in a tent for years. He was learning Irish; all the Killigrews were eccentric. (*She smooths* **Desmond**'s *hair.*) And how is my darling boy?

Desmond (*gloomily*)   Very depressed.

Mrs Millington   Why, darling? Are the lampshades not going well.

Desmond   Lampshades? (*He laughs.*) Listen, Mother, I've got something important to tell you.

Mrs Millington (*absently*)   Yes, dear? (*She fiddles amongst the ornaments on the mantelpiece.*) Really, Mary's dusting is a farce! I'll have to give her a good talking to.

Desmond (*going over to her*)   I had a letter from Derek Howard this morning.

Mrs Millington (*floating over to the piano*)   That nice boy! How is he?

Desmond (*following her*)   He's doing awfully well in London – you know, as designer in Forsytes. He says he can get me in there any time. The pay is small at first, but if Father would give me an allowance for the first year – until I get a rise . . .

Mrs Millington   Oh, but darling, surely you're not thinking of going to London?

Desmond (*eagerly*)   Yes, Mother – of course I am. Remember tomorrow I'll be twenty-one. It's time I got out of this place . . .

Mrs Millington   But your father says . . .

Desmond (*oblivious*)   I need a wider field. I know I'd do well as a designer; there's no scope for me here. Oh, I've got all sorts of ambitions and plans – stage-designing, interior decoration. Derek and I plan to have a shop of our own –

Mrs Millington   Do use an ashtray, Desmond; there are plenty of them on the mantelpiece. Why don't you speak to your father about this London plan?

Desmond   Father's impossible! He doesn't understand anything. I have to think before I speak to him. It's like talking to a foreigner.

Mrs Millington   Nonsense. He's anxious about your future. (*She notices the paints strewn around.*) I wish you'd tidy up your paints. The room is in a shocking mess.

Desmond (*groaning*)   It's nothing to the mess I'm in.

Mrs Millington (*twitching and pulling at the cushions on the sofa*)   Only the other day your father was saying that it was time you were definitely settling down. He wants you to go into the office almost at once.

Desmond (*desperately*)   Nothing on earth will make me go into the office! *Nothing*! Do you hear?

Mrs Millington (*clasping a cushion vaguely to her bosom*)   No dear . . . But your father says . . .

Desmond (*tearing his hair*)   Damn Father!

Mrs Millington   Desmond!

Desmond (*taking the cushion from her, and making her sit down*)   Sorry, Mother! But please listen to me. This is serious. Will you ask Father to consider this plan of mine? Will you?

Mrs Millington (*distracted*)   I really don't know what to do! You wouldn't go into Trinity.

Desmond   What was I to do there? I don't play games and anyway I couldn't have passed matric – I would have come down in maths. Compound long-division is only a name to me. You know that, Mother. I wanted to go on with my designing. I begged him to let me go to an art school, and all he said was, 'My God, I should have thrashed the art out of you long ago!'

Mrs Millington   Dear, dear! This is all very tiresome, and here I am not dressed and the dinner gong will go any minute.

Desmond   Mother, please take this seriously.

Mrs Millington   Really I don't know what to do. Your father will need help sooner or later. And he has his heart set on you going into the firm. It has been a question of father and son for over 100 years.

Desmond   Well, it's time it stopped. Tell Father I've got a chance of a job in London, and I'll only need a small allowance for the first year.

Mrs Millington   This is really most upsetting. Your poor father!

Desmond   Please, Mother – it's my future. The office would be death in life for me.

Mrs Millington   Well, I'll do my best, but I don't promise anything. (*She rises.*) I'll go down now and see if Father has had a good day in the office – and if he has I'll broach the subject this evening.

Desmond   God bless you! My old white-haired mother! (*He kisses her.*) And when I've made my fortune in London or Paris or New York I'll buy you a black silk dress and a gold chain like all the good boys in books. Let me know if Father shows any signs of coming round and if he does I'll wire Derek.

Dr Gerald Parr *comes striding in with every outward and visible sign of inward spiritual unrest. He is clean, hard and ambitious, with a soothing bedside manner.*

Mrs Millington   Oh Gerald!

Desmond   Your woman's working upstairs. Shall I call her?

Gerald   Do, old man. (**Desmond** *trips blithely out.*) I must apologise for coming at this unearthly hour, Mrs Millington, but I was late calling for Deirdre at the lab so I just came along to explain.

Mrs Millington (*collecting scarves and gloves*)   You're welcome at any time, Gerald. You and Deirdre are going to the RDS concert this evening, aren't you?

Gerald (*picking up her gloves for her*)   I believe that's the idea.

Mrs Millington   Someone with one of those extraordinary foreign names . . .

Gerald (*gloomily*)   Shinka Bachmann – she's a piano thumper.

Mrs Millington   That's it – Shinka Bachmann. I love a good concert; unfortunately I have to play bridge this evening, otherwise nothing would have kept me away. It has been such a disappointment to me, Gerald, that neither of my daughters plays the piano – It's so nice for a girl to be able to sit down and play some little pieces in the evening – or even accompaniments. Thank you, Gerald, you'll stay for dinner of course?

Gerald   No thanks, Mrs Millington. I have to call in at the hospital. I'm meeting Deirdre afterwards.

Mrs Millington   Too bad! While these hospitals can't keep regular hours passes my understanding. Surely they know everyone dines at 7:30? And it's so bad for these young doctors. Their digestions must suffer in the end.

Gerald (*opening the door for her*)   Very true, Mrs Millington.

Mrs Millington (*she drops her handbag*)   Well I must go down and see Father; he always locks himself into the library until the gong goes for dinner. He says this is a madhouse! I – oh, thank you Gerald – tiresome little bag. Goodnight, Gerald.

Gerald   Good night, Mrs Millington.

She trails out. There is a short pause while **Gerald** *warms himself uneasily at the fireplace.* **Deirdre** *enters – briskly of course. She still wears her huge horn-rimmed glasses and looks extremely grim and formidable.*

Gerald   Oh, there you are. You'd gone when I arrived at the lab.

Deirdre (*eluding him*)   Of course. I couldn't wait. My time is valuable.

Gerald (*disconcerted*)   I know, dear, but I was only five minutes late – and I couldn't help it.

Deirdre   Please don't bother to explain. You were late: you always are late, and I suppose you always will be late. (*She removes her glasses.*)

Gerald (*plaintively*)   I don't see why you need to be so cold to me, Deirdre, I had to see a patient . . .

Deirdre   I'm not in the least cold to you.

Gerald   But you are, dear. Very cold. (*He attempts to kiss her. She repulses him.*)

Deirdre   Please, Gerald, don't be so emotional.

Gerald (*sulkily*)   I really don't think I deserve this freezing, Deirdre, simply because I'm five minutes late calling for you. You'll have to resign yourself to all sorts of alarums and excursions when you become a doctor's wife. Come on, darling, kiss and make friends. (*He attempts to draw her to him.*)

Deirdre (*resisting*)   My dear Gerald, I'm beginning to think you suffer from sentimentality.

Gerald (*turning away*)   Perhaps I do . . .

Deirdre   Well, get rid of it – there's no room for it nowadays. Do as I do, and look upon it all as purely chemical.

Gerald   What's all chemical?

Deirdre   This thing called love.

Gerald   Really?

Deirdre   Yes. It's all so simple. If only we could make up our minds to eliminate romanticism and idealism and recognise that love is only a figment of the imagination; it simply doesn't exist. So-called love is nothing more or less than chemical attraction. For instance: our reactions to each other can be diagnosed as chemical attraction bringing us together for a biological necessity.

Gerald   Oh, so I'm a biological necessity, am I?

Deirdre (*airily*)   Oh, there's more in it than that. There is also a union of the mind. It's quite possible you may meet other chemical affinities. I wouldn't mind if you were what Mother calls unfaithful – I know it's just – er . . .

Gerald (*bitterly*)   One chemical calling to another.

Deirdre   Exactly. Your feeling for me, of course, is different. All the stupid little passions, such as jealousy, are, thank Heaven, unknown to me.

Gerald   That's very gratifying.

Deirdre   We must get a grip on ourselves.

Gerald   You seem to have a grip on yourself all right.

Deirdre (*with simple pride*)   Yes, I think I have. Well, I must go and get changed now.

Gerald   There's that god-awful concert this evening.

Deirdre (*surprised*)   But I thought you liked good music, Gerald?

Gerald   Oh so I do, so I do, but I feel more like performing seals this evening.

Deirdre (*going over to him*)   Gerald! (*She waits for him to kiss her but he doesn't respond.*) Oh, very well, if you must be so childish! (*She goes to the door.*) By the way, did you get the tickets for *Back to Methuselah*?

Gerald   Yes, do you really want to go?

Deirdre   Of course. It's the sort of thing one should go to. Intellectual stimulation. Call for me at twenty past eight. Don't be late. Goodbye. (*She goes.*)

Gerald (*rushing after her furiously*)   Just listen to me –

But the door is closed. **Gerald** *stands for a moment in impotent fury, then very deliberately goes to the piano and throws all the books on the floor. At that moment* **Desmond** *creeps in.*

Desmond (*grinning*)   Naughty temper! Deirdre *is* a little trying.

Gerald (*haughtily*)   Trying! What do you mean?

Desmond   Oh well – I've just passed her, looking like Lady Macbeth on the stairs; then I heard this crash, and I put two and two together. Another quarrel. You know my methods, Watson.

Gerald (*pacing up and down*)   If only she wasn't so damn superior . . .

Desmond   My dear!

Gerald (*irritably*)   Can't you drop that effeminate cliché!

Desmond (*unperturbed*)   My dear fellow! After all I *am* effeminate. It's my temperament. I was born that way. Now my reactions –

Gerald (*stopping in his stride*)   For God's sake don't mention that word.

Desmond   What word?

Gerald   Reactions. I've been hearing quite enough about them from Deirdre.

Desmond (*impatiently*)   Ah, you don't know how to manage Deirdre.

Gerald (*pathetically*)   It's all this damned unnatural science, chamber music, and all that. She doesn't believe in love. She's just called me a biological necessity, and left it at that. I'm damned if I'll stand it. It's all very well to laugh but I'm damned worried over the whole thing. Why can't we be happy like other people?

Desmond   Are other people happy? However, that's irrelevant. You love Deirdre, don't you?

Gerald   Oh God, yes. (*He starts pacing again.*)

Desmond   Yes, and I really think she loves you. She's a bully, of course. She's the kind of woman that needs to be beaten. She used to beat me when we were children until I stood up to her one day and gave her one on the jaw. She was all right after that. Of course she's full of culture and self-control, and she's afraid to show her feelings.

Gerald   Has she any feelings?

Desmond   We'll see. She'll react to one thing – jealousy.

Gerald   What?

Desmond   Jealousy.

Gerald   No she won't. She's above all those little petty passions – she doesn't believe in love, you know.

Desmond   Oh, she says that, does she? Well, we'll see. Gerald, I have a plan. Tomorrow night I'm having a party in my studio. Will you come?

Gerald   Yes – if I'm not wanted at the hospital.

Desmond   Deirdre will also come from a sense of duty, if nothing else. Toots Ellerslie is coming and bringing some American girl; I'm also asking Europa Wrench, and Pearl Harris – (*He ticks them off on his fingers.*) Then there'll be Harry the Big Hairy He-man from Kenya, George Gordon Byron Killigrew; his friend Horace Egosmith who's apparently deaf and dumb; my friend Willie Sullivan – you know Willie, the mountain echo; – and my beautiful sister Constance. Oh, I must ask Philip Pryce – he needs some organised shocking. At this party, Gerald, you must ignore Deirdre, treat her with cynical contempt –

Gerald (*uneasily*)   I'm not sure I like this –

Desmond   And you must seduce either Pearl Harris, Europa Wrench or the American girl . . .

Gerald (*horrified*)   I certainly will *not* . . .

Desmond (*airily*)   Oh, don't take me literally – flirt – get off, have a bit of gas. Pay her marked attentions, as great-aunt Agatha would say.

Gerald   I think I see what you're driving at.

Desmond   And mark Deirdre's reactions to that petty but important passion – jealousy.

Gerald   I don't want to do anything that might be misconstrued, you know I have to be very careful in my position – and you know what Dublin is –

Desmond   If she shows any temper – beat her.

Gerald   Good God, no!

Desmond   The Cause, Gerald, the Cause! Tame the Shrew! Remember Shakespeare. Remember Douglas Fairbanks.

Gerald   I'll think it over.

Desmond   Don't think – *act*. The psychological moment has arrived and Deirdre must be tamed.

Gerald   Very well, I'll do it.

Desmond   Splendid.

Gerald   Do you really think she'll react? Be jealous I mean, and all that sort of thing?

Desmond   I'm certain of it. Strange how women react to brutality. They love it. Until they reach the feverish forties and then they prefer my type, the soft, clinging, merely decorative she-man. Something that croons on the hearthrug at their feet. Gerald, d'you know any rich intelligent woman of forty? Somebody's got to take me in hand.

Gerald   Not at present, old man, I'll do my best. (*He pulls out his watch.*) Good Heavens, I'm late! (*He goes.*)

Desmond (*taking up telephone receiver at writing table*)   Hallo! 22934 please – thank you. No don't hurry, I'll be here all night – Hallo, is that 22934? May I speak to Willie, please? (*He whistles 'Today I am so Happy'.*) Hello, Willie, is that you? My dear, you sound pale – what is it? The weather – yes, too awful. Oh Willie, I'm so depressed . . . Oh just life, and my career, and my paternal parent, and one thing and another . . . this house, my dear, complete Bedlam . . . No, only the family . . . now listen, Willie, tomorrow is my twenty-first birthday, d'you hear? For I am to be Queen of the May, Willie, I'm to be Queen of the May! And I'm giving such a merry little party up in the studio . . . Yes, my dear, it's going to be divine, all the wrong people, everyone at daggers drawn . . . You'll come to the party, Willie? Good. Bring some drink. I have some news for you, Willie . . . No, I can't tell you over the phone. I'm so upset. Oh, Willie, Willie, how I long for the tea and toast of middle age! . . .

The dinner gong sounds somewhere in the depths of the house.

Farewell, rewards and fairies! And don't forget the gin . . . about nine-thirty, Willie, don't dress . . . no, Willie, I can't tell you now. The old family gong is sounding . . . nine-thirty . . . Gin!

The gong swells to a roar as

THE CURTAIN FALLS.

Act Two

Scene: **Desmond**'s *studio*

Time: The following evening.

Desmond's *studio. The decoration is modern and flavours of the macabre. The gramophone is to the extreme left of the stage. A cocktail bar has been constructed on stage left. There are no chairs. A seat cut out from the wall encircles the room. There is one light over the centre of the room and another over the cocktail bar; the rest of the room is in shadow. The dancers keep within the circle of light in the centre. All through this act nobody appears to be listening to anybody else, except where there is actual friction between two people.*

Connie *is standing by the gramophone, disconsolately turning over the records.* **Terence** *comes in hurriedly. He is wearing his usual polo jumper make-up.*

Terence   I seem to be indecently early.

Connie   No, it's nearly half-past. The others are late, and Desmond is downstairs collecting glasses and sandwiches. Where's your bodyguard?

Terence   Who? Oh, Horace. Horace is on his way.

Connie   Sit down. Help yourself to a cigarette. I rather wanted to see you alone for a few minutes.

Terence   But how delightful! You're looking very charming tonight, Connie. A little like Dolores of the Seven Veils – or was it Sorrows – anyway, Swinburne – (*He seizes her suddenly, and kisses her.*)

Connie (*repulsing him*)   Please sit down, Terence. I have something to tell you.

Terence (*sitting down beside her*)   This is very mysterious.

Connie   Life's pretty difficult.

Terence (*taking her hand*)   Aren't you being rather Russian?

Connie   Oh *please* – this is serious. (*She takes her hand away.*)

Terence   Marie Vassilivitch! I'm all attention.

Connie   I'm thinking of getting married, Terence.

Terence   Unoriginal, but economically necessary. Have you fixed on a suitable man?

Connie   Yes, I'm going to marry Harry Middleton.

Terence   Oh, that –

Connie (*defiantly*)   Yes *that*. He is sincere and reliable and physically attractive.

Terence   So I gathered. Mentally, of course, he is fourteen.

Connie   Oh, you may sneer! (**Terence** *laughs.*) But Harry's awfully nice. He's kind and sympathetic, he'll look after me, and take care of me –

Terence   Why not advertise for a male nurse?

Connie   I can trust him.

Terence   I see. You don't love this C3 Empire Builder[3] of course?

Connie   No, I don't love him.

Terence   Then why in God's name marry him? Do you want him?

Connie   No. – You know who I want?

Terence (*drawn by her gaze*)   Who, Connie?

Connie   You.

Terence (*in a half whisper*)   Me.

They stare at one another for a moment then slowly kiss.

Connie (*her arms around him*)   Yes, you. I know you love me, Terence, if you'd only let yourself, but you're afraid. Oh darling, I know it would be all right. Let me help you. I don't mind being poor – I'll work too – I'll work like a black, and you can write your novel. I believe in you. We'll be happy together.

Terence (*half-surrendering to her*)   Too late.

Connie (*fiercely*)   It's not too late. Why should it be too late? We're young. It's marvellous to be young together . . .

Terence (*laughing*)   How romantic you are, Connie.

Connie   You'll be a success. I know you will. (*He lifts his head and looks at her.*) I believe in you. I have you safe now. Say you love me; say it. Just tell me once you love me.

Terence (*slowly*)   Connie . . . I . . .

The door opens gently. **Horace Egosmith** *walks in and stands in the shadow.*

Terence (*breaking away*)   No.

Connie   Terence! Terence, stay with me. Don't leave me.

Terence (*rising*)   No. it's too late. (*Brutally.*) I thought I loved you for a moment, Connie, but I don't. I was going to tell you that I loved you as much as my egotism would allow me, but that's only another way of saying I don't love you at all.

Connie (*in anguish*)   Oh, Terence, don't speak to me like that – oh, Terence! (*She sobs.*) I can't bear it . . .

---

3   C3 indicates Terence's contemptuous view of Harry as mediocre and lower middle class.

Terence (*striking an attitude*)   Behold me, Connie! The real me. A hypocrite! A transparent poseur from puberty. For once I'll be sincere. I don't love you, Connie. I'll never love anyone. I can't even love myself. (**Egosmith** *coughs genteelly.* **Terence** *turns and sees him in the shadows*). Oh, you (*He laughs.*) for the moment – d'you know, Horace old man – I thought I saw myself, and behold, I was a very ordinary fellow.

Connie (*rising*)   Well, why did you make me think you loved me?

Terence   I never succeeded in making you think, Connie.

Connie (*hysterically*)   You did, you did! You never left me alone. Oh, why did you do it? Why did you make me love you?

Terence   Connie, for God sake be quiet. We're not alone.

Connie (*sobbing wildly*)   I don't care – let him hear. (*Voices are heard outside.*) Let them all hear! (**Terence** *approaches her. She waves him away.*) Go away – don't touch me! Don't dare to touch me! I despise you, I loathe you –

Terence   Connie, pull yourself together.

Connie (*half screaming at him*)   You rotten waster! That's what you are – a rotten Dublin waster! And you're a coward – you're afraid of everything! Coward! Coward! Coward!

Terence (*laughing at her*)   Now you're *thinking*! Sit down and be quiet. (*He pushes her back into her seat, then quietly wipes his mouth. She shrinks from him, sobbing. He turns to see* **Egosmith** *advancing on him rubbing his hands nervously and wearing the usual deprecating smile.*) I must end this sooner or later. (*He walks to the bar and leans his head on his hands.* **Egosmith** *continues to watch* **Connie** *nervously.*)

Connie (*in despair*)   Oh God, if only I could die now!

Laughter outside. The doors thrown open, and **Willie Sullivan**, **Desmond** *and* **Gerald** *enter, laden with bottles.*

Desmond   Come, let us be joyful! Mind the bottles, Willie! Now isn't this a merry party? Gerald, you know Killigrew and Egosmith? Willie, put the bottles on the counter. Doctor Parr – everybody –

Terence   Aha! The demon rum! I must drink deep tonight, Flossie! The only excuse for existing. (*He throws a swift glance at* **Connie**, *who is busy repairing the ravages with a powder puff.*) Come here, Horace, look at this – and this – (*He lifts the bottles lovingly;* **Egosmith** *joins him.*)

Desmond (*counting and sorting the glasses*)   Just give me a hand, Willie.

Willie (*in a pale imitation of* **Desmond**)   – a hand, yes. Two of gin. One of brandy. Two vermouth.

Gerald (*mopping his brow*)   Where is Deirdre, Connie? Isn't she coming?

Connie (*indifferently*) She's just pouring herself into a new dress.

Desmond Oh Gerald, come here a moment. (*He draws him aside.*) I want a word with you. Egosmith, give Willie a hand with the drinks like a good fellow.

Egosmith *quietly walks behind the bar and assumes the duties of bartender, which he retains for the rest of the evening.*

Terence (*lazily*) I feel I ought to be doing something. Can I help, Sullivan?

Willie (*one of those people who not only repeat the last word you say, but stare at your face intently as if their life depended on your next sentence*) – help me? Thanks awfully old chap. Just count the glasses, will you?

Gerald (*to* **Desmond**) Look here, I don't really feel I can carry this thing through. Really it's a little bit strong – you know what Dublin is!

Desmond Oh, don't be a bloody fool! Do as I tell you. Everything will be alright. Anyway it's too late to go back on it. Pearl Harris is coming. Isn't Pearl coming, Willie?

Willie Is Pearl coming? Yes she is.

Desmond Pearl is Willie's cousin and ever so innocent. She's just left the convent or whatever it was. She's sweet, Gerald. But on the other hand there's Europa Wrench. She's coming too. Isn't Europa coming, Connie?

Connie Mercy! So she is –

Desmond You know her, don't you? Her mother writes those books on economics and White Slaves and things? I think she raised the Age of Consent – or lowered it, or something like that. But Europa is very clever and awfully National, and runs an industry. Then there's the American girl Toots is to bring. Have you heard anything about her, Connie?

Connie Toots says she's ravishing and has the most wonderful pearls.

Desmond There! Three of them. Now which are you going to ruin – just for the evening, Gerald – just for the evening. Or why not all three – in rotation!

Gerald Good heavens! I think it had better be the first one –

Desmond Yes, perhaps Pearl is the safest. Yes, it had better be Pearl.

Willie We're two glasses short, Des.

Desmond Just run down and collect all the tooth mugs, then.

Willie *departs immediately, murmuring 'tooth mugs'.*

Gerald (*haunting* **Desmond**) By the way – what's the decoy duck like?

Desmond (*laconically*) Blonde. Arrested development.

Gerald This is frightful.

Connie Give me a cigarette, Gerald.

Gerald   Oh, sorry – here you are.

Desmond   Have a spot, Terence. Help yourself, Egosmith. Here you are, Gerald. Put on a record, somebody. Drink this, Gerald, and be quick. Ah, here's the Fairy Queen! Hello, Pearl darling –

Pearl Harris, *a childish blonde with an irritating lisp, trips in all of a flutter.*

Pearl   How sweet of you, Des, to ask me to your party. Many happy returns! Oooh Connie, what a lovely frock! Oh, I was so excited, Des, when Mummie gave me your message.

Terence   My! We are seeing life, aren't we?

Connie (*languidly*)   Oh Pearl, who do you know? Mr Killigrew, Mr Egosmith? You know everyone else. We haven't seen you for years. Sit down somewhere and somebody will bring you something to drink.

Pearl (*seating herself near* **Connie**)   Yeth, I've been in school in Switzerland for the last two years you know . . .

Desmond   Pearl darling! Cocktail? Smoke?

Pearl   No, thank you, Des. I don't drink any wine, Mummy doesn't like it. Have you any lemonade? I'd love some lemonade.

Desmond (*to* **Gerald**)   Now, are you ready? It's all right. She doesn't know who you are. She's been away for the last two years. Get busy before the others come. Take Miss Harris a goblet of Kia-Ora and make yourself agreeable.

Gerald *swallows his drink hastily, pulls down his waistcoat, and follows* **Desmond** *across the room to where* **Pearl** *is sitting.*

Pearl[4]   This is Doctor Edward Lushington Codd, the famous explorer. (**Gerald** *opens his mouth to speak but* **Desmond** *stills him with a look.*) He's just been up the frozen Amazon in an aeroplane, but no doubt you've read all about him in the papers.

Pearl (*appealingly*)   How d'you do, Dr – er – Codd? I'm afraid you'll find me very stupid. I don't know much geography. Do tell me all about your adventures.

Gerald   Well, there really isn't very much to say about it. (*He looks furiously at* **Desmond**.)

Desmond   Ta ta – enjoy yourself now! (*He goes back to the bar.*)

Terence (*raising his glass to* **Egosmith**)   *Morituri, morituros salutant.*[5]

Willie *enters carrying a strange assortment of mugs and carafes. He is followed by* **Deirdre**, *very demure in pink.*

---

4   Given as Pearl, but this line is clearly spoken by Desmond.
5   Those about to die, salute those about to die: gladiators to each other, before the fight.

Willie   Here you are, Des. It's all I could get. I ransacked all the bathrooms and bedrooms and things.

Desmond   These drinks will be completely dental.

Willie (*giggling*)   – completely dental.

Deirdre   Do you like my new dress, Desmond? (*She bows coldly to* **Terence** *and* **Egosmith**.)

Desmond   Hello, Deirdre darling. My *dear*, too marvellous! Willy, isn't it virginal?

Willy   Completely virginal.

Desmond   I designed it. Do you like Deirdre's dress, Gerald?

Gerald (*leaping up*)   By Jove! (*Remembering his part, he walks over to* **Deirdre**, *who stands with a complacent expression.*) Wait! No – no, I'm not quite sure. Isn't Deirdre too severe a type to wear pink?

Deirdre (*dismayed*)   But you suggested pink, Gerry!

Gerald (*walking back to* **Pearl**)   Oh yes, perhaps. I'd forgotten.

Deirdre (*following him*)   But Gerry –

Gerald   You know Miss Harris?

Deirdre (*coldly*)   Yes – but Gerald –

Pearl   Deirdre and I were at school together. Of course Deirdre was very senior to me. I was only in the kindergarten. Now go on about the polar bears! (*She turns to him, wide eyed, absorbed.*)

Gerald (*with an uneasy look at* **Deirdre**)   Oh yes, the polar bears – (*He turns to* **Pearl**.) The cold was terrific –

Deirdre *walks over to* **Connie** *and sits down beside her. At that moment* **Europa Wrench** *sweeps into the room. She is a plump young woman of twenty; a living, breathing mass of Celtic embroideries and hand-woven tweeds. She carries a sheaf of documents, wears glasses and her hair wisped in plaits over her ears. She speaks with an extreme cultured Anglo-Irish accent.*

Europa   I'm so glad I'm not late. I was so afraid I'd miss all the jollity.

Desmond   Europa, come to my arms! What will you have to drink? You know everyone, don't you?

Europa   Of course. No, I won't have anything to drink. I have to be up early while the Conference is on . . .

Desmond   What conference, darling? (*He hands her a drink.*) Oh, just a little one!

Europa   The Economic Conference, organised by the Women's International League for Open Windows and Closed Doors. Mother is the President, you know. We sent a note to Japan today, demanding an inquiry into the Manchurian question.

Desmond   How thrilling! Do you think they will answer it? Europa darling, sit down somewhere. Where did you get that wonderful tweed?

Europa (*sitting down near the bar*)   It is rather jolly, isn't it? It's handwoven by the bracken industries. I'm learning to weave there myself – Desmond, you simply ought to take up weaving . . .

Desmond   Europa! How could you suggest such a thing?

Willie   Shall I put on a record, Des?

Desmond   Put on anything. Drown the conversation, for God's sake . . .

Willy   I'll put on something nice . . .

Terence   I'm bringing you a drink, Connie. (*He sits down beside her. She stares blankly in front of her.*) So your Empire Builder is coming tonight. The situation will be amusing. You know, Connie, you're having a very interesting life at present. You ought to write a book about it.

Connie (*looking at him coldly*)   How I despise myself . . .

Terence   Nonsense! You're only suffering from wounded vanity. (*There is a burst of laughter from* **Egosmith** *and* **Desmond**. *They break a glass*. **Terence** *rises*.) They seem to want a steadying influence over there. D'you want another drink, Connie?

Connie   No, thanks. (*Turning away.*) I love your dress, Deirdre.

Deirdre (*looking at* **Gerald**, *who is getting on remarkably well with* **Pearl**)   I'm glad somebody likes it.

Terence *slouches over to the bar. He slaps* **Egosmith** *on the back and stares at* **Europa**, *who is busily replaiting her hair – which has become rather dishevelled with excitement.*

Europa (*to* **Terence**)   Are you interested in wheat?

Terence   Intensely.

Europa   Well, you must come to the Conference tomorrow. We're discussing the question of a world quota for wheat. *Do* come! We want everyone to ask questions.

There is shouting and laughter outside. **Toots** *bounces in, laden with bottles. She is followed by* **Priscilla Converse**, *an exquisite, frail creature in green.*

Desmond (*rushing towards* **Toots**)   My darling! God, how I love you!

Toots (*sentimentally*)   Take these bottles – they were my father's. Many happy returns. (*She kisses him.*) Getting a big boy now. Soon have to put a weight on your head. Is that Connie wilting in the corner? And Europa darling – I'm sorry I never got to the conference, but I had a toothache. Hallo, Deirdre! Harry Middleton is on his way up. Oh, I must introduce Priscilla Converse from Boston. Priscilla – this is Dublin's underworld . . .

Priscilla   I think it is perfectly marvellous of you to ask me to your birthday party, Mr Millington.

Desmond   I think it's perfectly marvellous of you to come – Have a cigarette – sit down. (*She sits down near the bar.*) Priscilla Converse! What a lovely Puritan, New England name – so divinely Quakerish – do you drink?

Priscilla   I certainly do. (*He hands her one.*) What a perfectly marvellous room!

Desmond   I like your dress –

Priscilla   I got it in Paris.

Desmond (*entranced*)   Paris! Paris in the Spring! Oh God, how I envy you. What do you think of Paris?

Priscilla (*vaguely*)   Paris? – oh – I got six pairs of shoes there. I'm crazy about shoes – I can't stop buying them –

Toots (*joining the crowd around the bar*)   Give me a drink, Des – I want to catch up on you. Oh, look at Egosmith behind the bar! Isn't he sweet? Listen to me, darling – your strategic position is perfect. In half an hour every soul in this room will be bared to you. They'll lean on this little counter and they'll tell you their little all! Am I right or am I wrong?

Terence   I rather think you're right.

Toots (*in a stage whisper to* **Terence**)   What's wrong with the party?

Terence   Mental and moral indigestion.

Desmond   Who hasn't come? Somebody hasn't come – oh, here's the Boys' Brigade.

Harry *enters, followed by* **Philip Pryce**, *a pallid, nondescript young man. They are both wearing dinner jackets.*

Harry   Cheeroh, everybody! What – oh, the festive scene! What a weird room. Bit gruesome – what? I met Pryce on the stairs – most extraordinary thing – we were both at school together!

Desmond   I'm sure you were, you know everybody, Harry. Philip, you haven't met Miss Converse?

Philip   How d'you do? Hallo, Toots, what have you been doing with yourself? Oh, hallo, Europa – I suppose you're very busy now?

Harry (*going to the bar –* **Egosmith** *looks at him questioningly*)   Irish for me – soda. When. Thanks, old man. Hallo, Toots! (*He nods coldly to* **Terence**, *takes his glass and goes over to* **Connie**.) I say, Connie, you're looking extraordinarily attractive tonight – extraordinarily attractive. (*He sits down beside her.*)

Connie   Am I?

Harry (*bemused*)   Yes. I love that white dress you're wearing. It's – it's – extraordinarily becoming, extraordinarily becoming –

Terence *watches them, smiling. He finishes his drink,* **Egosmith** *hands him another, and he turns to* **Toots**.

Terence (*lifting his glass*)   Your health, Toots! Why do they call you Toots? What's your real name?

Toots   Diana Fitzgerald Cunningham Ellerslie. Isn't it incredible?

Terence (*thoughtfully*)   Incredible – no! (*He lifts his glass to her.*) 'Queen and huntress, chaste and fair!'

Toots   Why did you tell me to read Saint Teresa?

Terence   I'll tell you why when I'm drunk. Marry, sweet wag! Let us be Diana's Foresters, Gentlemen of the Shade, minions of the moon. Behold me, a Gentleman of the Shade!

Desmond (*combing his hair in a pocket mirror*)   Translated into Neo-Georgian means shady gentleman!

Terence   Ah, the pocket of Narcissus! Beware of your own reflection. (*He slouches over to* **Connie** *and* **Harry**.) Salaams, white men all! Hail, Bwana Middleton! (**Harry** *stares at him coldly.*)

Priscilla (*to* **Desmond***, making a gesture towards* **Terence**)   What's the matter with that poor mutt?

Philip   He writes poetry. They're all like that; there are hundreds of them here!

Priscilla   I'm crazy about poetry. I plan to read a lot of poetry this year, if I can get round to it.

Willie (*coming over to the bar*)   Hallo, Toots. Why do you look so suppressed – I mean, depressed – (**Willie** *has had too much.*) Listen, did you hear about Mary Hammond?

Europa (*reprovingly*)   Now, *no* gossiping – there's far too much gossiping in this city – (*Eagerly.*) yes, what about Mary Hammond?

Toots   Be careful, the pure Pearl might hear – She's a bosom friend, isn't she?

Willie (*vaguely*)   Oh yes, completely bosom – (*He giggles.*)

Toots   Oh, get on with it! What happened to Mary Hammond?

Willie *is convulsed.*

Desmond   Put on another record, Willie, and stop being idiotic.

Willie   What'll I put on, Des?

Desmond   Anything you like. Make it snappy.

Willie   Make it snappy – very well. (*He breaks into laughter and wavers back to the gramophone.*)

Priscilla (*earnestly; she's reached the earnest stage*)   That's an awfully sweet little boy. Where did you raise him?

Toots   He's a cross-breed. We raise them under glass.

Gerald (*crossing to the counter*)   Look here, I've had enough.

Desmond   My dear, you've only had one.

Gerald   You know what I mean. I've had enough. Good Lord, why did you introduce me as an explorer? There's Deirdre looking at me as if I was a murderer, and I've got polar bears up the Amazon and can't get them down –

Desmond   Have another drink, and try gorillas.

Gerald   Damn you anyway. (*He takes his drink and goes back to his seat.*)

Desmond (*in a low voice to* **Toots**)   For God's sake, talk, talk, talk! This is a terrible party! Send somebody over to Deirdre. Oh God, why do I do it? Why do I do it? (*He walks centre.*) Gents, choose your partners for the next dance. Girls, be prepared! Dance, everyone. Love, live and laugh! (*He goes back to the counter.*) Oh God, I'm so depressed.

Toots   So am I.

Willie *puts on a raucous record. Only the group at the bar remains in the light. The dancers are in shadow.* **Harry** *and* **Connie** *dance.* **Gerald** *and* **Pearl** *follow them.*

Gerald   We had a very narrow shave with gorillas one day –

Pearl   Gorillas! How awful! What did you do? I would have been simply terrified. What did you do?

Gerald   Harpoons, you know. Very simple when you know how.

Deirdre (*crossing to the bar and addressing* **Toots** *and* **Desmond**)   What is the matter with Gerald? He's talking about gorillas. Is he mad?

Desmond   He's behaving outrageously with that innocent little girl.

Toots   Perhaps it's a nervous breakdown.

Desmond (*with sinister meaning*)   It's a breakdown, all right.

Deirdre *sits and watches the dancers with jealous rage written on every line of her face.*

Philip (*dancing with* **Priscilla**)   How do you like Dublin?

Priscilla (*vaguer than ever after her third cocktail*)   I think Dublin is perfectly grand. I'm crazy about Dublin.

Philip (*falling fast*)   Have you been here long?

Priscilla   We arrived yesterday. Mother has had a most terrible headache – it's candy, she can't stop eating it – takes it to bed with her. We're going to Killarney tomorrow. I'm crazy to see Killarney.

Philip   Have you seen the Book of Kells?

Terence (*joining the crowd of the bar*)   Well, how's the League of Nations?

Toots *and* **Desmond** *are leaning in attitudes of dejection against the bar counter.* **Deirdre** *with her back to them is watching* **Gerald.** **Europa** *is making notes in a vast exercise book.*

Europa   Terence Killigrew, you're clever. Why don't you join the MFL?

Terence   What is it? An army of some kind?

Europa   Gracious no! It's the March Forward League. An international organisation for cultural relations between the nations!

Harry (*to* **Connie**)   You seem pretty matey with that chap Killigrew. He's a nasty piece of work.

Connie   Yes, he's pretty awful! Harry, tell me do you love me?

Harry   Well, Connie old girl, I can hardly say it in this riot.

Connie   Yes you can. Do you love me?

Harry   You know I do, Connie.

Connie (*smiling triumphantly as they pass the bar*)   Harry, you're rather a darling.

Terence (*to* **Egosmith**)   You know, old man, I sometimes think of the world as a colossal animal, a sort of gargantuan cow. The trees, the rivers and the mountains are a skin disease which it unfortunately happens to be suffering from; and the inhabitants are merely parasites eking out a dreary existence from the pus-exuding scabs. In my more footless moments I can even explain God in this way. Curious, very curious.

Gerald   I may call you Pearl, mayn't I?

Pearl (*giggling*)   Yes, if you like. I'm always called Girlie at home.

Gerald (*as they pass* **Deirdre**)   Aren't you dancing, Deirdre? Splendid party, isn't it?

Deirdre (*looking murderous*)   Splendid.

Toots (*to* **Egosmith**)   This is a terrible party. Listen, Horace – I may call you Horace, mayn't I? (**Egosmith** *nods, and hands her another drink.*) D'you know, I think there is some curious attraction between us. I think we've both got broken hearts. Didn't you know I had a broken heart? I was in love once . . .

Priscilla (*coming back to the bar*)   Say, I'm kind of tired.

Toots (*politely*)   Have you met many people here?

Priscilla   I've got some introductions –

Toots   I wonder do I know them?

Priscilla   Maybe – I got one to the President – he looks cunning – and one to the Archbishop – and the other to Liam O'Flaherty. I'm crazy about his books. I guess I won't be able to get them all in though – I've got to do some shopping –

Philip   Have a drink. Sit here.

Willie (*calling across to* **Desmond**)   I can't find 'The Pagan Love Song', Des. D'you know where it is?

Desmond (*sleepily*)   What is it now? What are you playing now? (*He crosses carefully to* **Willie**.)

Willie (*who's had far too much*)   – playing now? I don't know. Why?

Desmond (*seriously*)   It's terrible. Simply terrible.

Willie   Oh, all right! All right! I only wanted to know if you had 'The Pagan Love Song' – that's all.

Desmond (*going back to the bar*)   Don't disturb me again.

Europa (*to* **Priscilla**)   What do you think about Prohibition?

Priscilla (*drinking*)   I think it's perfectly crazy.

Europa (*with intense solemnity*)   My mother wrote a pamphlet about it; it's been translated into six languages.

Priscilla (*idiotically*)   Your mother must be very, very clever; and I guess you're very clever too.

Europa (*owlishly*)   I'm not really. If you like, I'll take you round the slums tomorrow.

Priscilla   That would be divine.

Phillip   Hello, Toots! What have you been doing with yourself lately?

Toots   Phillip Pryce, if you ask me that again I'll slit your throat from ear to ear! Dance with me, Des.

Desmond   Darling, of course.

Deirdre   It's disgusting! Everyone's had far too much to drink.

Priscilla (*to* **Phillip**, *indicating* **Deirdre**)   I guess she's having a nervous breakdown.

Phillip   No, she's just brainy – they're always like that.

Terence   Each one wrapped in his or her little cloak of egotism. Each one going his own futile wavering road – Oh Lord, what a generation!

Desmond (*calling out*)   Deirdre, aren't you dancing?

Deirdre   I'm perfectly happy, thank you.

Harry   Do you really mean this, Connie? You're not fooling me?

Connie   Of course I mean it! Of course I do.

Harry   Darling!

Toots   There's a kind of Freudian depression hanging over this party – have you noticed it?

Desmond   Yes, love, things are coming to a climax. Deirdre looks like thunder.

Toots   What's the matter with your feet? They haven't gone flat have they?

Desmond (*offended*)   They're perfectly all right – at least, they were when I saw them last.

Toots   You know, I don't believe drink makes you forget anything. I never felt more depressed in my life. I just can't forget – I suppose I never will.

Desmond   You're probably going to be sick.

Gerald   I know exactly how you feel about it – deep down –

Pearl   As Mummie says – girls nowadays make themselves so cheap – they put no value on themselves. (*She nestles close to him.*)

Gerald (*pressing her gently*)   I quite understand.

The music stops. **Gerald** *and* **Pearl** *seat themselves. After a moment* **Deirdre** *drifts over and sits on the other side of him. He trembles visibly.* **Toots** *and* **Desmond** *join the crowd round the bar.* **Harry** *and* **Connie** *also go back to their seats.*

Gerald (*to* **Pearl**)   Do you mind if I tell you that you've got wonderful eyes?

Pearl (*giggling*)   Do you really think so? Really?

Deirdre (*trying to take his hand*)   Gerry, what's the matter with you? You're not sulking, are you?

Gerald (*jerking his hand away and standing up*)   Can I get you anything to drink, Deirdre?

Deirdre   No, thank you. (**Gerald** *goes over to the bar.*)

Pearl (*powdering her nose violently*)   He's rather sweet, isn't he? I *am* enjoying this party, aren't you?

Deirdre (*with an effort*)   Oh yes, it's lovely.

Pearl   Have you a headache, Deirdre?

Deirdre (*snapping*)   No thanks – why?

Pearl (*recoiling*)   I thought you looked pale.

Gerald *returns with the drinks. He devotes himself to* **Pearl**.

Willie (*drifting over from the bar*)   Another drink, please – I'm afraid to go home. (*He giggles and turns to* **Toots**.) Have you met my mother?

Toots   No, what's she like?

Willie   Terrible.

Toots   Is your father awful too?

Willie   We don't meet –

Toots (*sarcastically*)   It must be awful to have to take an allowance from him –

Willie (*pettishly*)   Well, it's his own fault – he brought me into the world –

Toots   Yes – he certainly ought to pay for that.

Priscilla (*looking amorously at* **Willie**)   I think that boy's awfully cunning. I'm crazy about him.

Willie *backs nervously from her, takes his drink from* **Egosmith** *and totters back to his old place beside the gramophone.*

Philip (*jealously*)   But, I say, you can't like that chap. He's – he's an awful little squit . . .

Priscilla   I'm crazy about pansies.

Philip (*shocked*)   Oh I say! – Good Lord! (*He shakes his head, and turns to* **Europa**.) Have you seen any good shows lately?

Harry (*rising*)   Connie, old girl, can I get you anything to drink?

Terence (*going over to them with a glass in one hand, a bottle in the other*)   Well Connie, how are you pushing along? Have a spot of something? (*Sitting down in* **Harry's** *seat.*) Thanks, old chap, don't let me keep you.

Harry (*glaring at him*)   I'll be back in a moment, Connie. (*He goes over to the bar.*)

Terence   The Empire Builder is displaying proprietary passion. You shouldn't encourage him, Connie. It's not fair to the poor chap –

Connie   Please go away.

Terence   Certainly. (*He goes back to the bar.*)

Harry (*returning with the drinks*)   I can't stand that fella Killigrew. Why doesn't he wash? What is he? A poet?

Connie (*wearily*)   Oh, nothing in particular.

Europa (*concentrating on* **Priscilla**)   I'd love you to see my hand-weaving industry. The workers are peasant girls from all over Ireland – most of them from the Gaeltacht. There are only two of them at present, but we hope to have many more. We're teaching them hand-weaving, Irish dancing, embroidery and harp. It's so vitally necessary to improve the peasant *culturally*, I think. My cousin Harold FitzGibbon – he's a Senator – has started a dandelion industry – it appears it's the quickest way of fattening chickens; you just stuff them with dandelions continuously, with *amazing* results. He's giving a demonstration tomorrow.

Priscilla (*dreamily*)   How perfectly marvellous.

Europa   My cousin Senator FitzGibbon is also leader of the Poultry Farmers' Defence League – you *must* meet him.

Priscilla   He sounds awfully cunning.

Willie   I can't find 'The Pagan Love Song', Des. You'll *have* to come and help me.

Priscilla   Oh, you cunning thing! Let me ruffle your hair!

Willie (*hastening away*)   No I won't! Des – come and help me. I can't find 'The Pagan Love Song'.

Desmond   Find it yourself! Find it yourself!

Gerald (*to* **Pearl**)   Well, what about a drive next Sunday?

Pearl (*clapping her hands*)   Oh, that would be lovely! (*She pauses.*) I *do* hope Mummie will let me go. They're so strict, you know. I'm not *out* yet.

Gerald (*tenderly*)   But I'd take such care of you. Shall I call for you? What about going to Woodenbridge?

Pearl   Oooh, lovely!

Deirdre *rises indignantly and goes over to the other side of* **Connie**. **Willie** *starts the gramophone. They all start dancing as before –* **Philip** *takes* **Priscilla***;* **Egosmith**, **Terence**, **Toots** *and* **Europa** *remain at the bar.*

Terence (*addressing* **Toots** *and* **Egosmith**)   There is not one drop of artist's blood in my veins. I tell you this because I know you will understand. Not a drop. I haven't even got technique. It takes me hours to write a letter – and why?

Toots   Why, Terence?

Terence   Because I'm constipated – mentally constipated. Too much Proust. Too much Joyce.

Toots (*to* **Egosmith**)   I want you to understand this: I didn't give him up without a struggle. I've gone through torture since, wondering if I ought to have married him and risked everything. I was a coward. The truth is, in spite of everything, I still love that man.

Terence (*to* **Egosmith**)   But oh – what material within me! To write one must be utterly miserable, utterly alone and hopeless. I'm all these things, but I'm indifferent. 'Warm, eager living life' – Oh God, I would give twenty years of my life for one year of it. You know, Toots, I like talking to you – there is a sympathetic alcoholic shine in your eye that draws me on . . .

Toots   I like you too – you're lousy, but I like you . . .

Terence (*to* **Europa**)   And what do *you* think of the present situation?

Europa (*very serious and very foggy*)   I'd rather not say. Don't ask me, Terence, I'd rather not say – my uncle's a Senator, I've got to be careful y'know and *really* I'm only interested in the international situation – but I must say I think de Valera *is* very sincere – I don't know what he *means* – but I think he's very sincere . . .

Desmond (*with tears*)   Darling, I think you ought to let him know – honestly I think you ought to let him know – it would *encourage* him.

Europa (*nodding like a mandarin*)   Yes, I really think he's sincere . . .

Deirdre (*to* **Egosmith**)   I'm speaking quite frankly to you, because you're the only sane person in the room – don't you think it's time this party came to an end? I don't care about myself, but really there are limits. No, I'm not a jealous person; I haven't a possessive nature, but a vulgar display of animal passion *does* rather disgust me – to say the least of it!

Willie *stops the gramophone with an appalling screech of the needle.* **Terence** *starts out of his reverie, and* **Toots** *wakes up.*

Desmond   What's the matter, Willie?

Willie (*very dignified*)   . . . the matter? Nothing's the matter. Everything's perfectly all right. Perfectly.

Desmond   You're playing the same record over and over again.

Willie   I'm not. I can't find 'The Pagan Love Song'.

Priscilla   Isn't he cunning? I'm crazy about that little boy.

Desmond (*removing the record*)   Here it is. You've played it at least three times already. Willie, you're drunk!

Willie (*passionately*)   I'm *not* drunk.

Deirdre (*rising*)   It's disgusting. Everybody's had far too much to drink. Connie – Harry – do stop those boys.

Philip   I say, this is rather – Oh, good Lord –

Desmond (*solemnly*)   Now, Willie, pull yourself together. I *insist* that you put on a new record. You heard what my sister said? She's very worried about you, Willie.

Willie (*snatching the record from* **Desmond**)   Oh, very well! (*He breaks the record.*) Now I can't possibly play it again.

Desmond (*slightly maudlin*)   Willie, d'you know that that's my favourite record?

Willie (*defiantly*)   Yes, but I don't care!

Desmond (*with quiet dignity*)   I'll have to slap your face. (*He slaps* **Willie***'s face.* **Willie** *retaliates by pulling* **Desmond***'s hair. They fall to the ground struggling.*)

Deirdre   This is awful!

Priscilla (*standing up on her seat*)   Whoopee! Attababy! Slap him down, Willie! Tear out his hair! Cut his heart out, baby! Whoopee!

Philip   I say, Miss Converse, do come down. Look here, Middleton, hadn't we better do something about it? Good Lord!

Terence   Part the warriors! They might hurt each other. (*He is helpless with laughter.*)

Connie   Oh Harry! – somebody *do* something!

Toots   Aren't we sweet! What a party!

Harry   Get up, you young ass! (*He pulls* **Desmond** *to his feet.*) Remember there are women present. Damn bad form.

Terence   Now kiss and make friends.

Willie   Shan't.

Desmond (*sulkily*)   It was Willie's fault. I'm going to have another drink.

Toots (*dusting him down*)   Aren't you ashamed of yourself? A big boy of twenty-one!

Egosmith *gives him a drink.* **Terence** *joins them at the bar.*

Europa   That's better. Now we can hold a little conference. It's so much better to talk everything out across the table, don't you think?

Connie   Don't let those boys drink any more.

Harry (*to the room at large*)   Be quiet, you young fools. (*He winds up the gramophone.*) Come and dance this, Connie. (*They dance.*)

Philip   Come down, Miss Converse. Dance this with me.

Priscilla (*she's reached the quarrelsome stage*)   Let me alone! Let my hand alone, don't touch me! How dare you touch me!

Philip   But Good Lord – I say Miss Converse, please don't mistake me – I was only trying to help you down.

Priscilla   Well, there's no need to develop hand-trouble.

Priscilla *climbs down very haughtily and sails across to the bar, followed by* **Philip** *exclaiming 'Good Lord' and 'This is awful!' at intervals.*

Deirdre   Gerry, aren't you going to ask me to dance?

Gerald   Well, as a matter of fact I'm engaged for this – but if Pearl doesn't mind –?

Deirdre   – If that's the case! – (*She turns away.*)

Gerald   Oh, but Pearl will forgive me, I'm sure! (*Tenderly.*) – I'll be back in a few minutes, little girl. (*They dance.*)

Deirdre   I'm sorry to tear you away from Pearl.

Gerald   Deirdre, I've had the most amazing chemical reaction to that little girl!

Deirdre   *Have* you?

Gerald   You know, Deirdre, it's awfully splendid of you not to mind. Now another woman would be frightfully jealous – you know what I mean – but, thank heaven, you've got a grip on yourself.

Deirdre   I think I'll sit down.

Gerald   What's the matter? You're not ill, Deirdre?

Deirdre   No, I feel splendid – just a little tired. You'd better finish this with Pearl. (**Deirdre** *goes back to the bar.*)

Gerald (*rejoining* **Pearl**)   Come on, little girl, we'll finish this together. (*They dance.*)

Desmond (*whimpering with his head on the counter*)   Nobody understands me.

Toots   Oh, come on – dance this with me. (*They dance.*)

Europa (*with intense politeness to* **Priscilla**)   And how do you like Dublin?

Priscilla   I'm crazy about Dublin. This afternoon we went out to some place with two lakes, and a bed. I can't remember the name. (*She giggles.*)

Europa (*giggling*)   Two lakes and a bed! There couldn't be –

Priscilla   And we had to climb miles and miles up into the bed – it belonged to a saint –

Europa   I know – Saint Kevin.

Priscilla   Right first time. D'you know I'm crazy about saints – I collect them – Lives, I mean –

Philip (*importunately*)   Won't you dance this with me, Miss Converse?

Priscilla   Dance with him, Europa. He gives me a pain in the neck.

Philip (*broken*)   You don't mean that! Good Lord!

Europa   Yes, I want to talk to you, Philip. I want to get you interested in world affairs. (*She takes possession of him and pulls him forth to dance.*) I want you to join the March Forward League – at once, you're just the type we need.

Philip   I'm playing a lot of golf at the moment, I'm afraid.

Priscilla (*to* **Egosmith**)   Say, I've been longing to get a word with you all evening. I guess you know what's the matter with me. I'm kind of worn out. Galloping across Europe with that old woman. I hate my mother – she's greedy, – eats too much, – she's a candy fiend. I wanna go home! There's the sweetest boy at home, but somehow he doesn't like me that way – it won't come right – d'you know what I mean? So I'm shopping here, there and everywhere – it takes my mind off things – shoes, shoes, I'm crazy about shoes. (*She weeps.*)

Terence (*to* **Egosmith**)   Look at us! Take a good look at us. Raised in gunfire. (*He speaks out towards the others.*) . . . one mysterious universe after the other . . . souls lacerated with psychoanalysis . . . censorship of literature . . . people putting their heads in gas-ovens all over Europe . . . the rest living from hand to flask . . . the Doctrine of Despair . . . the Philosophy of Hopefulness. Communism is coming . . . the Intelligentsia must die . . . Onward Christian soldiers marching as to war. Oh, Mickey Mouse, where are you? Take me home and bury me! (**Egosmith** *hands him a drink.*) Thanks, old man. Wormwood! Wormwood!

Toots (*coming back to the bar followed by* **Desmond**)   Well, Hamlet! Your health! (*She drinks to* **Egosmith**.)

Priscilla (*indicating* **Terence**)   Say listen – that boy's got something on his mind.

Terence (*oblivious*)   Death! Death! Why should Death grin at me suddenly out of the shadows? I greet it with the same complete indifference with which I greet Life. 'Let us endure' be damned! I'm living for nothing but the next drink. Born without guts and just enough wit to realise my own unutterable futility. Everything I have is borrowed, and though I may be able to convince a few, I'm certainly not able to persuade myself that I am anything but what I am. (*He laughs, turns and sees* **Toots** *perched on the bar behind him.*) Ah, Santa Teresa – do you remember Hortigosa?

Toots   Yes, I remember Hortigosa – where you won me from the world.

Terence (*holding her hand with mock earnestness*)   Teresa Cepeda D'Avila y Ahumada. Look on this Vanity and repent . . . Get out of this – before it's too late.

Toots   I hear you, Brother, I hear you – and I'm moved to obey your words.

Desmond (*who has been drooping against the counter*)   This is a terrible party!

Toots   Oh, for God's sake! – you've been saying that all the evening – (*She starts making up her face feverishly.*)

The gramophone stops. **Willie** *is sleeping peacefully. The others drift to various seats round the room.* **Europa** *leads* **Philip** *back to the bar.*

Europa   I can't get Philip interested in anything (*She slaps* **Terence** *on the back.*) – and I can't get Terence to take life seriously. I want him to study World Planning –

Priscilla   I guess he'd better get started on himself first (*She sees* **Willie**.) Whoopee! Aw, look at the sleeping beauty! Isn't he cunning? I must go and talk to my little Willie.

Philip (*yearningly*)   Oh, but I say, Miss Converse, do listen to me! I say – Oh good Lord –

Priscilla (*advancing on the sleeping* **Willie**)   I'm crazy about this boy! (*She flops down beside* **Willie***, who wakes up with a start and tries to wriggle away from her.*) Oh, you cute thing! (*She ruffles his hair.*)

Willie   Leave me alone! Desmond! Somebody! Tell her to leave me alone!

Priscilla   No, you stay right here. Now! That's fine. (*He quiets down.*)

Philip (*sitting near her*)   Miss Converse, I want you to believe that my intentions are absolutely honourable. Good Lord, you've got the wrong idea about me.

Priscilla (*to* **Willie**)   I think you're perfectly marvellous. I'll take you back to the States as a mascot. (*To* **Philip**.) Leave me alone – you're not safe. Now I'm going to take off my shoes – yes, right now. (*She takes them off and settles down for sleep.*)

Philip (*looking round*)   Dammit – it's awful. I've never been spoken to like this before.

Gerald (*holding* **Pearl**'s *hand – they are sitting in a remote corner*)   Pearl, you're adorable. May I kiss you? Just a little one on the forehead.

Pearl (*fluttering*)   Oh, really, Doctor Codd, you shouldn't! I don't know what Mummie would say – really, I think I'd better go home! (*She puts her arms confidingly round his neck.*)

Gerald (*slightly taken aback*)   She won't know. My dear child, I might be your father.

Deirdre *rises and goes towards them. The others watch the scene appalled.* **Gerald** *sees her advancing and instantly kisses* **Pearl** *with immense efficiency on the mouth.*

Deirdre (*tensely*)   Gerald!

Gerald   Yes, Deirdre? Going to bed so early? Well, perhaps you're right – all these exams take a lot out of you –

Deirdre   Have you anything to say?

Gerald   Why – er no, Deirdre.

Deirdre   I've had just as much of this as I can stand, but this is more than I can bear. You've insulted me in every possible way. (*She chokes with fury.*)

Connie (*going over to her*)   Oh Deirdre, do keep your temper!

Deirdre (*screaming at her*)   I *am* keeping it –

Europa   Come now, let's talk this over – much better really – we'll hold a little conference –

Gerald   But Deirdre, I'm only acting according to your own ideas. I thought you were above any feeling of this kind. After all, these little chemical attractions *will* arise –

Deirdre   Shut up! (*She slaps his face. There is an instant's horrified silence, and then* **Gerald** *seizes* **Deirdre** *and shakes her.* **Desmond** *claps his hands and slides to the floor.*)

Desmond   Up the repuberlick!

Gerald (*smacking* **Deirdre**)   You little bully! I'll teach you!

Philip (*shaken to his foundations*)   Good Lord! I say, this is perfectly awful!

Harry (*rushing forward*)   I say, old man, what are you doing?

Deirdre (*breathlessly*)   This finishes everything – everything, do you hear? (*She bursts into tears and makes for the door.*)

Gerald (*rushing after her*)   Deirdre – listen. (*The door is slammed in his face.*)

Desmond   This is a terrible party.

Pearl   Ooh, what have I done! I didn't mean to do any harm.

Connie (*viciously*)   Deirdre is engaged to Gerald, you know.

Pearl   I didn't know – nobody told me – oh, take me home somebody. I want to go home – oh, Mummie!

Philip   Yes, I think we'd all better go home.

Gerald (*aghast*)   What have I done?

Terence (*piloting* **Gerald** *over to the bar*)   Come and have a drink, old man.

Gerald (*suffering himself to be led*)   Good God – what have I done?

Desmond   You've overacted – simply overacted –

Gerald (*piteously to* **Egosmith**)   She'll never forgive me – never!

Desmond (*waving his hand vaguely*)   She will. Call tomorrow, not in the morning.

Terence   Really, I'm almost shaken out of my usual indifference. A most enjoyable experience.

Toots   Aren't you a cruel devil? (*She stares at him.*)

Europa   I'll really have to be going. The Conference is beginning at ten, you know. Dr Katteracts, the Czecho-Slovakian Representative, is to speak on 'Nationalisation of the Mushroom Industry', and I must be there. You know, there's a future for mushrooms in this country –

Connie   Harry and I are engaged. We're going to be married soon. (*She takes* **Harry**'*s hand.*)

Harry   Yes, Connie's coming out to Kenya with me.

The others gather round, all except **Willie** *and* **Priscilla**, *who slumber peacefully near the gramophone.*

Terence (*without turning*)   Where are you going to, my pretty maid? I'm going to Kenya, sir, she said.

Desmond (*weeping*)   My poor little sister!

Toots (*embracing her*)   And I'll be bridesmaid, the professional bridesmaid. I'm so glad, darling.

Gerald   I hope you'll be very happy. (*He buries his head in his hands.*)

Philip   Congratulations. That's very good news.

Europa   How jolly! This is delightful. Connie, I hope you'll get your trousseau handwoven from Bracken Industries –

Terence (*followed by* **Egosmith**)   Allow me to add to the chorus of congratulations!

Connie (*without looking at him*)   Thank you.

Terence (*swaying a little*)   'Love me little! Love me long,
    Is the burden of my song'

– eh, Middleton? Sound man, Middleton. Content with very little. Knows his place. (**Harry** *takes a step forward.*)

Connie (*between them*)   Please –

Terence   Reliable! Guaranteed unbreakable!

Toots (*nervously*)   Oh, let's dance! Put the gramophone on, somebody!

Philip   Time to be going home.

Connie (*hastily*)   Time to go, Harry – (*She pushes him towards the door.*) Go home now. (*She looks at him entreatingly. He gives in.*)

Harry   All right, Connie.

Terence (*laughing: possessed by a devil*)   Good dog, Tray! Always comes when his *mistress* calls! No, no – don't misunderstand me, Middleton.

Harry *pushes* **Connie** *away, and makes a step towards* **Terence**.

Connie   Harry! Please go –

Terence   I've always said – where would we be without the conventions? Consistently! Haven't I, Egosmith?

Harry   You'd better be careful, Killigrew.

Terence   Careful? Why should I be careful?

Harry   Because you've said enough.

Terence   Said enough! No, you can't be serious! (*He lurches towards* **Connie**.) 'Since there's no help for it, come let us kiss and part' –

Harry *knocks him down.* **Connie** *gasps and makes a quick movement towards* **Terence**. **Egosmith** *watches her, smiling.* **Terence** *sprawls against her dress. She jerks her skirt away contemptuously.* **Harry** *stands perfectly still, breathing hard.*

Connie (*going to the door*)   This is impossible.

Harry (*turning*)   I'm awfully sorry, Connie.

Connie   It's all right, Harry. It wasn't your fault. You couldn't help it. (*Her face works. Suddenly she bursts into tears.*) Everything's vile! I wish I were dead. (*She goes.*)

Desmond   Women and children first. I'll go down with the ship – whoopee!

Terence *sits up.* **Harry** *tries to help him. He waves him away with drunken dignity.*

Terence   No – the guard dies, but does not surrender. (**Egosmith** *helps him up.* **Terence** *faces* **Harry**.) No, don't apologise – say nothing – (*He turns and sees* **Philip***'s expression of shocked dismay.*) Get out of my way, you smug, smiling ape! Get out – the laugh is on you –

Philip *skips nimbly out of the way.* **Terence** *makes for the bar.* **Philip** *looks at* **Harry** *and taps his forehead significantly.*

Harry   If we were anywhere else I'd knock the head off you – you dirty . . .

Terence (*leaning against the counter and watching* **Harry**)   *Mortuum flagellas*.[6] Foolish fellow! Waste no more time beating the dead. Go and kick the negroes;[7] it's more profitable . . .

He turns.

Harry   Damned swine!

Philip (*restraining him*)   It's all right, Middleton, – the chap's off his head. It's the poetry; they all go like that!

Toots (*interposing fiercely*)   Leave him alone, can't you?

Pearl (*wailing suddenly from the background*)   Take me home somebody – take me home!

Toots   Shut up! or I'll strangle you.

Pearl *subsides with a startled hiccup.* **Toots** *gathers up her things.*

Europa (*enveloping herself in what appears to be a bathrobe of an early Irish Queen*)   Yes, indeed, we must *all* go. Well, it has been such a jolly party. (*She goes over to* **Terence**, *who is leaning on the bar-counter with his head in his hands.*) – and you, Terence Killigrew, I want you to help with my Rural Cultural Organisation. We want to get the Intelligentsia *interested*.

Terence   Give them all a bloody Revolution and blow the Intelligentsia to hell!

Europa (*taken aback*)   *Gracious!* Poor Terence!

Toots   Go home, Europa! Philip take Europa home – oh, and Gerald, do you mind taking Pearl?

Gerald (*making for the door*)   I will not –

Pearl   Ohhh – *Mum*mie!

Gerald (*in a stage whisper*)   And listen – don't let this outside the house – keep tonight's happenings to yourself – you know what Dublin is –

Toots, Desmond, Philip, Europa (*speaking all together*)   Yes! We know what Dublin is!

Desmond   It's been marvellous having you – come again soon.

He holds out his hand – **Gerald** *slams the door in his face.*

Toots   Harry, you take Pearl home –

Harry   Yes, oh yes, certainly. Come on, Miss – er –

---

6   The phrase refers to flogging something already dead; flogging a dead horse.
7   The original text uses a more offensive term, replaced here with 'negroes'.

Pearl (*sniffing*)   Harris. Oh, thank you so much. Mummie will be so anxious.

Harry   'Night, everyone.

He goes, **Pearl** *fluttering before him.*

Philip   By the way, I'll see Miss Converse back to her hotel –

He approaches **Priscilla**.

Toots   Splendid. I'm all right – I live next door.

Europa (*indicating* **Priscilla** *with a sweeping gesture*)   The results of Prohibition. Exactly as Mother predicted in 1927.

Toots (*shaking the Sleeping Beauty*)   Wake up, Priscilla! Wake up! We're all going –

Priscilla (*yawning and rising with perfect grace*)   Going? Is the party over? (*She looks at the sleeping* **Willie**.) Isn't he cunning? (*She stands up, swaying slightly.*) Where does the Archbishop live? I'm going to call on him right now. (*She makes for the door.*)

Philip (*following her, scandalised*)   Oh, you can't do that – I say, Miss Converse – you're coming with me. I'm driving you back to the hotel.

Priscilla (*with hideous meaning*)   Oh, no, you won't. *You're* not safe. (**Philip** *winces.*) I'm going to tell the Archbishop what I think about you.

Europa (*consulting hastily with* **Toots**)   We'll *pretend* we're going to the Archbishop, but we can take her to the hotel instead –

Philip (*to* **Europa**)   Yes, you go ahead, and wait in the car.

Willie (*struggling over to* **Desmond***, who's wandering round shaking hands with everyone*)   Des, that's a terrible woman – I'm afraid of her, Des.

Europa (*shaking hands with* **Desmond**)   Goodbye, Desmond – it's been delightful.

Desmond   Darling, it's been marvellous having you – come again soon.

Europa   Remember you're taking a Designing class at the MFL rooms for me. Don't forget. Oh what a head I'm going to have at the Conference! Goodbye. (*She goes.*)

Priscilla   I'm going to the Archbishop. I'm going right now. Where's Willie? He's coming too.

Willie (*clinging to* **Desmond**)   I'm not! I'm not! Take her away!

Philip   I'll drive you there – now, Miss Converse, Europa is coming too – she's waiting in the car.

Toots (*whooshing her towards the door*)   If you don't go quick the Archbishop will be in bed.

Priscilla (*giggling*)   Oh, the cunning thing! (*To* **Philip**.) Lead on, you big ham. (*She reaches the door piloted by* **Philip***; at the door she suddenly becomes immensely* *dignified and polite.*) It's been perfectly marvellous. I'm crazy about Dublin. If you're ever in Boston do come and see me, please –

Desmond (*shaking hands*)   Goodbye, darling – it's been marvellous having you – come again soon –

Priscilla (*pointing to* **Willie**)   I'm crazy about that boy.

Philip (*opening the door*)   Quick now – come along, Miss Converse –

Toots   For pity's sake, be quiet going down. Don't wake up the parents. Desmond's future hangs on his father's temper.

Desmond (*almost sobering up*)   Yes, darling, my future –

Priscilla (*sailing into the passage*)   Whoopee! Hotcha!

Philip (*with a look of agony*)   Goodnight. It's been a splendid party – (*He closes the door.*)

Toots   We are alone. Peace at last. (*There is a tremendous crash off.*)

Desmond   There goes my future. Oh, God!

Toots   I think Priscilla fell downstairs. It's all right; there's the hall door. They're gone. (*She closes the door again and sails over to the bar.* **Egosmith** *is sitting beside* **Terence**. *To* **Terence**.) Well, you've made a nice mess of things!

Terence   Nothing in us endures! In three months she will have forgotten all this –

Toots   Who? Connie? No – there are some things time can only cover with a little dust. Well, I'm off – goodbye.

Terence   No, don't go for a moment. (*He takes her hand and looks at her.*) We should have met before –

Toots (*melodramatically*)   We shall meet, I trust, in Heaven –

Terence   Tomorrow I shall die. But you must save yourself. Cease running hither and thither seeking in others that which you should find in yourself. Withdraw now before it is too late. Stand alone. Be independent of these follies.

Toots   Brother, your words pierce my very soul.

Terence (*ironically*)   Sister, the libertine invariably moralises in his cups.

Toots   I must go. Already the sun rises in the East. (*She turns to* **Egosmith**.) Farewell, ghost. See your companion safely to his rest. (*She goes slowly to the door.*)

Terence (*watching her*)   Nymph, in thy orisons be all my sins remembered.

Toots   Brother, something tells me we shall meet again.

Terence   Once this side of Hades.

Toots   Brother in misfortune; weary fellow-traveller; last of a dying race. One whom I might have loved – Hail, and Farewell. (*She goes.*)

Desmond   Willie, isn't this a terrible party?

Willie   I'm afraid to go home, afraid to go home.

Terence   And now I *must* go. There is no apparent reason why I should prolong the disgusting business of living. A speedy exit is clearly indicated. Horace, come here. (**Egosmith** *comes over to him.* **Terence** *puts his hand on his shoulder.*) Shall I leap into the surging waters of Dublin Bay in the darkest hour before dawn and finish with a flourish? Or shall I blow my brains before the looking-glass, and bespatter the surrounding plush with my good red blood? We shall see – Open the door, old man. (**Egosmith** *does so.*) And now into the night that covers me. (*He turns to* **Willie** *and* **Desmond**, *who watch him open-mouthed.*) Farewell, Brothers; remember the password – *Morituri, morituros salutant.* (*He goes.*)

Desmond (*vacantly*)   It was marvellous having you – come again soon. What does he mean? I'm not dead yet.

Willie (*hilariously*)   Goodbye – whoopee! Oh, I'm afraid to go home!

Desmond   Well, if you stay here you'll have to sleep in the bath – so there! Come and tidy up.

Willie (*singing to himself*)   Come and tidy up. Come and tidy up.

Desmond (*staring hopelessly in front of him*)   My future – I must think of my future! (*He drinks the remains of a glass, and starts singing – 'Youth's the season made for Joy, Love is then a Duty' –*) Come here, Willie. (**Willie** *trots over to him obediently, carrying a load of bottles.*) Listen, Willie. (*He sings the first two lines again.*) Listen, Willie, if you hear anyone singing that song, strike him across the face.

Willie (*stupidly*)   . . . strike him across the face.

Desmond   Yes, because it's a bloody lie. Do you hear, a bloody lie.

Willie (*repeating it mechanically*)   . . . a bloody lie.

Act Three

Scene: The **Millingtons**' *sitting room.*

Time: Four o'clock in the afternoon of the following day. It is blustering March weather outside. Throughout the act rain is blown in gusts against the windows. **Desmond** *is lying on the sofa half covered in rugs. He is half asleep.* **Toots** *peeps furtively round the door; she is carrying her hat in her hand and looks considerably worse for the wear.*

Toots (*in a hoarse whisper*)   Where's everybody? Are you alone?

Desmond (*starting up*)   Is that you, Toots? Come in and close the door. The house, as you can see for yourself, is under a cloud. Deirdre is upstairs crying her eyes out over the sex-life of crabs or something equally scientific and depressing –

Toots (*creeping over to the fire*)   . . . and Gerald's outrageous behaviour. (*She looks in the glass.*) The Living Corpse! (*She lights a cigarette.*) Last night finished me!

Desmond   Last night! – Oh God! I didn't get up till one. I couldn't look at lunch, so Mary brought me a cup of Bovril a few minutes ago. Would you like some?

Toots   No, thanks! I'll wait for tea. You're very bad. Can I do anything for you? Rub your head, or sing you to sleep?

Desmond (*rising on his elbow*)   Don't touch the piano till I'm unconscious. (*He falls back.*) Oh God, I'm so depressed. (*The telephone rings, he springs up.*) That damn thing has never ceased today.

Toots   Hallo! Oh, hallo! Is that you? Do you want Desmond? Yes, he's here. It's Europa.

Desmond (*grimacing*)   Oh God! (*He takes the receiver.*) Europa, my angel, how are you? What – who? Priscilla? No, I don't know anything about her. I hope she's dead. I tell you I don't know who the people at my party were. I hope they're all dead. I hoped *you* were dead. No, Europa, I never promised anything of the sort. No. I won't, I *won't*. My darling, I'll be in London next week. Pray God. Goodbye, darling. (*He bangs down the receiver.*) That bitch has finished me! My dear, it appears Priscilla promised to meet some moth-eaten old uncle of hers at the Dail or somewhere, and when they went round to the Shelbourne to call for her she'd gone to London by the morning mail. Papa cabled or something.

Toots   What an escape for Priscilla!

Desmond (*settling down again*)   And that appalling Europa said I promised to take a class for Design in her industry. I must have been awfully drunk. (*He sits up.*) Was I very drunk?

Toots   We all were. I have a terrible feeling that I told Egosmith *all* my past. I remember leaning on that counter and baring my soul to him –

Desmond   My dear, I'm perfectly certain he's gone away loaded with guilty secrets. Oh God, I've got a vague idea that dreadful things happened last night and I feel worse things are about to happen –

Toots   Nothing worse could happen. Connie got engaged to Harry –

Desmond   Out of pique. Bad enough for Harry. What else? Oh Lord – Gerald! What happened? Tell me quick –

Toots   Gerald was disgraceful. He treated Deirdre like dirt, and got off with the Snowy-Breasted Pearl –

Desmond   Good. I put him up to it – to make Deirdre jealous, and teach her a lesson.

Toots   How divinely old-fashioned. It always works, of course.

Desmond   Yes, it was all carefully planned. I rehearsed Gerald for it myself. He overacted a bit, but that's unavoidable with Pearl.

Toots   She's rather awful.

Desmond   She's got a mother-fixation.

Toots   What's that?

Desmond   I don't know, but she's got it. Mark my words, Diana Ellerslie, Gerald will come crawling round this afternoon wanting to kiss and make up. He hasn't enough courage to carry the thing to its logical conclusion.

Toots   Deirdre will have a wonderful time. (*She imitates* **Deirdre***'s cultured voice.*) 'As far as I'm concerned, Gerald, the thing is over and done with. We'll say no more about it.' But she'll refer to it every day regularly for the next ten years.

Desmond   No, I'll have a few words with Doctor Parr, before the interview takes place.

Toots   You think yourself very clever, don't you?

Desmond   Brilliantly superficial! Brilliantly superficial!

Toots   Oh, why do we go on giving these awful parties?

Desmond   You're looking like a female Savanarola, darling. What's wrong?

Toots   I'm sick of my life. Running aimlessly here, there, and everywhere. Chattering, forever chattering. I wish I was a farmer's daughter.

Desmond   . . . and starved on yon green. Idyllic in theory.

Toots   But it's real. We're not real people, Desmond; we're only imitation. That party last night finished me –

Desmond   Every party finishes you for a day or two, until your liver settles down.

Toots   It's not liver.

Desmond   It is. Everything in life boils down to your stomach.

Toots   How disgusting! Oh, you don't understand!

Desmond   Oh, God – don't I?

Toots   I want to get out of this and be alone somewhere, and work out my own salvation.

Desmond   Get thee to a nunnery –

Toots   Not a bad idea. (*The telephone rings. She picks up the receiver.*) Hallo! Who? Oh, Desmond – yes, he's here. Come on, it's Philip.

Desmond   My dear, he acts on me like an emetic. You talk to him.

Toots   In that case perhaps I'd better. Hallo! It's Toots Ellerslie speaking. Desmond says he's too ill to come to the phone. Yes, they're all out. Who? I don't know where she is. Oh, wait, yes I do. She's gone to London. Went this morning. Yes, I could let you have her address. No bother. Goodbye! (*To* **Desmond**.) My dear, Philip has called at the Shelbourne to take Priscilla down to the vaults of St Michans[8] to see the corpses, and he found she'd gone. He's heartbroken. He wants her address.

Desmond   What that girl has missed! The Corpses of St Michans and Senator FitzGibbon. Well, they might easily change places, and you'd never know. Have you ever met the Senator?

Toots (*yawning*)   No, what's he like?

Desmond   Like something left over from the eighteenth century, undergoing a slow process of decay.

Toots   Philip's not a bad little boy.

Desmond   So commonplace, and oh, so happy. I wish I were Philip.

Toots   But darling, there are so many Philips.

Desmond (*solemnly*)   They are the backbone of the bourgeoisie.

Toots   Where's Connie?

Desmond   Didn't you know the engagement's all fixed up? Harry came round at eleven and staged the He-Man stuff. I wasn't there, but I can imagine it –

Toots (*imitating* **Harry**)   Extraordinarily passionate, extraordinarily passionate.

Desmond   They're to be married in haste next month and go straight to Kenya.

Toots   Poor Harry!

---

8   St Michan's is a medieval church in Dublin, near the river Liffey. Its crypt is home to a number of mummified corpses, who are clearly visible because their coffins have disintegrated. The main four corpses are called the unknown woman, the nun, the thief and the crusader.

Desmond   Aye, aye. He's got a bad time ahead with that selfish bitch. Anyway, Lousy Leopold's got the push.

Toots   Who?

Desmond   Terence, Tormentor of Himself.

Toots   What's going to be the end of Terence Killigrew?

Desmond   My dear, he's one of the many minor poets, whose names are writ in whiskey.

Toots   Egosmith is queer. He gets on my nerves with that timid smile and perpetual silence. Have you ever heard him speak?

Desmond   No, but Terence makes up for it. Toots, I'm frightfully worried about my future. I have to let Derek know finally tomorrow whether I'm going or not, he can only keep the job open till then –

Toots   Has your mother spoken to the male parent?

Desmond   I don't know. She never came near me this morning. I was sick in bed. There's an atmosphere of disgrace. I'm only hoping Connie's engagement will keep Father fairly normal. I expect Mother in any moment. She's lying down.

Toots   Terence didn't show himself here today, did he?

Desmond   No, thank God. What's the matter. You're not falling in love with him, are you?

Toots   Ah, don't be a fool! I'm only worried about him.

Desmond   Worried about him – why?

Toots   People who talk about committing suicide never do, do they?

Desmond   No, of course not.

Toots   I wonder –

Desmond   Surely you don't think –

The door opens cautiously and **Gerald** *peers in. He looks ghastly.*

Gerald (*timidly*)   Is Deirdre in?

Desmond   Enter First Murderer.

Gerald (*coming in*)   Hello, Toots –

Toots   You brute!

Gerald (*timidly*)   Don't rub it in. I hardly slept last night –

Desmond   You did very well last night, Gerald, very well indeed. Continue on the same lines and you'll live happily ever afterwards.

Gerald (*sitting down*)   I couldn't do that.

Desmond   You don't mean to tell me you're going to apologise?

Gerald   There's nothing else for me to do.

Desmond (*sitting up and throwing off the rugs*)   My dear Gerald, don't you see the game's in your hands? Don't attempt to apologise. Strike her again if necessary.

Gerald (*rising excitedly*)   Now look here –

Desmond   Ah, don't be a bloody fool! You have her where you want her – Oh, don't mind Toots – she knows all! Besides she's one of the family.

Toots   That's right, Gerald. Of course she gave herself away last night –

Gerald   But –

Desmond   Ask to be released from the engagement –

Gerald (*in a frenzy between the two of them*)   This is –

Toots   Say there's somebody else.

Desmond   You needn't mention names. Just imply it.

Gerald   Listen! I will not.

Toots   She'll eat out of your hand.

Desmond   – hold you to the engagement.

Toots   – you'll do the forgiving and live happily ever afterwards.

Gerald (*sinking into a chair and wiping his forehead*)   Well, I'm damned!

Desmond   Well, that's settled. I'm glad you've seen reason. Now everything will be all right.

Toots (*powdering her nose*)   If you'd gone and cried in her lap now, she'd have the whip-hand for ever.

Gerald (*weakly*)   But this is awful – awful!

Desmond   Now, Toots, come on downstairs. I'll send Deirdre down to you. She's reading in her room. We'll leave you to it – only ten minutes, mind. We're both very weak and need the comfort of the fireside. (*He sails majestically to the door, followed by* **Toots**.)

Gerald (*jumping up*)   Look here, Desmond, this is impossible. I can't do it –

Desmond   Didn't Deirdre react to my plans for last night? Didn't she?

Gerald   Yes, I suppose she did.

Desmond   Well, carry on. Now listen, I know Deirdre. I've lived with her for twenty-one years. She's a self-righteous bully –

Toots   A self-satisfied shrew –

The door opens and **Deirdre** *comes in. She is wearing a navy-blue dress of extreme severity. Her face is pale and shows signs of recent tears. She is staggering under a load of books. For a moment she stares in surprise at* **Desmond** *and* **Toots**, *who are both considerably taken aback. Then she looks at* **Gerald**, *who shuffles his feet nervously and looks at the floor.*

Toots   Deirdre darling, have you recovered from the party yet? We were just saying how marvellous you looked.

Deirdre (*icily*)   Good afternoon, Toots. Are you both going out or coming in?

Desmond   Going out, sweet sister mine. (**Gerald** *looks at him imploringly.*) Goodbye for the present, Gerald. (*He frowns at* **Gerald**; **Toots** *makes a hideous face at the unfortunate man behind* **Deirdre**'s *back. The happy couple exit laughing.*)

Deirdre   Please sit down, Gerald. I've something to say to you.

Gerald (*remaining standing*)   Yes, yes – dear . . .

Deirdre   Sit down, Gerald. There is no need to look so frightened.

Gerald (*stung*)   Frightened! What should I be frightened about? (*He comes down.*) I've something to say to you.

Deirdre (*coldly*)   I suppose you mean to apologise.

Gerald   Certainly not. I want you to release me from our engagement.

Deirdre   What do you mean, Gerald? (*She is completely taken aback.*)

Gerald (*looking straight ahead*)   For some time past I have been convinced that our chemical attraction for each other was not working out as it should –

Deirdre   Chemical attraction?

Gerald (*glibly*)   Chemical attraction. You mentioned it the other day. I've been thinking things over, and really, Deirdre, it would be better to end the thing at once. You will easily find another chemical affinity – so shall I. Now my time is valuable and I would be grateful if you would let me have the ring before I go.

Deirdre   Are you mad?

Gerald   Come, come. Let us have no stupid sentimentality about it. The ring which you now wear on the third finger of your left hand cost me a considerable sum of money.

Deirdre   You can't be serious!

Gerald   Serious, of course I'm serious! You don't think I'm joking, do you? The ring please – it will be useful later on.

Deirdre   How dare you! How dare you!

Gerald   Deirdre! You surprise me! I thought you were above this kind of thing – sentimentality and passion! Good Lord – you made me feel like a criminal if I tried to kiss you. You were so damn superior I sometimes wondered how I ever had the courage to propose to you. But then I thought you were a real person worth winning – now I know you're just an ordinary jealous –

Deirdre (*almost screaming*)   I'm not! I'm not!

Gerald   You are. You're jealous of Pearl.

Deirdre   That little fool! She's mentally deficient.

Gerald (*with a bland smile*)   She's very attractive.

Deirdre   She's got fat legs.

Gerald (*delightedly*)   There you are – obviously jealous.

Deirdre   Of course if you *prefer* that type –

Gerald   It's more pliable.

Deirdre   You really want to break our engagement?

Gerald   Frankly, I do.

Deirdre   You mean you don't love me any more?

Gerald   I'm afraid –

Deirdre   Please don't bother to explain – (*She takes off the ring and hands it to* **Gerald** *without looking at him.*)

Gerald   Thanks very much. Well now – I'd better go. I hope, of course, you'll be very happy.

Deirdre   I hope you will too.

Gerald (*from the door*)   Er – goodbye.

Deirdre   Goodbye.

Gerald   Well, I'm going now.

Deirdre   Oh, Gerald! – just a moment.

Gerald (*coming back*)   Yes, Deirdre?

Deirdre (*gulping*)   Is there – is there anyone else?

Gerald (*shrugging his shoulders*)   Oh, just a mere passing chemical attraction – it stirs me biologically for the moment – and then –

Deirdre   If you say that again I shall scream!

Gerald   Say what?

Deirdre   Chemical – (*She bursts into tears.*)

Gerald (*hovering*)   But I'm only quoting what you said!

Deirdre   I didn't say passing – (*She sobs.*)

Gerald   It was your hatred of sentimentality. I'm rather a romantic person – possibly it's stupid, but there you are!

Deirdre (*desperate*)   Oh, Gerald!

Gerald   Yes, Deirdre.

Deirdre (*flinging her arms around him*)   I am sentimental! Oh, I am sentimental!

Gerald (*releasing himself*)   Deirdre, come – you must get a grip on yourself.

Deirdre   I won't get a grip on myself. Gerald, don't leave me! Please say you love me!

Gerald   Now Deirdre, do you still look upon me simply as a biological necessity?

Deirdre   No, you know I don't. (*She attempts to embrace him again. He wards her off and walks towards the piano.*)

Gerald   This is very difficult.

Deirdre (*following him*)   Oh, please forgive me, Gerald! Please forgive me.

Gerald   Very well, Deirdre, I forgive you. But it must never happen again. Never, do you hear? (*He advances on her threateningly.*)

Deirdre (*cowering*)   No, Gerald. I promise.

Gerald   And for heaven's sake stop filling me up with all this super-culture.

Deirdre   Oh, yes – no, I mean.

Gerald (*kissing her condescendingly on the forehead*)   Now I must go – it's late. I have to go out to the hospital.

Deirdre (*humbly*)   We're still engaged, aren't we?

Gerald   Yes, of course.

Deirdre   What about the other woman?

Gerald (*forgetting his part*)   What other woman?

Deirdre   Oh, then – there isn't anybody else?

Gerald   No, of course not – (*he succumbs*) – darling!

Deirdre   Oh, what a lie!

They embrace fervently. **Mrs Millington** *enters unobserved. She is dressed for going out. Furs, feathers, liberty-scarves and old lace twisted round her in all directions.*

Gerald (*fiercely*)   But I'm very violent when aroused, Deirdre, and if you behave like that again I won't answer for the consequences –

Deirdre (*shrinking*)   Oh Gerald, you wouldn't hurt me –

Gerald (*demoniacally*)   I would! I'd thrash you within an inch of your life. (*He sees* **Mrs Millington***'s horrified face.*) Of course not, darling. (*He releases her.*)

Mrs Millington Oh, I'm so sorry. Is that you, Gerald? Has anyone seen Desmond?

Deirdre He was here a moment ago.

Gerald I think he's in the library. Shall I call him, Mrs Millington?

Mrs Millington No, don't bother – yes, please do – it *is* rather important. So sorry to trouble you, Gerald – so tiresome – (*She sits on the sofa.*)

Gerald Not at all, Mrs Millington. (*He goes.*)

Deirdre Mother, your hat's on crooked. (*She straightens it.*) Are you playing bridge?

Mrs Millington Yes, and I can't tell you the agonies I am going through. I never slept a wink all night, just thinking – thinking –

Deirdre Why on earth? Are you ill?

Mrs Millington (*dramatically*) Contract, dear, contract. This is my first outing since I started contract bridge – you know I've been taking lessons.

Deirdre You gave me a fright. I thought it was something to do with Connie's engagement.

Mrs Millington (*laughing*) Gracious, no! Deirdre, I'm not going to allow anything to worry me in the future. I've been reading such a wonderful book; it has changed everything for me. (**Gerald** *comes back.*) Thank you, dear Gerald –

Gerald He's coming up now.

Mrs Millington I've just been telling Deirdre about a wonderful little book I'm reading – *In Tune with the Infinite*. Deirdre, you should read it out to Gerald in the evenings. I often think it's very sad how you young people neglect the spiritual side –

Gerald I quite agree with you, Mrs Millington. Only too true. Well, I must be off to the hospital. I'll look in on my way back about six o'clock. We might go to a picture, darling –

Deirdre That would be marvellous, Gerry.

Gerald Six o'clock sharp.

Mrs Millington Don't drive too fast, Gerald. The roads are shockingly slippery with all this rain. What the Government is thinking of I don't know –

Gerald You can blame the Government for almost everything *but* the rain –

Mrs Millington They should do something about the scandalous way people drive –

Deirdre Your tie's crooked, Gerald. (*She straightens it.*)

Mrs Millington (*flowing gently on*) That was a terrible thing in the papers this morning.

Deirdre What was that, Mother?

Mrs Millington   Poor old General Ritchie knocked off his tricycle in Killiney, and left unconscious on the road. A dear old man; I used to meet him at Our Dumb Friends League –

Gerald   Thank you, darling. Yes, I've got a clean handkerchief, and I washed behind my ears.

Toots and **Desmond** *appear in the doorway. They stand there grinning at the lovers, who are quite unconscious of their appearance.*

Gerald   Goodbye, darling – six o'clock then.

Deirdre   And I don't mind if you're late, darling.

Gerald   I'll do my best, sweet. (*He catches sight of the intruders.*) Damn! Blast! I beg your pardon, Mrs Millington – (*He bolts self-consciously from the room.*)

Toots (*entering*)   And so those two found at last their little-cottage-of-dreams-come-true.

Desmond (*going eagerly over to his mother*)   Yes, Mother – you wanted me?

Mrs Millington (*ignoring him*)   Toots, dear – how's your mother? Better, I hope?

Toots   She's still rather rotten.

Mrs Millington   Poor dear! She does suffer so! I do wish she'd try one of those new diets, Christian Science, or Theosophy. I must lend her a little book which has been the greatest help to me . . .

Desmond   Mother, have you spoken to Father?

Mrs Millington (*making a tour of inspection*)   Your soup, Desmond. Why do you leave it there? And one of the good cups too. Very tiresome of you.

Desmond   I'm sorry, – I'm sorry. Now listen, Mother –

Connie *comes in, dressed in picturesque black and looking like death.*

Toots   Here comes the bride!

Mrs Millington   Oh, there you are, darling. I got these patterns for you. (*She fumbles in her bag.*)

Desmond   Oh my God! (*He stalks over to the piano, sits down, plays a crashing chord and then buries his head in his hands.*)

Connie (*in a dead voice*)   Hello, Toots.

Toots   Change and decay all around I see.

Connie   Harry's coming to dinner, Mother.

Mrs Millington   I'm so glad about all this. Father is so pleased – dear Harry is so suitable in every way.

Connie   Yes – isn't he?

Desmond (*back to his mother*)   Mother, did you ask Father about letting me try my luck in London?

Mrs Millington   Just a moment, Desmond. Don't be so impatient. Deirdre, put the soup cup on the mantelpiece.

Desmond   If you don't answer me I'll go mad!

Connie   What's the matter with you?

Mrs Millington   You needn't show temper, Desmond – it's all your own fault. I cannot describe what I went through last night. I went to bed with neuralgia and then your father was in one of his worst tempers. We were kept awake till dawn by drunken screams – yes, I repeat, drunken screams – coming from the studio – and I do depend on you, Deirdre, to keep some kind of order. It was all I could do to keep your father from rushing upstairs in his dressing-gown. And then some girl fell down the stairs just outside our door and, really, the language –

Desmond (*tearing his hair*)   Purgatory! Purgatory!

Mrs Millington   And then to crown everything, when your father went into the bathroom this morning he found a strange boy asleep in the bath –

Desmond   Willie! – oh God!

Mrs Millington   Yes indeed, as I afterwards found out, Willie Sullivan. I'd like to hear what his mother has to say. She's a very sweet woman, but she won't play contract –

Toots   And after that?

Mrs Millington   Your father removed him forcibly, and Mary gave him a cup of tea and sent him home – mercifully, he only lives a few doors down. Then do you think we could find a tooth-glass or a carafe? – and the *studio* – words can't describe the studio! What kind of drunken orgy took place there last night? I may as well tell you, Desmond, your father went off to the office this morning more like a fiend than I've ever seen him. Thank God you didn't appear –

Desmond   Yes, the party was a mistake. It was all a mistake. Did you ask him about London?

Mrs Millington   *In tune with the Infinite* – rather a beautiful title, I think.

Desmond   What did he say?

Mrs Millington   Don't badger me, Desmond. Really, one would think it was a matter of life and death.

Desmond   It is.

Mrs Millington   I'm afraid it will be a disappointment to you –

Desmond   Oh, so he turned it down?

Mrs Millington   Wouldn't hear of it. He said you are going to work in the office next year, or he'd throw you out on your neck to find your own living –

Desmond   But I *want* to earn my own living. It's only a question of getting started –

Mrs Millington   He said he never heard of anybody earning a living by Art –

Desmond   Oh God!

Mrs Millington   Don't be silly, Desmond. Your father has had frightful expenses this year, and now Connie's wedding –

Connie   Please leave me out of it – I'm going to be married in a registry office.

Mrs Millington   Now, Connie, don't be ridiculous –

Deirdre   I think it's an excellent plan.

Mrs Millington   I call it indecent. Think of your relations!

Connie   That's just what I am thinking of.

Toots   Think of your enemies – and I want to be a bridesmaid!

Mrs Millington   What would people say?

Desmond (*turning round violently*)   What would people say? What the hell does it matter what people say? Now, Mother, concentrate for one moment on what you were going to say. Did you explain everything to Father?

Connie   Damn my relations anyway. It's *my* wedding and I'll have it anyway I like –

Deirdre   Have you spoken to Harry about it?

Connie   Mind your own business!

Toots   The bridesmaids should wear cloth of gold and carry bouquets of dark red roses. (*She examines her face in the glass.*) At the moment I look like a bad case of leprosy.

Deirdre (*to* **Connie**)   Personally, I think you should take an aspirin and lie down.

Desmond   Circles! Circles! Everyone revolving in their own narrow little circle. (*He sits down.*) But what does my future matter? No, there are more important things – Connie's wedding for instance. Let's talk about Connie's wedding. She'll be married at St Anne's and all the traffic will be stopped. She'll have twelve bridesmaids, and one dear little trainbearer, who'll have to be taken out hurriedly in the middle of the solemn ceremony –

Mrs Millington   Desmond!

Desmond   Mother, what a mind you have – he was overcome with emotion –

Deirdre   Desmond, don't be silly. It's not Mother's fault, and you've nobody but yourself to blame for that terrible party.

Desmond (*turning on her savagely*)   And Deirdre, dear antiseptic Deirdre, will have a brisk ceremony at dawn. The church will be sprayed with carbolic and she'll wear a string of pure white pearls! Pearls! Pearls!

Deirdre   You deserve anything you get!

Desmond   *You* deserve anything you give, which won't be much!

Mrs Millington   The whole thing was disgraceful, and your father says quite firmly – *no more parties* –

Desmond   Mother, what made you marry that man?

Toots (*giggling*)   Desmond!

Deirdre   Really, Desmond, after all he is your father –

Desmond   I don't believe it – I don't believe it! D'you hear?

Mrs Millington   You are extremely coarse.

Desmond   Coarse! Don't make me laugh. Listen, how many times has that old man said I was no son of his? In this very room two nights ago he roared out he didn't know why to God he'd been cursed with such a ninny for a son! *Damn* him. Damn him to Hell! I hate him! I'll go into the office – (*He paces wildly up and down the room.*) I'll disgrace him! I'll forge cheques! I'll drink myself to death! (*He nearly collides with* **Mary**, *the maid, who is bringing in the tea.*) I'll (*He sinks into a chair.*) – have a cup of tea.

Mrs Millington   *Prenez garde!* (*She looks meaningly at the maid and then at* **Desmond**.) Toots, I've been reading such an interesting life of King Edward. I must send it to your mother – it's really quite scandalous –

Toots   Thank you, Mrs Millington – I'm sure Mother would adore it.

Mrs Millington (*floating over to* **Desmond**, *who is sitting with his head buried in his hands*)   Poor dear boy – it's all very tiresome.

Desmond (*ironically*)   It's not a headache, Mother. Listen, Mother –

Mrs Millington (*warningly*)   As I was saying – King Edward –

Deirdre   I won't be in for dinner, Mother. I'm going out with Gerry.

Desmond   I won't be in either.

Mrs Millington   Why, dear? There's your favourite dinner –

Desmond   I couldn't sit opposite that man who calls himself my father while there's a carving knife about! No, I'm going out to get drunk, vilely, helplessly drunk, then I'll stagger home and make a scene on the doorstep.

Mrs Millington   *Prenez garde, s'il vous plait.* Mary, tell Cook there'll only be four for dinner.

Mary   Yes, m'm. (**Mary** *goes.*)

Mrs Millington   Desmond, there's a time and a place for everything. I do beg that you control yourself before the servants –

Connie   Oh, do shut up, Desmond. You're not the only one with a shady future.

Desmond   Poor Harry – you'll put him in the white man's grave all right –

Mrs Millington (*gaily*)   Desmond, you'll break my heart. (*She inspects the tea-table.*) You're all driving me into my grave. Oh, I see Cook has made some of those shortcakes you like, Des! Deirdre, do look for my gloves and bag. Toots, are my glasses on the writing table? So tiresome – I can't see a thing without them. Oh, I'm so nervous! My first bridge party since I started contract, you know – (**Deirdre** *recovers the gloves and bag;* **Toots** *hands her the glasses.* **Connie** *throws another scarf around her.*) Thank you dear. Enjoy your tea, children. I won't be home till half-past seven. (*She reaches the door.*) Deirdre, try and make Gerald take a nerve tonic, he looked quite wild when I came in this afternoon. (*She turns to go and drops her bag.* **Toots** *retrieves it.*) Thank you, dear, tell your mother I'm sending in that book about King Edward. What an eye-opener; I wonder if they should –?

Toots   Should *what*, Mrs Millington?

Mrs Millington   – have all those Ladies-in-Waiting – it does seem so unnecessary. The neglect of the spiritual – that lies in the root of all this modern unrest. If only we could keep in tune with the infinite. Gracious, I'm late! Goodbye, darlings – (*She goes, murmuring 'Contract, contract'.*)

Desmond (*after a short but pregnant silence*)   The Mother of the Gracchi![9] That woman goes through life with her eyes firmly fixed on Two, no Trumps!

Connie   Nothing has ever really penetrated her consciousness. If I told her I was going to have a baby next week, she'd simply murmur 'how tiresome' and say what a pity she'd have to give up bridge for some time –

Deirdre   It's her upbringing – tight lacing, sealed windows and the Book of Genesis.

Desmond   She hands me my death-warrant, and talks about short-breads.

Toots   Don't take this so hard, Des. Life isn't altogether futile. You can go on with your painting as a side-line.

Desmond   Thanks, there are enough amateurs here already. No, you don't understand – how could you? You're normal. It's the loneliness that's driving me mad. I can't deceive myself, you know. I'm a very sensitive person. I know I'm unpopular. I know exactly what people say about me here – it all goes round in a vicious circle. But I can't help it – I haven't the guts. I'm a coward, I'm soft. The Lord helps them who help themselves and quite right too – (*He stands at the window looking out. The wavering sound of a cornet playing 'Let Me Like a Soldier Fall' comes from the street below.*) There's the cornet man playing in the rain – God help him!

---

9   The mother of the Gracchi was Cornelia, daughter of Scipio Africanus. She was known for her interest in the arts and her involvement in her sons' political careers. Desmond's comparison of his own mother to Cornelia appears to be an ironic comment about her detachment from her children and their lives.

Connie   You should resign yourself to the inevitable, Desmond.

Desmond   And what have you resigned yourself to?

Connie (*sighing*)   Harry –

Toots   Very nice too.

Desmond   Look at her radiant face!

Connie   Oh, shut up! You're not in the Sunbeam Class yourself!

Desmond   Twenty-one years have I looked out on this square, and I see us all here, struggling to escape from our environment, fighting against it, refusing to conform; and Life, like a big sausage-machine, descends upon the raw material, grinds it up, moulds us into the required shape, and throws us out again as nice, pink, conventional little sausages –

Connie   I *won't* give in!

Desmond   You'll be the first to give in – you weak piece of voluptuous affectation.

Connie (*viciously*)   At least I'm normal.

Desmond   True, Jezebel! You are distressingly normal. But fear not, the machine will twist me into the required shape, and I shall become as normal as Philip Pryce, as normal as Egosmith –

The cornet breaks uncertainly into 'Scenes That Are Brightest'. It grows perceptibly darker.

Toots   Egosmith isn't normal.

Connie   Don't be ridiculous.

Toots   He's an unquiet spirit. He's Terence Killigrew's *Doppleganger*. Listen, there's his voice in the wind.

Connie   Don't!

Deirdre   Who is Egosmith?

Toots   Egosmith is Terence. Terence is Egosmith; the two in one, Dr Jekyll and Mr Hyde; and it's war to the death between them. I wonder which will win? (*Pause.*) Perhaps even now the battle is over.

Connie   What do you mean?

Toots   Oh, I'm talking nonsense –

Connie (*hysterically*)   I know what you mean! You think Terence has killed himself. Go on say it!

Toots   Sit down! Make her sit down, Deirdre.

Connie   I won't sit down – I *won't*. Listen, I don't care if he *has* killed himself because he's a beast, d'you hear me? – a *beast*, and I hate him – I never want to see him again. If he comes near me I'll get Harry to thrash him –

Toots   Most satisfactory indeed. Well, why worry? You've got Harry. Sit down and be quiet.

Connie   I don't want Harry – that's the awful thing. Oh, what have I done? I'm caught; I can't get away!

Toots   Tell him that you've made a mistake. Get out of it now.

Connie   I can't, I haven't the courage. Oh, that party – that awful party!

Desmond   Why did I ever have it?

Connie   My punishment is only beginning; when I think of the future I wish I were dead.

Desmond   Nonsense! You'll settle down, and be very happy.

Harry *enters, wearing plus fours and looking the picture of health.*

Harry   What a day! I've just been for a breather; walked to Rathfarnham and back. I'm pretty well soaked. How's everyone? (*He goes over to the fire.*)

Desmond   Extraordinarily jolly. Extraordinarily jolly.

Connie   Sit down anywhere. Deirdre will give you tea. (*She starts making up her face.*)

Toots   I'm sorry about this wedding scheme of yours, Harry. Connie tells me you're going to be married in a registry office.

Harry   Not really! I say, good work! Do you really mean it Connie? (*He goes over to her and takes her hand. She withdraws it impatiently and moves away from him.*)

Connie   Of course.

Harry   Thank God! I was beginning to get all shaky at the thought of the church. That's splendid! (*He chuckles.*) The governor will be scandalised, but I'll bring him round.

Connie   You mean you'd rather be married in a registry office?

Harry   Of course! The job's done in a few minutes.

Connie (*slowly*)   Of course, if your father wouldn't like it –

Harry   Nonsense! I'll bring him round to it.

Connie   No, I couldn't think of it. It had better be in church. After all, I have to think of my relations.

Harry   Oh, look here, I thought you said –

Connie   Sit over there and take your tea – don't argue, please. I have a headache.

Harry   Headache? Good Lord, isn't there anything you can take for it?

Connie   No, nothing. Just leave me alone.

Harry *strolls over towards the window. The cornet player fades into the distance.*

Desmond   I suppose you haven't an old bowler hat you don't want, Harry?

Harry (*startled*)   Good God, no – why?

Desmond   Tomorrow I'm going to my father's office and I must wear the uniform –

Harry   By Jove! Congratulations! Good work!

Desmond   You're optimistic.

Harry   You're damn lucky. I wish I had a chance of a job here.

Toots   Good heavens! What words to I hear from a loyal servant of Empire?

Harry   I'd never have left Dublin, but the governor's only got his pension, you know, and when I left Trinity there didn't seem to be much chance of an opening here for my type. Practically all the chaps I knew were going abroad, so I just drifted out.

Connie   But I thought you just loved the wide-open spaces?

Harry   Well, I don't exactly give three rousing cheers, you know! It's damn lonely sometimes – However, 'needs must' as the poet Johnny says. (*He turns to the window.*) It's the mountains I miss the most.

Desmond   You can have them as far as I'm concerned.

Harry (*oblivious*)   I went to school up there. Extraordinarily fine view of the bay from Kilmashogue – extraordinarily fine. When I retire I'm going to buy a house near Rathfarnham. It's first-rate country.

Desmond   And a third-rate city.

Toots   Ah, no!

Harry   I'd like to be buried here.

Desmond   So we are. Buried alive.

Harry   Oh, hang it! I can't explain, but you know what I mean; it's part of us, somehow.

Toots   Yes, I know. We all revise it and run it down and run away from it – but we always drift back sometime. Dublin never lets a Dubliner go.

Desmond   Oh, God, the self-consciousness, the gossiping, the bigotry, the Imitation Chelsea, the Imitation Mayfair, the Imitation Bright Young People! And such *un*original sin!

Toots   Forget it! Try living in Manchester. Anyway I know what Harry means by Dublin. He means Merrion Square on a Spring morning, with the hawthorns breaking over the railings like the sea.

Deirdre   Yes, but what about this cathedral? So unhygienic.

Toots   Rathfarnham! Those green hills, and forlorn old houses scattered in the fields! It's all ours! And the chimes – the chimes of St Patrick on Christmas Eve! Don't you love those chimes, Desmond?

Desmond   Glory be to Guinness! To me it means another year gone by in this accursed city.

Toots   Wretched Youth! Doesn't the sweep of Killiney Bay mean anything to you? Have you ever stood on Baggot Street Bridge and thought you could sail straight up the canal into the sunset?

Desmond   No, but I've often stood on Baggot Street Bridge and thought I could throw myself straight into the canal!

Connie   Why didn't you?

Desmond   Because there was nobody kind enough to sew me into a sack and do it for me.

Harry   Come on, old chap – never say die.

Desmond   No, Life is just a colossal sausage-machine –

Toots   Oh, he's back to it again!

Desmond   And if you don't go through the machine, you're thrown out on the dust heap.

Harry (*going over to* **Connie**)   You look pale, old girl.

Connie   Please don't call me 'old girl'.

Harry   'Old Thing' then! Listen, darling, I think you ought to lie down. You look pretty fagged out. It was that damn party. That dame swine Killigrew upset you –

Connie   No, he didn't. Nobody upset me. Don't hang over me, please. You're making me nervous.

Harry   I'm sorry, darling.

Deirdre   If anybody wants any more tea say so now because I'm going to have these things taken out – (*She rings the bell.*)

Harry   If I may mention a painful subject, that madman Egosmith walked down to the Forty-Foot[10] last night after the party.

Toots   What on earth for?

Harry   I met Pryce this morning. Apparently he had some trouble getting that American girl to go home quietly, and when he was persuading her, Killigrew staggered out of your house, and gave them to understand he was going to sober up in the waters of that icy hole.

---

10 The Forty Foot is a promontory on the southern tip of Dublin Bay, from which people have been swimming in the Irish Sea all year round for more than 250 years. The water is deep, even at low tide.

Deirdre   Suicidal on a night like last night.

Connie (*starting*)   Suicidal!

Mary *comes in to clear away the tea things.*

Toots   Let's talk about anything but that party. Anything. Harry, have you ever tuned in to the infinite? So charming I think, and really the only solution to the sex problem . . . (*She becomes* **Mrs Millington**.)

Deirdre   Well, I'm going to get some reading done. When Dr Parr comes, will you tell him I'm in the library, Mary?

Mary   Yes, Miss Deirdre. (*She goes out with the tea-things.*)

Deirdre   And I really think it would be better if we all forgot about last night. Wipe it out. It's over and done with now. I for one will never refer to it again. (*She goes, with immense dignity.*)

Desmond   Smug little piece that!

Connie   It's awfully stuffy in here. (*The room is growing darker.*) Do you think we could have a window open?

Harry   There is a bit of fog. Wait a minute, dear, I'll do it. (*He goes to the window nearest the door and opens it. The sound of rain flowing in the gutter is heard.*)

Toots   Are you all right, Connie?

Connie   Yes, I'm perfectly all right.

A boy's voice calling 'Stop Press!' is heard in the distance. **Connie** *and* **Toots** *exchange swift looks.*

Harry   Hallo! There's a Stop Press.

Desmond (*jumping up and going to the window*)   'News of battle! News of battle, hark! 'Tis ringing down the street!'

Toots   I hate Stop Presses. They always remind me of wars and rumours of wars.

Connie   What – what do you think it could be?

Toots   I've no idea what it could be. Nothing sensational, I'm sure.

Connie   You're lying! You think just the same as I do – Terence –

Toots   Pull yourself together.

Harry   Shall I get a paper?

Connie (*in a stifled voice*)   No.

Harry   It's probably the result of the Nottinghamshire Plate.

Connie (*hopefully*)   Were there races today?

Desmond   Races! How banal!

Connie (*agonised*)   No, I don't believe it! I *won't* believe it!

The boy's voice dies away in the distance. There is a sudden guest of wind, the door opens and **Terence** *comes in. He is soaked to the skin, almost unrecognisable, haggard and wild-eyed.* **Harry** *shuts the window with a bang. There is a sudden silence except for the wind and rain outside. They all face* **Terence** *in amazement. He stands for a moment leaning against the door, breathing fast. His eyes search the room.*

Connie (*struggling between relief and contempt*)   You! I might have thought it.

Terence   Has Egosmith been here?

Toots   No.

Terence   Thank God! There's still time. (*He walks towards the sofa.*)

Harry (*blocking his way*)   Get out of here, you infernal scoundrel.

Connie   No, Harry. (*To* **Terence**.) I think I told you I didn't want to see you again.

Terence (*ignoring her and addressing* **Toots**)   I called at your house, but they told me you were out.

Toots (*uncomfortably*)   Oh!

Harry   Shall I kick him out?

Connie   Harry, please – no more. Leave this to me. You go now and come back later for dinner. (*She puts her arms around him with a defiant look at the others.*) Goodbye, darling.

Harry   All right. But I don't altogether like –

Connie (*stopping his mouth*)   Please darling – for my sake – (*She kisses him.*)

Harry (*melting*)   For the present then. Ring me if you want me – (*He goes, with a last resentful look at* **Terence**.)

Connie (*spitefully*)   Toots, before you rush headlong into an affair with Terence Killigrew, let me warn you –

Toots   What do you mean?

Desmond   Connie, don't be a fool!

Connie   I'm not a fool. I saw her trying to get off with him at the party. (**Terence** *laughs.*)

Connie   I warn you he's no good.

Toots (*on the brink of tears*)   I'm going home. Let me out – this is disgusting.

Terence   Wait a minute. (*He goes up to* **Connie**.) I thought we finished with each other last night. (*He seizes her wrist.*)

Connie   I won't keep you any longer. Desmond, when Terence has finished his interview with Toots perhaps you'd get rid of him before Harry comes back. I don't want another scene.

Terence   Listen to me, you contemptible jade, we know each other pretty well; we have no more to say to each other – that's all finished. Everything is finished as far as I'm concerned. Toots just happens to understand the situation. I have a few words to say to her before I go, and I must keep my promise to Flossie. (*He stares into her face.*) Do you understand?

Connie   It's all over then?

Terence (*turning away from her*)   Yes.

Connie (*brokenly*)   I'm sorry, Toots – I didn't mean it really –

Toots   That's all right.

Connie   No, don't come near me now. I can take what's coming to me – goodbye. (*She goes.*)

Desmond   I think I'll go up and work. (*He sidles towards the door.* **Terence** *turns on him snarling.*)

Terence   Keep away from the door. Come back here. I've something to say to you.

Desmond *comes down nervously. He flashes a look at* **Toots**. *For the first time, they notice* **Terence***'s peculiar manner.*

Terence   Listen! Don't talk too loud. I've got rid of Egosmith.

Toots   Have you?

Terence   Yes, last night. You know I went down to Sandycove – I don't know where I slept. I've been walking ever since.

Toots   You're ill. Let me get you something to drink.

Terence   No, I'm all right. Yes, I've got rid of Egosmith. What's the time?

Desmond   Nearly six.

Terence   I must get away before six. If he finds me here I'll have to stay. (*He rises and listens intently.*) Sh! There's someone outside the door.

Desmond *goes to the door and looks out.*

Desmond   There's nobody there, really.

Terence   Shut the door. Lock it. Nobody must come in.

Desmond (*frightened*)   Must I lock it?

Terence   Yes.

Desmond *locks the door with an imploring look at* **Toots**, *who never takes her eyes off* **Terence***.*

Desmond   What do you want to say to us, Terence?

Terence   You think I'm mad. I can see you both think I'm mad. I have moments of insanity that are the very breath of life to me. Last night I was mad – down there alone with those melancholy waves, those eternal rocks, eternal pain – something did snap in my brain. Suddenly I felt as light as air . . . I realised it was finished. Egosmith had left me – I was free. Oh, how could I ever explain to you the boundless depths of my freedom?

Toots   Don't you think you should go home and rest?

Terence (*sitting down suddenly on the sofa*)   If I could only get away from those footsteps. Up and down, up and down . . . You can hear them now. Listen . . . I can no longer endure the intolerable agony of living.

Toots   No, don't say that – there's always hope.

Terence   I've lost the habit of hoping. It's only a habit, you know. And what are you going to do? You must get out of this, you know –

Toots   I am going – at least I think I'm going.

Terence   Alas! It will need a stick of dynamite to get you out; but we'll see what can be done. And what of friend Flossie?

Desmond   I've resigned.

Terence   Resigned from what?

Desmond   I – I don't know . . .

Terence   You've nothing to resign from. You've achieved nothing. You probably never will achieve anything. But you must first cast out of yourself the illusion of nonconformity, and be a human being; just a nice, goddam, little human being.

Toots   Where are you going?

Terence   I don't know. In a few minutes you'll hear my voice howling on the wind with all the lost souls. All that I say must sound incomprehensible to normal human beings like Middleton, who'll shout – 'He is mad, tie him up, drag him to a nursing-home, his nervous system's out of order . . .' Mad! My God, my mind is crystal clear. I see what I've missed. I see how disgusting I've been. I realise the utter futility of what is gone and what is to come. I am a void. There is no desire in me, no desire for anything but death, and for that I am impatient.

Toots   The only thing to do is keep quiet.

Terence   You ask me to keep quiet when eternities of silence stretch in front of me!

Desmond   It's getting late. I think I'll put on the light.

Terence   Come away from that door. Leave the light alone.

The clock strikes six. A door bangs somewhere in the house. **Terence** *stands up suddenly.*

Terence   There he is, that's Egosmith trying to stop me. This time he's too late. Flossie, come here. I shall shoot myself through the heart. It's just a fad; I've always preferred it to the head. Do you remember my promise? Do you?

Desmond (*shivering*)   No – yes –

Terence   Come now, you remember? I said if I ever met myself face to face I'd shoot myself. Well, Flossie, I met myself last night, and I saw, what do you think, that I was just a picturesque windbag! (**Toots** *laughs.*) – a book of handy quotations – a melancholic misfit.

Desmond *and* **Toots** *both laugh.*

Terence (*taking out a revolver*)   It's so damn funny I almost made up my mind to take Egosmith's advice and sell insurance policies – (**Toots** *laughs again;* **Desmond** *creeps closer to* **Terence***.*) – but I disdain the dustheap. Now I hope you don't mind – I'm bumping myself off here, because I think this house needs to be shaken to its bourgeois foundations. I swear that if anyone attempts to stop me I will take them with me. Terrible is he who has nothing to lose! (*His voice grows louder.* **Toots** *realises his intention too late, and rushes towards him.*) Santa Teresa, pray for this sinner now, and in the hour of his death! (*He shoots himself through the heart, and very slowly falls forward off the sofa.*)

Toots   Oh, God! (*She stands still for one terrified moment, then rushes to the door and beats on it frantically.*) Let me out! Let me out! I want to get out! Oh, let me out of this! (*Footsteps and voices are heard. The house is roused. The cornet man starts playing 'The Stein Song' in the street below.*)

Desmond (*creeping over to* **Terence** *and staring down at him*)   Morituri, morituros salutant!

Toots (*sobbing*)   I can't unlock the door! Help me, Desmond! Somebody! Let me out!

Desmond (*piteously sinking on to a chair and staring at* **Terence**)   Tomorrow, Terence – tomorrow I'm going to buy a bowler hat, and an umbrella –

CURTAIN

Witch's Brew

A Drama in One Act

Dorothy Macardle

Dorothy Macardle (1889–1958) was immersed in the political and cultural life of the Free State: she was a writer, teacher and journalist; a revolutionary and political prisoner; and author of *The Irish Republic* (1937), a history of Ireland, 1916–23, commissioned by de Valera. Born in Dundalk, County Louth, Macardle went to Alexandra College in Dublin and graduated from University College Dublin in 1912. She later returned to Alexandra, where she taught Mary Manning, and she also served as the drama critic for the *Irish Press* newspaper. Macardle was imprisoned from 9 November 1922 to March 1923 for her Republican involvement. She was an anti-Treatyite and supporter of de Valera's newly formed Fianna Fáil party which came into power in 1932. However, her support was not uncritical and she keenly felt the betrayal of revolutionary ideals, including women's equal participation. Macardle wrote to her friend de Valera: 'As the Constitution stands, I do not see how anyone holding advanced views on the rights of women can support it, and that is the tragic dilemma for those who have been loyal and ardent workers in the national cause' (quoted in Lane 2019: 225).

Attention to this 'tragic dilemma' and the threat posed by idealized femininities underlies Macardle's literary and theatrical output. She had her first Irish production with *Asthara* (Little Theatre, Dublin, 1918), followed by several plays at the Abbey: *Atonement* (1918); *Ann Kavanagh* (1922); *The Old Man* (1925). Cathy Leeney suggests that in Macardle's Abbey plays, 'the conventions of melodrama and realist form are appropriated, exploited, and finally disrupted, if not entirely overturned' (2010: 106). This is further developed through the supernatural frame of *Witch's Brew*, submitted to the Abbey in 1929. The play was rejected but it was published two years later; to date, it has not received a professional production. *Witch's Brew* is located at a crossroads within the theatrical heritage of women theatre makers, 'as a marker between the formal daring of Gregory and Gore-Booth, and the coded, elliptical explorations of Manning and Deevy' (Leeney 2010: 125). Leeney notes the detrimental loss of the script of Macardle's play *Dark Waters* (1932, Gate), which also inhabits a supernatural realm and offers a closing scene which 'must be read as intentionally discordant, a disturbing, transgressive image of happiness and release in the wake of a murderous move against the patriarch in the play' (2010: 124). *Witch's Brew* culminates with the reassertion of order and of normative relationships: the self-sacrificing mother with her son; the dependent wife with her husband as saviour. However, this does not adequately smooth over the unease that has been generated and Macardle deploys this to feminist ends.

In contrast to the cultural nationalists' use of myth in the early twentieth century, Macardle evokes pagan times and the supernatural to reflect her complicated position as supporter of both women's rights *and* the national project in which women were increasingly side-lined. Women were scapegoated by the newly founded State and the battle over a woman's body in *Witch's Brew* is an all too familiar Irish cultural text. The forces of the pagan Gods clash with a Christian God over Una, who is lying unconscious in the opening of the play as a storm batters the hut. Una's husband Phelim has gone in search of 'blest water', while Phelim's mother Aine and his sister Nessa, remain with Una. Aine appeals to the old Gods for help before deciding to go and find Blanid, 'the witch-girl'. Aine returns with Blanid who prepares her witch's brew which, when given to Una, reanimates her. Yet, the woman who is revived invokes a horrified response: Nessa shudders when she looks into Una's face.

Possession is featured in Macardle's collection of short stories *Earth-Bound* (1924; Swan Press, 2016); tales which were shared with her fellow inmates during her time as a political prisoner in Mountjoy and Kilmainham Gaols. In 'The Return of Niav' a changeling entrances the narrator and her daughter, who both transgress normative femininities, and in 'The Portrait of Róisín Dhu' the life of a young woman is leeched away as her portrait is painted; a damning indictment of the consequences of idealized myths of femininity. Transgressive, monstrous and 'unnatural' women feature in Macardle's later work, notably upending expectations of who we understand to be the ideal mother in her gothic novel *The Uninvited* (1942; Tramp Press, 2015). In *Witch's Brew*, Blanid is presented as both a vigorous and threatening figure, and the dangers of the potion are implicated through the reference to Cáit na Poul, whom we are told was revived by the brew, only to murder her children.

When Una is lifeless, she is described as beautiful and passive, but following her eager drinking of the brew, she refuses to conduct herself as a loving daughter-in-law, sister-in-law and wife. As in O'Leary's play, women are construed to be 'difficult' when they fail to uphold appropriate gendered behaviour. The energies of the pagan world are invoked through Blanid's striking entrance, the brew and the storm. Yet, the play concludes with the blood sacrifice of the monk Kiaran and assertion of Christian redemption. Una's body is once again revived from lifelessness and this time she fulfils gendered expectations: she speaks 'joyfully' and 'lovingly' as a wife. The figure of an enervated, deathly, beautiful woman resonates with *Bluebeard* and Macardle 'presents powerful femininity as liminal, pathological and finally defeated' (Leeney 2010: 122). The final image of everyone joined in prayer condemns Una's sinful actions. Yet, as in *Bluebeard*, the thrill of unleashing repressed energies cannot be fully contained. Through exploitation of the uncertainty of the state between life and death, the play captures the anxieties and fears triggered during a period of transition, namely between revolution and state-building.

5 Group photograph of members of the Women Writers' Club with Dorothy Macardle at a banquet given by the club for the publication of *The Irish Republic*, 1938. UCD Digital Library. Reproduced by kind permission of UCD-OFM Partnership.

Characters

Phelim, *a young woodman*
Aine, *his mother*
Nessa, *his sister*
Una, *his wife*
Blanid, *a girl of the forest*
Kiaran, *a hermit*

The action takes place in Ireland in early Christian times, in **Phelim**'s *hut in the forest, on a night of storm.*

The names are pronounced approximately: Faýlim, Awnya, Oóna, Bláhnid, Kée-arawn.

The scene is the interior of a one-roomed wattle hut. The room is well cared for and is furnished with stools, trestles, a bed, skins and earthen vessels. There is a pile of logs in a corner. Hunting knives and axes hang on the wall. A low brazier stands at the centre, full of smouldering logs; an iron tripod stands over it. The door is at the back and it is barred against the storm which rages outside. There are no windows. The bed stands at an angle, the head towards the wall, left, the foot below the centre of the room. **Una**, *a young and very beautiful woman, is lying on it, unconscious. She holds a crucifix made of two sticks in one hand.* **Nessa**, *a girl of about fifteen, is kneeling at the foot of the bed, praying with intensity.* **Aine**, *an ageing woman, is sitting on a low stool above the bed, bent forward, her eyes fixed on* **Una**'s *face. After a long pause, in which only the moan of the wind and the monotonous murmur of* **Nessa**'s *prayers is heard,* **Aine** *speaks to her without turning her head.*

Aine   How long, now, are you at your prayers?

Nessa *sighs wearily, says 'Amen' and lifts her head, looking anxiously at* **Una**.

Nessa   A long time, maybe.

Aine   There is no change.

Nessa (*rising and standing above the bed*)   She is quieter, surely? Isn't the fever gone?

Aine   The fever is gone, and the last of her strength with it.

Nessa   She is scarcely breathing at all!

Aine   Life is leaving her.

Nessa   Don't be saying it, Mother!

Aine   At dawn, when the pulse of the world is faint and sluggish, she will die.

Nessa   It is not right to be saying it! The blest water will save her. She told Phelim herself it would make her well.

Aine   He will not be in time.

Nessa   The storm should pass over soon, and the moon will be rising. I was praying to God to guide him and quiet the wind.

The wind swells and roars, shaking the door.

Aine (*lifting her head*)   You were praying; aye, for an hour. Phelim prayed, too, to the God of Patrick, and he lighting the lantern setting out. And a storm burst out of the sky that would slaughter an army and rain that'd drown the world.

The sounds of the storm rise deafeningly.

Nessa (*agitated*)   We must have faith.

Aine (*brooding*)   Seeking Kiaran out in the black darkness, in the far place he does go to, to pray. Crossing over the lake and it raging. Tearing a path where there is no path, through the forest, and the trees crashing down! . . . To win home in the end with the water, and find her dead!

Nessa   Her forehead is cold, and her hands.

Aine   He will change to a thing of stone. He will say, 'You let her die on me. You sat idle.' He will look at me with a face of hate.

Nessa (*crying*)   Oh, dear God!

Aine   Let you pray to your God to kill Phelim, if he has Una marked for death.

Thunder roars and trees are heard crashing down.

Nessa   Oh why, at all, did He send the storm?

Aine (*brooding*)   Ay. Who sent it?

Nessa (*controlling herself*)   It was maybe to try Phelim, would he risk life itself for his love?

Aine   The God that would not know without tricks that Phelim is burnt up with his love for Una is a poor, powerless God.

Nessa   Mother! It is blasphemy you are speaking, and death at the door! Oh, you will anger God!

Aine   I am wondering, Daughter, is the God of Patrick listening. Is he minding my blasphemies or your prayers?

Nessa   He sees everything! He hears all!

Aine   I am wondering.

Una *sighs. The fire sinks low.*

Nessa   She sighed as if her soul was leaving her! Oh, Mother, pray!

Aine   To a God that has maybe no care for us, or no power?

Nessa   You are bringing darkness into the house!

Aine   Put wood on the fire.

Nessa *takes up logs, watching* **Aine** *with dread.*

Nessa   I am afraid.

Aine   It is no time for fear. No time to be sitting idle for fear of a God that is maybe an empty tale.

She rises.

Nessa   Mother! What will you do?

Aine   I will do for Una what was done for others.

Nessa   Oh, what is in your mind?

Aine   It is in my mind that Cait na Poul was as sick at Samhain, and she did not die.[1]

Nessa (*in horror*)   Cait na Poul!

Aine   Murroch Mór was as near death as she is, and he came back!

Nessa   Murroch Mór!

Aine   They were clay-cold in their beds; I saw them; and they lived.

Nessa   Murroch Mór lived to kill his brother! Cait na Poul cut the throat of her own child! Do not be naming those names!

Aine   They lived; and it was not the God of Patrick that gave them life!

Nessa   It was Blanid, the wickedest thing in Ireland, with her witch's brew!

Aine   It was Blanid.

She lights a lantern.

Nessa   It would be better to let her die!

Aine   No, Death is the worst.

Nessa   God will smite you with his thunderbolts, Mother!

Aine *wraps a cloak about her and goes to the door.*

Aine   If your God has thunderbolts let him smite me, and spare the young girl!

Nessa   Oh, you will lose your soul!

Aine   She is more than his life to Phelim, and my son is more to me than my own soul.

She unbars the door.

Nessa (*praying*)   Holy Mary, Mother of God, pray for us sinners! (*To* **Aine**.) Oh, you have sinned! You have sinned.

Aine *has opened the door, a crash and the noise of the storm stream in. Standing erect, the lantern in her hand, she speaks strongly, like one freed from fear.*

Aine   Ay, we have sinned! But it is against the old Gods we have sinned! We have denied them, and they are living! We have mocked them, and they are strong! Their

---

1   Pronounced Koytch-na-Poo-ul and Sah-wen (All Hallows E'en).

anger is shaking the forest and making shreds of the sky! It is Mananaan is drowning the world with water! It is the Dagda is shouting out in the wind! – It is Baal, it is Baal,[2] is smiting the earth with fire!

Nessa (*imploring*)   Mother, in the name of Christ!

Aine   Let me call on your God, daughter, and I will call on mine! Phelim will come first, maybe, with the blest water, If 'tis between God and a witch-girl, God should win.

She goes. **Nessa**, *leaning, faint with dread against the doorpost, looks out into the darkness.*

Nessa (*despairingly*)   No light! No sign! . . . No sign? . . . No God, maybe . . . No God . . .

She closes the door, then flings herself in anguish down on her knees by the bed.

Oh, Una, Una, where are you? . . . I am afraid! . . . I am alone! . . . Una! . . . Una!

Una *stirs and opens her eyes; she moves weakly, but smiles at* **Nessa** *and lays a hand on her cheek.*

Una   I am here, darling!

Nessa (*incredulously, gazing at her*)   Una! . . . Oh, you came back to me! . . .

Una   You called in such anguish, Nessa; it drew me down!

Nessa   I had lost God.

Una   And I . . . I had almost found him! I heard the music pouring from Heaven's gate.

Nessa   I thought you were dying!

Una (*joyously*)   So I am! I am dying, Mavourneen.[3] It is more beautiful even than Kiaran told us! . . . do not be keeping me, with your tears!

Nessa   You cannot leave us! We love you!

Una   I will be thinking of you in Heaven. I will be saying prayers for you in Mary's ear. I will ask her to give you your heart's desire!

Nessa   My heart's desire is you to stay with us, Una!

Una   I cannot stay. My soul is a wild bird; it is craving for the air and the light! Pray for me Nessa! Help me to go!

---

2   This sentence calls upon a number of deities, all of them associated with fertility and with natural forces. Manannán mac Lir is the 'son of the sea' in Irish and Manx mythology, and is a ruler of the supernatural world. The Dagda is a deity associated with fertility and agriculture, and Baal is referred to in the Old Testament and is a Canaanite god of fertility.

3   My beloved.

Nessa   I cannot. I am afraid!

Una   Nessa, there is nothing to be afraid of. Nothing anywhere in the world. Phelim will take care of you – and of Aine. Aine is growing old. If God lets me, when she is dying . . . I will come . . .

Nessa   Do not leave Phelim alone!

Una   Now, for this night, Phelim and I are parted – we will never be so far from one another again. I will be with him in the air and the sunshine and the shadows and the light of the stars. He will feel my love in his heart, till he comes.

Nessa   I am afraid of death!

Una   To die is to escape from sorrow and dread and pain.

Nessa   You that were never sad!

Una   I thought that life was happy, but it is mournful, Nessa. There is heaviness over everything. All the sweetness and gladness are after death. It is like . . . Do you remember, Nessa, when we woke on the Hill of the Rivers, at dawn?

Nessa   I remember. Phelim and Martin were lighting a fire.

Una   Yes; it was summer, but it was cold. There was a silver light on the fields, and the stars were fading; you said it was beautiful . . .

Nessa   We were happy.

Una   And then the sun rose, breaking out of a cloud, and the sky and the fields and the rivers shone out in a thousand colours; the gorse was like gold, flaming, and the air was warm.

Nessa   And the larks began singing.

Una   Dying is like that.

Nessa   Then die, my darling; but my heart will break.

Una   No, no, for you will remember. I will give you something to remind you always . . . Look Nessa! My silver ring!

Nessa   Your ring, Una?

Una   See it shining! Take it from my finger, Acushla, and wear it for a sign . . . a sign that l am praying for you and loving you; that God loves you, and you will come.

Nessa (*trying to put ring on her finger*)   It is too small.

Una (*faintly*)   Your smallest finger. Try for me. There; do not forget.

The ring is on **Nessa**'*s little finger.*

Nessa   I will remember, my darling. I will have faith.

Una *raises herself with momentary strength, in ecstasy.*

Una   They are singing together, all the morning stars! . . . . Pray for me.

Her eyes close. She sinks down and lies still, her hands crossed over the crucifix on her breast.

Nessa (*praying*)   . . . Now and at the hour of our death . . .

She listens, startled. There is knocking on the door. She goes to it.

Phelim! . . .

She unbars the door, then recoils. It is **Aine** *who comes in.*

Nessa   You! . . . You are alone?

Aine   Did he come?

Nessa   No!

Aine   Then it is time! – Come!

She stands aside and beckons. Out of the darkness, her black hair and streaming rags wet and dishevelled, **Blanid***, the witch-girl, runs in, noiselessly, as though blown by the wind. She is laughing. Her apron is full of herbs. A gust of wind is heard.*

Blanid   They are pleased, Aine! They laugh!

Nessa   God has saved her from you! She is dead!

Blanid *runs to the bed, looks at* **Una***, listens and laughs.*

Blanid   Her soul is like a wild bird, hovering. I will catch it before it flies! I will thrust it back in the cage!

Nessa   Oh, where is Phelim? . . . He is in the forest! He is coming! Wait, Mother, wait! In the name of God!

Aine   Your God moves too slowly. The witch has won!

Nessa   Give me the lantern! I will find him! . . . Phelim!

Nessa *seizes the lantern and rushes out calling 'Phelim!' farther and farther away. The witch-girl is mixing her herbs in a pan over the brazier. Red fumes rise from the cauldron.* **Aine** *comes over and looks fearfully in.*

Aine   I think life is gone from her. She lies with her hands crossed, like the dead.

Blanid   Lay her arms straight by her sides.

Aine (*hesitating*)   Why should I do that?

Blanid   Straight by her side, Aine.

Aine (*obeying*)   It is done . . . She has a crucifix in her hand.

Blanid   Burn it under my cauldron.

Aine   It is Phelim's . . . He will be asking where it is.

Blanid   He will not fret for two sticks if his wife is living, or ask for it if she is dead.

Aine   Kiaran blessed it for their marriage.

Blanid   Put it in the fire.

Aine   If it is her life . . .

She drops the cross, trembling, into the brazier. Red flames rise. **Aine** *recoils.*

Blanid (*laughing*)   The old Gods love fire, and it burns well.

Aine   Your brew has a bitter smell.

Blanid   Ay, it is bitter.

Aine (*looking into the cauldron, though afraid*)   It is the colour of blood.

Blanid   Blood is life.

Aine   It is writhing like serpents.

Blanid   Like snakes . . . They say Patrick has put the snakes out of Ireland, but there are snakes in Ireland still.

Aine   It is horrible.

Blanid   Death is more horrible yet, Aine, hugging a young man's bride.

Aine   I would sooner not give it to her, at all.

Blanid (*laughing*)   You would sooner see hate and death in your son's eyes!

Aine   Phelim is terrible when he is angered . . .

Blanid   You neither love nor fear him, may be.

Aine   My son is more to me than my own soul.

The wind roars outside.

Blanid (*laughing*)   You speak bravely! The Gods are pleased.

Aine   It will not wither her beauty?

Blanid   Her skin will be as white and smooth.

Aine   Make haste! Make haste!

Blanid   'Tis seething! The bubbles are frothing at the brim . . . Milk to cool it . . . Give me a cup, Aine, and raise her in your arms.

Aine (*hesitating*)   Phelim will maybe come . . .

Aine *gives* **Blanid** *a cup with milk in it.*

Blanid   And will his kisses put breath in the dead?

She fills the cup.

Aine   The blest water . . .

Blanid (*screaming*)   Silent! Say that word again and I spill my medicine on the ground! . . . Obey, Aine! . . . Raise her in your arms!

Aine   She is cold.

She raises the limp body of **Una** *in her arms, and* **Blanid** *brings the cup.*

Blanid   One drop is enough.

She dips her fingers in the brew and puts them between **Una**'s *lips.* **Una** *stirs and moans.*

Aine   She moved!

Blanid (*softly*)   Drink, Una! Drink!

Una *sips the brew and opens her eyes.* **Blanid** *lays down the cup, drops down, hiding, and steals into the shadows.*

Una   Give me more, more!

Aine (*lifting the cup*)   Drink, then! Deep! Drain it! . . . You came back to us! You came back!

Una *drinks, then looks into the cup.*

Una   It is sweet and heady! It is the colour of blood!

Aine   Drain the cup! It is life! I have saved you from death. You will live now!

Una (*putting down the empty cup*)   Ay; I will live now.

Blanid (*laughing, unseen*)   Ay!

Una (*sitting erect and tense*)   Who laughed?

Aine   Your eyes are bright!

Una (*offended*)   Somebody laughed when I said, 'I will live now'!

Aine (*exultant*)   You have your beauty and your strength!

Una *rises, wraps a covering from the bed about her, and stands swaying.*

Una   I have my strength and my senses; the pain is gone. Why did you not give it to me sooner, the healing drink?

Aine *is silent;* **Una** *speaks in a weak, complaining tone.*

Una   You left me in my pain and my sickness. Where is Phelim? Why did he leave me alone?

Aine   He went to find Kiaran, Daughter.

Una   He left me alone and I in dread of death!

Aine   He went to seek Kiaran, through the storm.

Una   To go out in the storm, and I dying.

Aine   He went for the blest water to make you well.

Una (*shuddering*)   The blest water! . . . He knew that would not cure me.

Aine   You yourself asked for it, Daughter. You said it would make you well.

Una   I was raving in fever when I said it. If he loved me he would not have gone.

She is standing over the brazier, warming her hands.

Aine   Man never loved woman, Una, as he loves you!

Una   He loved me while I was laughing and beautiful. A man tires of a woman that is ailing and sick. I do not blame him that he wished me to die.

Aine   Do not be thinking evil of Phelim. Do not be doubting his love!

Una (*bitterly*)   You also . . . I loved you and served you like your own child, while I was able; but I was a trouble to you and I lying helpless. You thought I was living too long.

Aine   I gave you life at the price of my own soul.

Una (*turning, despairingly*)   I have no wish to live in a world that is without kindness! You should have let me die.

She sinks down by the bed and hides her face, weeping. **Blanid** *laughs.*

Aine (*turning on* **Blanid**)   You laugh!

Blanid   My medicine was powerful, Aine! She will live long.

Aine   Child of Hell! . . . Go from me! Go!

Blanid   My gold, Aine, my gold! (*Spreading her fingers.*) Nine pieces of silver and one of gold! I have earned it well!

Aine (*thrusting money into* **Blanid***'s hands*)   That the curse of the old Gods and the curse of Patrick's God follow you to Hell!

Blanid (*smiling*)   Another for my silence, lest Phelim hear!

Aine (*giving her another coin*)   Go, now, out to the darkness where you belong!

Aine *pulls open the door. Laughing,* **Blanid** *runs into the darkness and is gone.* **Aine** *looks out.*

Una   Shut the door! It is cold! Oh, the wind is howling like lost souls!

Aine   Ay, like lost souls!

Una   Shut it!

Aine   Nessa is coming!

Una (*rising, imperiously*)   Shut the door! Shut the door!

Nessa *runs in.* **Aine** *shuts the door.* **Nessa** *stares at* **Una**, *in love and dread.*

Nessa   Una! . . . Una! . . . You are living!

Una   It is not you who saved me! . . . You went away.

Nessa   Something passed me in the darkness, laughing!

She looks into **Una**'s *face and shudders.*

Nessa   Mother, what have you done?

Aine (*heavily*)   I do not know what I have done.

Nessa   Una! Let me look into your face! Oh. I thought you were dead!

Una *hides her face.*

Una   Leave me! Leave me! I want only to be alone!

Nessa   Phelim is coming. There are two lights moving among the trees.

Aine   Oh, God have mercy!

Nessa   To what God are you praying for mercy now?

Una (*wildly*)   Do not let him come to me! Do not let him look at me! He wanted to see me dead!

She sits on a chair, hiding her face.

Nessa   No, Una, no! Do not believe the black thought that is in your mind!

Una   My thought is my thought.

Nessa   No, no, it is false, Una, it is evil! Oh, Una, she has given you poison! You have drunk the witch's brew!

Una   Why did she not give it me sooner, the sweet, healing wine?

Aine   Nessa said it was evil . . .

Una   Nessa is a foolish child . . . You should not have heeded her.

Aine   I was afraid.

Una (*looking with contempt at* **Aine**)   Ay, you were afraid for your own soul! You tell me you love me, but you loved your own soul better!

Nessa   It was the devil's medicine, Una!

Una   It was sweet and strong.

Nessa (*to* **Aine**)   Phelim will kill you!

Aine   He will not know.

Nessa   I will tell him.

Aine   If you tell him I will throttle you! I will strangle you in your sleep!

Nessa   Murderess!

Una   Murderess! Murderess!

There is a loud, impatient knocking on the door.

Nessa   Phelim!

Aine   Do not open it!

She lifts the cauldron from the hook and hides it in a corner.

Nessa   Maybe there is some help still in Heaven! Maybe Kiaran would come.

Nessa *opens the door.* **Phelim** *strides in, a young strong man, storm-beaten; after him* **Kiaran** *comes in, a tall grave man, worn with fasting, habited as a monk. They carry lanterns.* **Nessa** *takes* **Phelim**'s *lantern and shuts the door.* **Kiaran** *sets his lantern down.* **Una** *runs to* **Phelim** *and he clasps her in his arms, her face hidden on his breast.*

Phelim   My love! . . . O my love! . . .

Kiaran   God bless this house.

Nessa (*faintly*)   You are welcome, Kiaran.

Phelim   I thought it was death I would find before me and it is life. Oh Una, my love, my thousand treasures! Let me see the sweet new life in your eyes.

Una (*still hiding her face*)   Why did you leave me alone?

Nessa   Put your blessing on this house, holy Kiaran, for it has need!

Kiaran   It has need, surely.

Phelim   Is there fear on you still, my darling? Your breath burns my cheek.

Una   I was near death, and you left me! You left me alone with these!

She looks up, and looks with bitterness at **Nessa** *and* **Aine**.

Phelim   My Mother and Nessa, who love you!

Una   You were deceived, Phelim! She does not love me, your Mother! Did an ageing woman ever love the bride her son brings to the house?

Phelim   You are like her own!

Una   She made you believe it. She was afraid.

Phelim   Mother! What have you done?

Una   She gave me a slow poison, Phelim, to kill me. You did not know.

Phelim   It is not true!

Una   Have I ever lied to you, my husband? Why should I lie?

Phelim (*staring at* **Aine**)   Mother!

Una   Poison! Ah, do you see the guilt in her face?

Aine   No!

But she shrinks like one overwhelmed with guilt.

Phelim   God in Heaven! . . . Nessa! What has she done?

Nessa   She gave her the witch's brew!

Kiaran   Oh, it was sin!

Phelim   Blanid! The witch-girl! . . . Poison! It is poison that Blanid brews!

Aine   It brought her back from death!

Phelim   Oh, Kiaran, what have they done?

Aine   I bought her life at the price of my own soul!

Kiaran   That price is paid to evil for evil only. You sold what belonged to God.

Phelim (*to* **Aine**)   I will not forgive you.

Aine   Phelim! She would have died!

Phelim   I will never forgive! . . .

Nessa   It would have been better to let her die!

Una   Yes, Nessa wanted me to die.

Nessa   Phelim, do not believe her!

Aine   It is true! Nessa said it. She said, 'It would be better to let her die.'

Phelim   Nessa said it?

Nessa   Phelim, can you not understand?

Phelim   Understand! No! I understand nothing! . . . Oh, Una, my love, tell me the truth! The truth!

Una (*softly*)   Yes, Phelim, I will tell you. You have been foolish, Phelim. You were deceived. You thought these two loved me. They feared you, Phelim, and so they pretended. They spoke to me with soft, smooth words. But they were all the time plotting together against me. They wanted me away, Phelim. They wanted me dead.

Phelim   God in Heaven!

Una   Aine was giving me slow poison and I fell sick. She sent you away in the storm, seeking for Kiaran; she thought I would die. Then she became afraid. She went for Blanid to save me. But Nessa said 'twould be better to let me die. They quarrelled about it; I heard them, and I half dead.

Nessa   Oh, Kiaran!

Phelim   I will kill them! I will kill!

Una   Do you know why Nessa wished me to die, Phelim? I had given her my silver ring. She stole it from me, with sweet, lying words. She was afraid that I would take it again.

Nessa *clenches her hands in anguish, hiding the ring.*

Phelim   Your silver ring!

Una   Look, she is hiding it! It is on her finger! Look! You will see!

Phelim *seizes* **Nessa** *by the hands roughly, and tries to pull off the ring.*

Phelim   I will have it if I tear off your finger!

Nessa   Phelim!

Una   Here is a sharp knife!

Nessa (*in terror*)   Kiaran!

Una *is filled with the strength of madness.* **Phelim** *holds her. She struggles, the knife in her hand.*

Una   Blood! Red and shining! I will have blood!

Phelim   She is crazed!

He holds her. She stands panting, staring at **Nessa***, the knife in her hand.*

Nessa   Oh, Kiaran, the blest water!

Kiaran   The hell-broth is in her veins. If I sprinkle the blest water she may die.

He holds a flask of water in his hands.

Nessa   Will blood take the curse away?

Kiaran   Murroch shed blood, and Cait, and they repented . . . I do not know.

Una   I myself must spill it! I myself!

Nessa   Let her, Phelim! Blood will take it away!

Phelim   I dare not!

Una   I am too strong for you, too strong!

She wrenches herself free, and rushes upon **Nessa***, who holds out her hand, trembling and hiding her eyes.* **Kiaran** *covers* **Nessa***'s hand with his own.* **Una** *stabs, and his hand is cut. He stands still and holds his bleeding hand before* **Una***'s eyes. She drops the knife, screams and shudders as though a possessing demon was leaving her body, and falls.*

Una   Ah, the blood of a saint!

She lies in **Phelim***'s arms, apparently lifeless. He lays her down on the bed.*

Aine   She is dead!

Phelim   I do not know.

Kiaran   Peace! (*He sprinkles the blest water on* **Una**.) *In nominee Patris et Filii et Spiritus Sancti.*[4]

Phelim   She is breathing!

Una (*waking slowly*)   Phelim!

Phelim   O my love! Do you hear me? Do you see?

Una (*joyfully*)   Phelim! . . . You came back with the blest water, through all the storm!

Phelim   I would go for you through all the storms of the earth or of the ocean! I would go for you through death or Hell!

Una   And I have come back from Heaven for love of you!

Nessa   Oh, Una, you have come back to us from Hell!

Una (*lovingly*)   Do not be crying any more, Nessa, my treasure. I will stay with you now . . . How wild and grey your face is, Aine! . . . I think the love of a bride is light and joyous, but the love in the heart of a mother is a weight of pain. (*She smiles at* **Kiaran**.) Kiaran will comfort us all.

Aine   There is no forgiveness for my sin.

Kiaran   Your sin was too much love for the life of the body, and too little care for the soul; but it was love. There is forgiveness for that sin.

He leans over **Aine**, *giving her absolution, while* **Phelim** *tries to sooth* **Nessa**, *who is still shaken with weeping.*

Phelim   Hush, little Nessa. All's well. I think it is you, maybe, who brought her back.

Una *raises herself a little, resting against the pillows.*

Una (*wistfully*)   Kiaran, you told us, long ago, that those are happiest who die while the wings of the soul are eager, and strong enough to carry them straight to God.

Kiaran   Be content to stay longer with those who love you, Una. Love strengthens the wings of the soul.

Una   I am content.

Phelim   Give us your blessing, Kiaran. There has been trouble on this house. Death and worse than death has been near us, and we have sinned.

---

4   In the name of the Father, and of the Son, and of the Holy Spirit.

Phelim, **Aine** *and* **Nessa** *kneel, and say the responses while* **Kiaran** *prays.*

Kiaran   *Agnus Dei qui tollis peccata mundi,*
Misereri nobis!
Agnus Dei qui tollis peccata mundi,
Misereri nobis!
Agnus Dei qui tollis peccata mundi,
Dona nobis pacem![5]

THE CURTAIN FALLS.

---

5   Lamb of God who takes away the sins of the world / Have mercy on us! / Lamb of God who takes away the sins of the world / Have mercy on us!/ Lamb of God who takes away the sins of the world / Grant us peace! This is a well-known prayer and part of the Roman Catholic Mass.

Bluebeard

A Ballet-poem

Mary Devenport O'Neill

Premiere: Tuesday 25 July 1933. Ran for six performances at the Abbey Theatre, Dublin. The programme included: W. B. Yeats's *At the Hawk's Well*, Lady Gregory's *Hyacinth Halvey* and Arthur Duff's *The Drinking-Horn*.

Ilina	Ninette de Valois
Baron Bluebeard	J. V. Wynburne
Sister Ann	Ria Mooney
Cyril	Joseph O'Neill
Ilina's Brother	Robert Francis
Ilina's Brother	Bartholemew Lynch
Ghost of Bluebeard's Former Wife	Cepta Cullen
Ghost of Bluebeard's Former Wife	Doreen Cuthbert
Ghost of Bluebeard's Former Wife	Margaret Horgan
Ghost of Bluebeard's Former Wife	Thelma Murphy
Ghost of Bluebeard's Former Wife	Muriel Kelly
Ghost of Bluebeard's Former Wife	Chris Sheehan
Director	Arthur Shields
Choreographer	Ninette de Valois
Composer & Musical Director	Dr John F. Larchet

Mary Devenport O'Neill (1879–1967) was an active figure within the literary world of the Free State: she was a poet and playwright, and held her own salon in Dublin (see Collins 2012). O'Neill published her collection of modernist poetry, *Prometheus and Other Poems*, in 1929 and this volume included a verse-play titled *Bluebeard*. O'Neill sent *Bluebeard* to the Abbey and W. B. Yeats 'requested the author to revise the play so that it could be produced in dance form without sacrificing the poetry'.[1] In the ballet-poem, O'Neill transferred Ilina's and Bluebeard's lines (revised as third-person narration) to Sister Ann and Cyril, so that Ilina and Bluebeard express themselves solely through gesture, dance and movement.[2] The premiere of O'Neill's ballet-poem, was included in the last programme of the Abbey School of Ballet on 25 July 1933. *Bluebeard* was performed through the 1930s and 1940s with the first revival in 1938: this production by the Payne School of Ballet was choreographed by Sara Payne, who

---

1 'An Irishman's Diary', *Irish Times*, 14 October 1943, p. 3.
2 The script included in this anthology is the ballet-poem (National Library of Ireland MS 21,440). The manuscript held in the NLI belonged to Ria Mooney, who played Sister Ann. Mooney would later serve as artistic director of the Abbey. See http://marydevenportoneill.org/bluebeard-2/ for the text of the verse-play.

also played Sister Ann. Thelma Murphy, a member of the chorus of ghosts in the 1933 premiere, performed as Ilina. Under the direction of Austin Clarke, the Dublin Verse Speaking Society presented the verse-play of *Bluebeard* in 1943. Clarke's Lyric Theatre Players then produced the ballet-poem in 1948, as well as premiering O'Neill's dance play *Cain* in 1945.

From Pina Bausch to Caryl Churchill, stage adaptations of the traditional folk tale Bluebeard have focused on the gendered violence inherent in a story where women are punished for breaking patriarchal rules. Through verse and movement, *Bluebeard* articulates women's experiences within the confines of the Free State's 'architecture of containment' (see Hill 2019). The repetition of Ilina's stock gesture, whereby her arms hang by her side, together with moments of aimless movement, present her as the living dead; a fate which foreshadows the dead women of the bloody chamber. Following Ilina's confrontation with the bodies of the dead wives, she runs off-stage, 'as if things had become unbearable'. This is juxtaposed with O'Neill's notable addition to the tale: the defiant appearance of the ghosts of the murdered wives who refuse their containment off-stage as a chorus of voices and within deathly tropes of femininity. The final dance sees the chorus enact their fatal revenge on Bluebeard, yet their collective agency is dispersed as they are 'scattered' and 'crumple' in the closing moments of the play. Defiance, enervation and stagnation pervade the movement of *Bluebeard,* pre-empting the legacy of the Free State with regards to women's cultural representation and participation.

Bluebeard is an important, and neglected, part of the history of Ireland's experimental and dance theatre which evidences European modernist influences. The involvement of Ninette de Valois (1898–2001), who choreographed the ballet-poem and danced the part of Ilina, is key to this legacy. De Valois' experience as a dancer in Europe shaped her work, notably her time at the Ballets Russes (1923–5) where she encountered the choreographers Michel Fokine, Leonide Massine and Bronislava Nijinska (McGrath 2013: 47). De Valois' subsequent period at the Cambridge Festival Theatre saw her development of what she termed 'abstract expressionism', as well as notable success working with groups. Richard Allen Cave describes 'her new-found ability to place groups of figures meaningfully within a performing space in accordance with a visual aesthetic that does not rely on traditional geometrical formations and which accepts that asymmetry has not only a powerful dynamic but also its own particular decorum' (2011: 43). This asymmetry is evident in the photo of de Valois as the Maiden flanked by groups of Sun Worshippers in a performance of *Rituelle de Feu* (Abbey, 1928, see Figure 6; also Walker 1984–5: 400). In *Bluebeard* the dynamics of repetition animate the haunting verse of the off-stage chorus and, despite the absence of any choreographic detail in the reviews of *Bluebeard*, it is a tantalizing possibility that this anticipates their movement on-stage as choreographed by de Valois. De Valois choreographed the chorus of Furies in *The Oresteia* (Festival Theatre, 1926) and Cave describes the production's expressionist aesthetic and 'the chorus's elongated bodylines and stabbing gestures' (2011: 27). Utilizing repetition and deploying distorted, angular qualities would certainly enhance the power of the chorus of murdered wives in *Bluebeard*. Furthermore, Arthur Shields, who directed *Bluebeard*, had engaged with expressionist techniques through his work with the Dublin Drama League. Conceivably, de Valois' choreography heightened the nightmarish reality of women's experiences as the living dead, both within Bluebeard's castle and the Free State.

6 Photograph featuring Ninette de Valois, Abbey Theatre, Dublin, 1928. Arthur Shields Archive, Hardiman Library, NUI Galway.

Characters

Baron Bluebeard
Ilina, *Bluebeard's seventh wife (a very young girl, newly married)*
Sister Ann, *Ilina's sister (very much older)*
Ilina's Two Brothers
Cyril, *a manservant*
Ghosts of Bluebeard's Six Former Wives

*The scene should represent a bare corridor in **Baron Bluebeard**'s castle. The door of the secret room should be at the back of the stage straight in the centre, facing the audience. When the curtain rises **Sister Ann** and **Cyril**, a serving man, are seen seated one on each side of the stage, right in front close to the footlights, facing each other. They should sit throughout the ballet in specially designed positions, changing their positions slightly from time to time, but all their positions should be dance positions and their movements when changing from one position to another should be dance movements taken to the beat of music. In fact, though these two actors remain sitting all the time they should be completely a part of the ballet. Also, their words when not actually sung or chanted to music should be spoken to the beat of music, slowly, giving full value to each word and to the vowel sounds. There should be no conversational speech and no unconsidered movement throughout the ballet.*

Sister Ann
> This castle's filled with silence,
> All around me like gigantic spiders' webs
> It hangs, so thickly I can scarcely move,
> I talk in whispers too.

Cyril
> I'll try to shout – ha – ho
> Ha-hi-ho-hoo.

Sister Ann
> You can't, it won't go through;
> The layers of silence are too old and tough,
> Your loudest shout is a little mouse's squeak.
> Look, here's Ilina.

Minuet.

Ilina *comes in walking with small creep steps, turning to look over each shoulder in turn. She moves to rhythm – the same rhythm that the others speak to.*

Sister Ann
> The silence wraps her feet so she creeps like this –
> Creep, creep, creep with little steps.
> She looks behind her,
> Over her shoulder though there's nothing there.
> She's listening now

She tries to hear the rain
All day it falls straight down and down
Straight down without a break.
(**Ilina** *lifts her hands above her head and lowers them letting her fingers hang.*)
And yet no sound of it comes through these walls;
It might be painted rain for all the company it is.

Cyril

And painted woods –
Tall inky pines
And bare grey beech-twigs scribbled on the sky.

During this speech and the next, **Ilina** *moves with her head lifted as if looking through little windows high up in the thick stone walls.*

Sister Ann

No wind at all.
Not even a little gust to make a noise –
I dream of noises –
And yet I used to hate the wind and storm.
But now – ah, now –
Bluebeard is always muffled in a dream,
And I have always toothache from the damp;
Yet the day must pass
Our brothers come to-night.

Ilina *during the last four lines has been in front of the door of the secret room, her back to the audience. Now she turns looking from the door to* **Cyril** *as if asking a question.*

Cyril

The door is locked, yes, lady, always locked;
That room is full of lovely precious things
From all the farthest corners of the world.
Carvings of amber, embroideries,
Ivory boxes full to the brim with pearls
And blocks of jade that look like big sea waves
I used unpack them, then I brought them here
But I always was made blindfold at that door.

Ilina *sinks to the floor, her dress is spread round her, she leans forward her chin in her hand and slowly, to the rhythm of* **Cyril**'s *speech, she moves gently from one attitude of rapt attention to another till the speech is finished.* **Sister Ann** *also leans forward and listens, very slightly changing her pose once or twice during the speech.*

Cyril (*singing*)

And perfumes, there was one big jar of scent,
I brought it in, and there in the still air
It was too much,
It overpowered me,
I was so happy that I could lie down,

I could have died there –
Not come out again
And gone about my work.
For days the scent of it stuck in my clothes,
Mostly if I stood beside the stove
Or in the sunlight;
Then I used to sniff,
I'd try to get the feeling back again,
I'd nose along my sleeve as a cat or dog does.
But you can feel it still
If he unlocks that door for only a moment
Going in or out, the scent of it escapes
And lumps of it will hang on the damp air,
And when the wind stirs
Blunder on to you.

Ilina *rises slowly and begins to dance the scent dance.*

Cyril

Ilina got that scent on winter days,
She thought it was because she dreamt of gardens
Down in the plains, far south and giddy with flowers.
And the scent comes from that room. 'Tis strange, so strange,
Strange, yet to-night her brothers come,
And surely sometime it will be to-night.

Ilina *goes out. The music starts again. It is slow, expectant, slightly ominous. Presently* **Bluebeard** *comes in. The music becomes meditative.* **Bluebeard** *moves to the music.*

Cyril

He's very changed, he has grown strange and slow.
They say he thinks about Jaspar's drug,
A drug that kills all change and all decay,
It fixes beauty for ten thousand years;
Perhaps it fixes beauty even for ever,
BUT IT KILLS LIFE TOO.

The words of this last line should be spoken very slowly with emphasis on every word. The music stops. **Bluebeard** *stands and listens; a low murmur like a chant is heard. It seems to come from the secret room. It becomes more distinct and low; clear voices are heard singing.*

Chorus

We are so still
Stiller than the dead.
We lie in the sun's light,
Our hair is long and bright,
But we are dead,
Stiller than the dead.

While this is being sung, **Bluebeard***, staring at the door of the secret room, recoils in horror, moving rhythmically backwards. The song dies down to a murmur.*

Cyril (*singing*)
    He heard that song again
    Does it sing in his head
    Or come from there?

The song grows louder again; **Bluebeard** *continues to stare and recoil.*

Chorus
    The worms that writhe and creep
    About the dead
    Are not such ill,
    As this beauty we must keep
    Who are so still
    Stiller than the dead.

The song dies away, and **Bluebeard***, trembling as he walks, goes out to the left.* **Ilina** *looks in at the right.*

Sister Ann
    Come here, Ilina, did you hear a noise?

Cyril
    There was a gust
    That made the rain blow sideways for a moment.
    (*Here* **Ilina** *dances a few steps, running sideways on her toes leaning at a slight angle, her arms flowing out slightly from her sides – to represent the rain blown sideways by a gust. Then, standing quite straight, her arms hanging at her sides,* **Ilina** *continues dancing while* **Cyril** *speaks the next line.*)
    Now it falls straight again.

Ilina *turns and moves aimlessly to the music till she comes in front of the door of the secret room, then she suddenly stops and looks down at the floor.*

Sister Ann
    What is it?
    A key?

Cyril
    It cannot be –

Sister Ann
    It is.

Cyril
    The key of that! (*Pointing to the door of the secret room.*)

Sister Ann (*to* **Ilina**)
    Go in and wrap the embroideries about you
    And dive your arms into a trough of pearls

And smell the scent and try the jewels on.
(**Ilina** *holds the key above her head, and dances, spinning round and round.*)
Old woods, old walls, old silence, go on, defy them all
What lovely pastime for a rainy day.

Ilina *springs to the door, opens it, and, going in, closes it behind her. Music plays while she goes in, then after a suggestion of discord, it suddenly ceases. After a few minutes she comes out, crouching as if hurt. There is a great clash of cymbals.* **Cyril** *and* **Sister Ann** *lift themselves up from their seats and, craning their necks, look towards the door which* **Ilina** *has left open.*

Cyril and **Sister Ann** (*together*)
Six mummy women in six long glass boxes.

Cyril
And there's an empty space, a space for her.

Sister Ann
I see no single inch of empty space
On walls, or floor, or ceiling. Quick, the key
The key, child, lock the door and drop the key.

Ilina *picks up the key, locks the door, drops the key on the floor and creeps slowly out, crouching down as if hurt.*

Sister Ann
We must be deathly quiet till to-night,
Quiet and let the very air forget us
Until to-night. To-night our brothers come.

Ilina *having reached the right side of the stage, goes out.*

As **Cyril** *sings,* **Bluebeard** *comes in and walks round the stage very slowly, his eyes fixed on the door of the secret room. From time to time he pauses, and when* **Cyril** *has got as far as 'This room must be walled up'* **Bluebeard** *has ceased to move, and stands motionless, sunk in thought in front of the door, his back to the audience. His figure shows between* **Cyril** *and* **Sister Ann**, *and the three of them should form a tableau during the latter part of the song.*

Cyril (*singing*)
That door wide open and the window too,
And the wind passing through it,
Ilina walking idly in and out,
And he all careless, having no concern.
I like that picture;
But they'd be in graves;
Buried in graves as if they were dead people;
And nothing left –
Beauty nor even life –
Without their beauty they should have their lives

As common people have
He took their lives to spare their beauty,
But if that beauty's gone he will have killed them
They'll be dead people, he a wicked man.
'A wicked man', is that what they would say
Down in the village, or in any town?
No, it can't be like that:
This castle's large:
Ilina'll walk through all the other rooms,
All through the woods:
This room must be walled up
Made fast as solid stone,
As if it had no hollow space within.
(*Here the music and singing becomes more lyrical.*)
They shall be beautiful in secret there
In that deep-scented darkness
With all their treasures;
They must have all,
He must bequeath them all;
They'll be luxurious and rich.

A low murmur is heard coming from the closed door. It grows louder and voices are heard singing. **Bluebeard** *rouses himself from his dream and recoils.*

Chorus
    We have no graves
    Like the dead
    Who spend their lives and die
    And lie in graves.
    We have no graves.

The song dies down to a murmur.

Cyril (*spoken*)
    Each time it grows more loud
    And the words are clearer
    It can't be in his head.

The song grows loud again.

Chorus
    Is there no bed
    In the ground
    Where we might lie
    Under the sound
    Of the grass that waves,
    The long grass overhead
    Upon the graves
    Of the dead?

Bluebeard, *shrinking backwards and trembling, goes out at the left.* **Ilina** *comes in from the right, walks a few steps, starts and looks round as if something touched her, listens, walks again, turns and stands peering round in every direction and listening as if trying to penetrate some mystery with her eyes and ears, and moving to the rhythm of the music while* **Sister Ann** *and* **Cyril** *speak.*

Sister Ann
To-night will come, but she will have gone mad.

Cyril
These six inside most likely remained sane.

Sister Ann
Ilina, you should rest.

Ilina *turns round and, in doing so, she totters.*

Sister Ann
You're weak, eat something, come
This sugared cake.

Cyril
A cake. It could be hidden in a cake
In any mouthful, she not knowing which.

Sister Ann
Then let her leave the cake,
But drink some wine.

Cyril
Wine, wine, how many drops are in a cup!
One drop perhaps enough:
No, no, not wine.

Sister Ann
Be calm and quiet, Ilina, this short time
This nearly dusk; to-night our brothers come.

Music expressing trouble, mostly between these speeches.

Cyril
All these separate moments till to-night,
When any single moment may be it,
The next one now, the sixth, the ninety-ninth –
No, no, don't let me guess, I might guess right;
But Lady Ann
Look through the window while there is still light;
Tell us what you see.

Sister Ann, *turning round towards the audience, lifting her head and looking as through a window.*

Sister Ann

I see
The shapes of pines
And the grey sky
And the straight falling rain.

Cyril

What do you hear?

Sister Ann

Not a sound.

Cyril

How little one can hear or see or smell,
Yet death is all around us,
We are deaf, we are blind.

Ilina, *as if things had become unbearable, rushes out to the right, and music stops.*
Music begins again, expectant, ominous as before. **Cyril** *begins to sing. Presently*
Bluebeard *comes in. He walks slowly to the music, deep in meditation.*

Cyril (*singing*)

They shall be beautiful in secret there,
But can they be?
In that dark space?
What will be left there?
We know if he breaks the walls again he'll find them –
Their beauty too,
Brought back to the light or made new
By his eyes in the light,
Made new, made new;
(*spoken*) [direction added in MS] Then what will have been in the dark?
Material precise and ready,
Measured and weighed and gauged and strained and sifted,
Waiting for eyes and light.

Here **Bluebeard** *becomes more active and excited as if he had found a solution.*

Cyril

What should he do?
Shall he build a tower in a lonely place
And set relays of sentinels to look at them –
Eyes on them night and day
Making their beauty moment upon moment.
Eyes, mere eyes?
(*Here* **Bluebeard** *becomes depressed and meditative again.*)
But eyes could pay
In minus quantities or small instalments.
No, no, this room must stay
His eyes alone can pay them their life's worth.

The dusk is beginning to gather, the corridor grows slightly dim. The door of the secret room opens slowly and, one after another, six beautiful **Women** *come out. They glide rather than walk; they are otherwise motionless. They wear brilliant dresses and jewels; their arms hang straight by their sides; their hair is spread on their shoulders or hangs in plaits. Slow, solemn music plays – very soft and low as in a dream;* **Bluebeard***, moving to the music, puts out his hands as if to press the* **Women** *back.*

Cyril
Go back, go back again
Till to-morrow, even,
He'll do what is most right,
He'll think again!
He'll think to-morrow!
No, to-night he'll think;
This moment now he'll think;
He'll think, but he is weary,
He must sleep.

Ilina's Two Brothers *rush in from the right.*

Sister Ann
Our brothers come,
Yes, he shall surely sleep.

Ilina's Brothers *draw their swords,* **Bluebeard** *draws his and then, while the slow, solemn music continues to play very softly, and dreamily, and the six beautiful* **Women** *move to it; quick, sharp, excitable music is played at the same time for the sword dance.* **Bluebeard** *pivots round and round defending himself while the* **Brothers** *dance round him attacking. They turn and turn like a kaleidoscope till very suddenly the dance music stops.* **Bluebeard** *falls, and the* **Brothers** *rush out. The slow, solemn, faint march music continues all the time. The six* **Women** *slowly glide forward one behind another. They begin to move round* **Bluebeard** *in a wide circle.* **Bluebeard** *keeps turning his eyes to look at them. Slowly, with an almost imperceptible movement beginning with the first and passing from one to another, their heads turn towards him. In the same way their bodies begin to lean towards him. Their necks stretch towards him. The circle they make round him grows smaller. Their expression grows tense. Their eyes grow eager.* **Bluebeard** *still turns his eyes to look at them, but feebly. He dies. They cease to stretch towards him. Their bodies relax. They seem to be about to glide away as they came, when suddenly the music changes. It becomes wild and free and then, as if a string connecting them snaps, they separate; like pieces of crumpled paper caught in a gust they scatter, each with a different movement in a different direction. The curtain begins to fall and has fallen before they come to rest.*

Bibliography

Bank, J., J. P. Harrington, and C. Morash, eds (2017), *Teresa Deevy Reclaimed Vol 1 & 2*, New York: Mint Theater Company.

Case, S. (1988), *Feminism and Theatre*, London & New York: Routledge.

Cave, R. (2011), *Collaborations: Ninette de Valois and William Butler Yeats*, Alton: Dance Books.

Collins, L. (2012), *Poetry by Women in Ireland: A Critical Anthology 1870–1970*, Liverpool: Liverpool University Press.

Connolly, L. (2003), *The Irish Women's Movement: From Revolution to Devolution*, Dublin: The Lilliput Press.

Cronin, M. (2010), 'Kate O'Brien and the Erotics of Liberal Catholic Dissent', *Field Day Review*, 6, 28–51.

Deevy, T. (1947), *The King of Spain's Daughter and Other One-Act Plays*, Dublin: New Frontiers Press. Available from the Deevy archive, digitized at https://repository.dri.ie/catalog/5999vb55x

Enloe, C. (1990), *Bananas, Beaches and Bases: Making Feminist Sense of International Politics*, Oakland, CA: University of California Press.

Ferriter, D. (2009), *Occasions of Sin: Sex and Society in Modern Ireland*, London: Profile Books.

Gale, M. (1996), *West End Women: Women and the London Stage 1918–1962*, London: Routledge.

Gore-Booth, E. (1930), *The Buried Life of Deirdre*, London: Longmans, Green & Co.

Grein, J. T. (1926), 'Criticisms in Cameo', *The Sketch*, July 21.

Hill, S. (2019), *Women and Embodied Mythmaking in Irish Theatre*, Cambridge: Cambridge University Press.

Hogan R. and M. O'Neill, eds (1968), *Joseph Holloway's Irish Theatre Volume 1*, Dixon, CA: Proscenium Press.

J. W. G. (1929), 'Distinguished Villa', *Irish Independent*, January 28.

Lane, L. (2010), *Rosamund Jacob: Third Person Singular*, Dublin: UCD Press.

Lane, L. (2019), *Dorothy Macardle*, Dublin: UCD Press.

Leeney, C. (2007), 'Interchapter 1: 1900–1939', in M. Sihra (ed.), *Women in Irish Drama: A Century of Authorship and Representation*, 23–7, Basingstoke: Palgrave Macmillan.

Leeney, C. (2010), *Irish Women Playwrights 1900–1939: Gender and Violence on Stage*, New York: Peter Lang.

Luddy, M. (2007), 'Sex and the Single Girl in 1920s and 1930s Ireland', *The Irish Review*, 35, 72–91.

Macardle, D. (1924, 2016), *Earth-Bound*, Dublin: Swan Press.

McGrath, A. (2013), *Dance Theatre in Ireland: Revolutionary Moves,* Basingstoke: Palgrave Macmillan.

Moran, J. (2018), 'Kate O'Brien in the Theatre', *Irish University Review*, 48:1, 7–22.

Motley (1932), The Gate Theatre Digital Archive, NUI Galway, Nov 1932, p. 5.

O'Brien, K. (1926), Letters of Kate O'Brien about *Distinguished Villa*. O'Mara Papers (P40), University of Limerick archives.

O'Dowd, C. (2018), 'Magic Windows: Ria Mooney at the Gate Theatre', in D. Clare, D. Lally and P. Lonergan (eds), *The Gate Theatre, Dublin: Inspiration and Craft*, 131–45, Oxford: Peter Lang.

O'Leary, M. (1929a), 'September Letter from Margaret O'Leary to Lennox Robinson', National Archives, Dublin. NL Box 32 LR/289/1-2.

O'Leary, M. (1929b), 'December Letter from Margaret O'Leary to Lennox Robinson', National Archives, Dublin. NL Box 32 LR/289/1-2.

O'Leary, M. (1939), *Lightning Flash*, London: Jonathan Cape.

Pine, R. (2018), 'Micheál mac Líammóir: The Erotic-Exotic and the Dublin Gate Theatre', in D. Clare, D. Lally and P. Lonergan (eds), *The Gate Theatre, Dublin: Inspiration and Craft*, 63–96, Oxford: Peter Lang.

Reynolds, P. (2016), 'The Avant-Garde Doyenne: Mary Manning, the Poets' Theatre, and the Staging of "Finnegans Wake"', *The Canadian Journal of Irish Studies*, 39:2, 108–33.

Rudd, J. (1988), 'Invisible Exports: The Emigration of Irish Women This Century', *Women's Studies International Forum*, 11:4, 307–11.

Ryan, L. (2002), *Gender, Identity and the Irish Press 1922–1937: Embodying the Nation*, New York: Edwin Mellon.

Schroeder, P. (1996), *The Feminist Possibilities of Dramatic Realism*, Madison, NJ: Fairleigh Dickinson University Press.

Sihra, M. (2018), *Marina Carr: Pastures of the Unknown*, Basingstoke: Palgrave Macmillan.

Sisson, E. (2018), 'Experiment and The Free State: Mrs Cogley's Cabaret and the founding of the Gate Theatre 1924–1930', in D. Clare, D. Lally and P. Lonergan (eds), *The Gate Theatre, Dublin: Inspiration and Craft*, 11–27, Oxford: Peter Lang.

Smith, J. (2007), *Ireland's Magdalen Laundries and the Nation's Architecture of Containment*, Indiana: University of Notre Dame Press.

Valiulis, M. (1995), 'Power, Gender, and Identity in the Irish Free State', *Journal of Women's History*, 7:1, 117–36.

Valiulis, M. (2019), *The making of inequality: Women, power and gender ideology in the Irish Free State, 1922–1937*, Dublin, Four Courts Press.

Walker, K. (1984–5), 'The Festival and the Abbey: Ninette de Valois' Early Choreography, 1925–34, Part One', *Dance Chronicle*, 7:4, 379–412.

Walsh, I. (2018), 'Hilton Edwards as Director: Shades of Modernity', in D. Clare, D. Lally and P. Lonergan (eds), *The Gate Theatre, Dublin: Inspiration and Craft*, 29–45, Oxford: Peter Lang.

Ward, M. (1995), *In Her Own Voice: Women and Irish Nationalism*, Dublin: Attic Press.

Ward, M. (2017), *Hanna Sheehy Skeffington, Suffragette and Sinn Féiner: Her Memoirs and Political Writings*, Dublin: UCD Press.

Ward, M. (2019), *Fearless Woman: Hanna Sheehy Skeffington, Feminism and the Irish Revolution*, Dublin: UCD Press.

Milton Keynes UK
Ingram Content Group UK Ltd.
UKHW022009281124
451744UK00004B/77

9 781350 234635